HYPOTHESIS-DRIVEN DEVELOPMENT

A GUIDE TO SMARTER PRODUCT MANAGEMENT

BY ALEX COWAN

Edited by Stephanie Ray
Cover design by Ian Groulx

For information on buying this title in bulk quantities,
or for custom editions please email: books@alexandercowan.com

ISBN   979-8-9878733-0-4
ISBN   979-8-9878733-1-1

DEDICATION

To my parents, JoAnn and Bruce

ACKNOWLEDGEMENTS

There's a version of a writer that captures our imagination–a solitary figure exploring the depths of something unknown and bringing it to life. Thankfully, those writers do exist. But that's not me. I'm just here to tell you what I've learned about building great products in digital.

I didn't learn any of it alone. As a startup founder, I was building with a team based on what we were learning about our customers. As an instructor, I've been supported by the team at Darden, my faculty colleagues, my collaborators in industry, the hundreds of students I've had the pleasure of working with in the classroom, and the 400,000+ online learners, only a few of whom I've had the chance to meet.

I'd like to thank anyone that has ever worked with me. Thanks for putting up with my mania and all my questions. Thanks to all the students I've ever had for all the inspiring questions you asked and also for telling me kindly but clearly what you did and didn't like about the teaching so I could keep getting better.

Thanks to Ian and Jane Groulx for creating, stewarding and helping me with just about every visual communication I've done since my first book in 2012. Thanks also to Ron Wiener and Saravanan Ponnaiyan for helping to bring that material to life.

I'd like to thank Laura Klein for the thoughtful, provocative, insightful correspondence we've had over the years, and also for her advice on the publishing process. I'd also like to thank Christina Wodtke for her help on the book design and publication process.

I'd like to thank all my faculty colleagues at Darden for their support, encouragement, and expertise in the classroom and elsewhere. In particular, I'd like to thank Mike Lenox for his early reviews of this book, Jeanne Liedtka for her insight on what works in teaching design, Casey Lichtendahl & Eric Tassone for their help and relentless curiosity about how businesses can improve their use of data analytics, and Yael Grushka-Cockayne for her help on early versions of this material. Thanks also to Michael Albert, Sasa Zorc, and Ahmed Abassi for their patient responses to all my questions about data science and applications of statistical reasoning.

I'd like to thank Darden's Batten Institute for Entrepreneurship and Innovation, where I'm a fellow, for supporting my faculty career from the very beginning. In particular, I'd like to thank MJ Toms and Sean Carr for their unwavering encouragement and support. I'd also like to thank the instructional design and media teams at Darden for their expertise and diligence in the hundreds of hours we spent together creating and recreating a set of courses that, as of this writing, have been taken >500,000 times.

Thanks to Drew Hammond and Jason Starkey for their early reviews of the book.

I have been particularly fortunate to work on this book with my longtime friend and collaborator, Stephanie Ray. As a gifted writer, content strategist, and practitioner in tech (currently as VP of Product at ProjectManager.com), I can't imagine a better editor for the whole of this book.

I'd like to thank Alex Hughes Capell and Anna Bellury for their ability to pair their expertise on book production with the specific point of view and audience I wanted this book to serve.

I'd especially like to thank my lovely and patient wife Sarah, and my two children, Elyse and Emilia, for their encouragement, care, and support.

While they have their own mentions throughout the book, I'd like to thank and acknowledge the guest editors who generously contributed their perspective and experience to the book's chapters. They are: Jeanne Liedtka, Laura Klein, Rob Zuber, Casey Lichtendahl, Eric Tassone, Darren Bauer Kahan, Conor Sibley, Colin Zima, and Nir Eyal.

Finally, to everyone who I should have mentioned explicitly and didn't, I apologize in advance and, at a bare minimum, I owe you a drink.

Contents

1

YOU, AND THE BUSINESS OF 'DIGITAL'

"Is it working?" If you're a techy, or you've been around software applications and the stuff that stitches them together, this is a question you've either asked or been asked plenty. Code has errors, systems don't come together right, and sometimes you're not entirely sure why something isn't working.

Analytically debugging your work becomes a matter of habit.

It's not surprising, then, that techies started asking the very same question about the business of technology. Arising out of a newfound inquiry-based approach to business, we got practices like agile, Lean Startup, OKR's, lean UX, and design thinking. Today, as tech has gone from relative obscurity to a notable sector to the dominant economic force in business, and as organic growth through innovation increasingly moves stock prices, these practices have gone from something the techies are doing to something managers in general want to apply. It's still challenging to build great products, but these approaches are working.

Predicting the future excites us, but none of us are very good at it. Here are a few heralded predictions about tech:

> *"The potential world market for copy machines is 5,000 at most."*   —IBM: 1979[1]

---

1   John Kennedy, "10 Of the Worst Business Predictions," Think Business (Think Business, August 2, 2016), https://hdd.works/3aOxQ9x.

"There's no chance that the iPhone is going to get market share."
—Microsoft: Steve Ballmer (2007)

No one knows what's next, and that's what keeps the work in tech so interesting. You're the limit, not the possibilities, and this book is about expanding those possibilities for you.

What And Where Is "Tech"—And Where Do I Fit In?

This is a great question, and I'm not sure I have a nice, simple answer. That said, you probably don't need one. Tech and the people that get it are everywhere and they're ascendant. Traditionally, this has been people with some kind of 'technical' skill—software developers, systems/ops folks, and, more recently, designers.

If you pay attention to 'business', you've probably noticed the world's changed a lot. A McKinsey consultant who might have been creating a competitive strategy for AT&T in 1998 is now leading a team that's part of their digital transformation effort, building a new application to improve the company's performance and extend its future. And that same MBA who had McKinsey at the top of their list of possible employers in 1998 is now just as likely to be angling for a product management job at Google or Facebook. The star analyst is now a data scientist, a PE associate is tasked with reinventing a company's IT instead of engineering its finances, and the marketer is now a 'growth hacker' running A/B tests.

Regardless, the exciting thing about 'tech' is that it no longer takes a corporate empire to make a billion dollars—Instagram had just 13 employees when it was acquired for that amount. While most startups need to scale to somewhat larger organizations for that kind of outcome, the work of tech usually has to do more with getting the right team of 7–12 people together and giving them the autonomy they need than it does with building a large command and control organization.

This is where you come in.

The digital applications these teams build change the way we live and work, amplifying us. They may amplify our recreation, like Instagram, or take the repetitive grunt work out of our jobs, like the way your calendar application helps you find the best time to do a meeting, or how you can ask Alexa to do any arithmetic you need. A more nerdy, more forward-looking explanation is that we're becoming a distributed intelligence, distributing part of our intelligence to automation. For example, when I walk out the door in the morning, rather than having to have watched the news or generally thought much about the weather, I can just ask Alexa what the temperature will be and make a decision at the moment.

As I jokingly tell my MBA students: 'Computers are the wave of the future.' In the 70's this statement was visionary, in the 80's it was popular, in the 90's it was conventional, and after that it was inevitable. If you're a businessperson, for better or for worse, it's no longer possible to be categorically 'non-technical'. And even if you're a technical dynamo in some form, given the amount of waste in software development across new products, features on successful products, and even enterprise software, if you want to make your product successful, a lot of the upside probably has to do with making sure users care about what you're building.[2]

But enough about you. A little about me.

Professionally speaking, I'm kind of a weirdo. I get asked by my students all the time: "Do you come more from the design side or engineering side or sales or what?" I don't know what to tell them.

Not knowing much of anything about anything, I dropped out of college and started my first company way back in 1995 at the age of 19, fixing computers and later working on internal IT systems for companies. A day in the life in my first job ranged from learning how to replace the disk drive on an Intel 386 computer to selling door-to-door in downtown Santa Barbara, seeing if anyone wanted their computer fixed. There were no departments, and while my partner was more experienced, we had a lot to learn, and we did. That company, now GovPlace, went on to be quite successful. I tried to finish college at Stanford, but dropped out again in my final year to do another startup, which failed, but then I managed to go on and found and advise a few ventures that were successful.

---

2   Mkrigsman, TechRepublic Staff, Ray Fernandez, Franklin Okeke, Brenna Miles, Cory Bohon, and Marc Librescu. "Study: 68 Percent of IT Projects Fail." TechRepublic, December 16, 2008. https://hdd. works/3ogNWMB/; Griffith, Erin. "Startups Are Failing Because They Make Products No One Wants." Fortune. Fortune, March 2, 2015. https://hdd.works/3PoL37W.

After running the professional services business at a unified communications software company, BroadSoft, I left and started a company called Leonid Systems to focus on the enterprise software part of what our joint customers were doing. These were communications operators like Verizon and Comcast. In 2015, BroadSoft acquired Leonid and then itself was acquired by Cisco a few years later. After that, I started teaching at UVA Darden while still working off and on in tech. I invested in and started advising a security startup, Singularity Networks, which was also sold to Cisco in 2019.[3] Currently, I'm working on a virtual reality language application with the team at Jedburgh Technologies, while writing this book.

Today, I'm on a university faculty and I still don't have a college degree, but I'm still learning plenty of new things. I don't see myself as mainly an engineer, a manager, or a designer, and, honestly, I think that's helped me figure out overall what works for a given company, product, or team.

Personally, I think being a generalist who's not afraid to dig into new topics is now a kind of a superpower. After selling my last company in 2015, I went to teach at UVA Darden to test that idea. Darden is the University of Virginia's graduate business school, and there, working with my colleagues, we help prepare interested MBAs for careers in tech. These are not your father's MBAs or the kind you see on TV. They're extending their understanding of 'general management' to work in design thinking, data visualization, software design, software coding, data science, and prototyping.

Teaching relative to my new "generalists are superheroes theory" was working well, and it was consistently improved by what I (and others) now call Hypothesis Driven Development, so I tested some online courses for the public. Today, I'm proud to say I've had the chance to work with 400,000+ learners who have collectively taken 500,000+ courses on taking a hypothesis-driven approach to creating wins in digital. Many of those students started out as generalists, like the MBA's at Darden, but I've been thrilled by the mix of designers, generalists, and engineers.[4]

---

3 "Singularity Networks - Crunchbase Company Profile & Funding," Crunchbase, accessed July 21, 2022, https://hdd.works/3yWRZ5w.

4 Cowan, Alexander. "Alex Cowan, Instructor." Coursera. Accessed July 12, 2022. https://hdd.works/3O6qmfP.

OK, Back To You: The Generalist Superhero.

I have a deep and abiding interest in how to equip interdisciplinary generalists to do high impact work in tech, work that moves the needle on product and business model economics. In the tech world, we sometimes call these 'traction roles'. In the MBA world, we call it 'general management'. For me, the basic test is whether someone in the role has meaningful responsibility for driving revenue while investing in certain costs to make that happen. The most common job title in tech with this responsibility is 'product manager', but it's also the job of entrepreneurs and increasingly, consultants and various other types of managers.

I've seen fantastic growth into these roles on the part of both non-technical generalists as well as technical specialists. For the 'non-technical', their big blocker was answering the question, 'Do I need to learn how to code?' It wasn't so much that they had tried to code and failed. While coding well is at least as hard as doing anything else well, if you're reading this book you can almost certainly go to a site like Codecademy and, over a couple of Sundays complete, as an example, their basic Javascript course.

Learning to code itself wasn't the blocker—the blocker was that they had trouble connecting their coding to the work they wanted to do. Ultimately, getting over that blocker has a lot to do with creating a testable point of view on what they wanted to happen, and then working from there to find the technical facilities to make that happen. In practice, this meant knowing how to learn just enough about the 'technical' matters at hand to focus their ideas and facilitate 'technical' collaboration on them.

As I often tell 'general management' students in my coding classes: "You don't have to know everything. But you have to know *how* to know everything."

Odds are, the team you end up on won't be a 10/10 across all the disciplines it takes to make a great product, from design, through development, test, deploy, and analytics. The world is changing fast and we all have life-changing opportunities to improve and try new things. And the great thing about being a generalist is that you have the opportunity to substantially improve interdisciplinary collaboration across all those areas.

I'm convinced practice can get much better for more practitioners, both for non-technical and technical types. However, I've noticed two big problems in the real world of digital.

The first problem I've observed has to do with onboarding generalists—for example, general managers like the MBAs that I teach at UVA Darden. A lot of the really great on-ramps for being some kind of manager or leader in tech assume prior experience in some technical discipline, like coding, data science, or design. At the same time, the cost to deliver a software application has plummeted, there are now 'NoCode' options, and by many measures most software that's written ends up in the cybertrash, lightly used or not used at all.[5]

Second, most of us want a go-to practice, something we're all in on—design thinking, Lean Startup, or agile, for example. However, all of these approaches have areas where they perform well and others where another practice is a better fit. For example, Design Thinking and customer interviews are great for figuring out who your customer is and what's on their A-list. However, showing users' prototypes and asking how they like them is much less effective at testing demand than Lean Startup. Agile is excellent, but test and deploy practitioners made it even better by iterating to the body of practice we now call DevOps.

Introducing Hypothesis Driven Development

What I've learned is that Hypothesis-Driven Development (HDD) does a nice job on these two big issues. Like agile, Hypothesis-Driven Development (HDD) is a loose body of work with a central purpose and set of principles. Central principles for HDD are to:
1. explicitly focus your intent, which is a long-standing feature of product design
2. link that intent to specific observations for making specific inferences, which is a long-standing feature of science
3. make crisp decisions based on the above with a focus on iteration and small batches, which is a long-standing feature of lean and agile.

---

5   Michael Krigsman, "CRM Failure Rates: 2001-2009," ZDNet, accessed July 12, 2022, https://hdd. works/3P552c1; Krigsman, Michael, TechRepublic Staff, Ray Fernandez, Franklin Okeke, Brenna Miles, Cory Bohon, and Marc Librescu. "Study: 68 Percent of IT Projects Fail." TechRepublic, December 16, 2008. https://hdd.works/3azAqQT;Martin Fowler, "The XP 2002 Conference," martinfowler.com, accessed July 13, 2022, https://hdd.works/3o04urP; S, http://www.gartner.com/newsroom/id/2648515; Erin Griffith, "Why Startups Fail, According to Their Founders," Fortune (Fortune, March 2, 2015), https://hdd.works/3PoL37W.

What I've observed is that just being great at a single discipline like product design, design thinking, Lean Startup, A/B testing, or agile doesn't by itself reliably, consistently produce great results. What I love about HDD is that it calls attention to what all the prevailing disciplines have in common and how that anchors back to a shared point of view on outcomes. It helps generalists of whatever sort engage with their peers around a shared view of how they'll test their way to a good outcome. And importantly for a field that changes a lot on the margins, it helps lifelong learners think about where they're headed next. In tech, it's generally frowned upon to use the term 'best practices' and the reason is that we've learned there's so much variation from company to company, product to product, and even team to team, that the idea there's a single approach that will always work often does more harm than good. HDD offers a useful solution to this in that progressive adaptation is built into the core of how it approaches the work of teams.

Testing Your Way To Success

HDD is *not* about 'analysis paralysis' and waiting for complete certainty before taking action. Particularly in tech, fortune favors the bold. HDD starts with the proposition that customer behavior is hard to predict. The untold story of just about every successful startup is that they had to kill or 'pivot' from lots of ideas before they got the outcome they were after. If the age old take on new ventures is something like 'let's build a lemonade stand', then HDD just amends that a little to something like: 'let's build a lemonade stand at the intersection of 4th and Main this Saturday and if it makes over $50, we'll consider that a win.'

In tech and in innovation, good ideas are testable ideas. This diagram of an agile Product Pipeline shows these different areas in the context of how a modern, digital team might loop through in a week-long agile 'sprint' or iteration:

Figure 1-1: The Product Pipeline

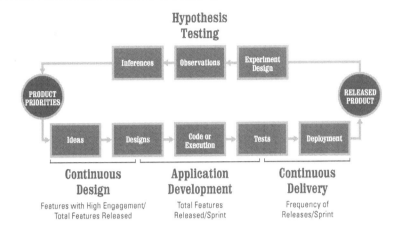

Whether or not you're 'technical,' to get reliably good outcomes you need to get in the habit of working in discrete batches of testable ideas. In practice, that means defining a testable view of the economic result you want for your product or company, and being able to cascade that to facilitating discussions with your team about which programming language to use, where you might find wins with machine learning, and how to automate your product pipeline.

Business Strategy & HDD

Historically, strategy is the bottom line on why a given action may or may not be a good idea for a particular business. Currently, in tech at least, strategic planning as a mainstay of management is out of fashion. As Guy Kawasaki says, "Ideas are easy. Implementation is hard."[6]

The whole idea of long term strategic advantage is much more relevant when you're, say, making multi-decade investments in building a cement plant than it is when you're a digital disruptor.

---

6 "Ideas Are Easy, Implementation Is Hard," Forbes (Forbes Magazine, June 6, 2013), https://hdd. works/3IMOKBX.

However, at the heart of HDD is acting intentionally. Particularly in the highly uncertain environment of digital innovation, a company needs some kind of anchor point for what it's trying to achieve. Without this, a company can easily have a number of beautifully executed initiatives that add up to an economically irrelevant mess—and this happens all the time.

Personally, I've participated in more than one such mess. In the salad days of the early 2000's, I dropped out of college for the second time to be the first employee at Scout Electromedia. We spent millions building proprietary hardware, proprietary device software, a proprietary networking infrastructure, and a proprietary city guide, each beautifully executed, if I do so say so myself. But our funders lost their appetite to fund the venture around the time we finished the product.

While my colleagues have gone on to do great things, including starting and selling several successful startups, I don't think any of us would hold up Scout as a model of how to proceed, strategically. The strategy, such as it was, was to build something cool (at scale) and take it from there. Could we have gotten there another way? Quite possibly, yes. Are today's early stage investors still game for such an adventure? Generally not, no.

Figure 1-2: The Modo!

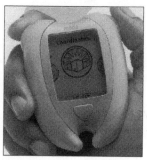

Startups and the practice of innovation in general have come a long way in the last 20 years. Most centrally, we've learned the difference between creating a valuable innovation and scaling it. As startup pioneer Steve Blank puts it:

> ... startups are not small versions of big companies. Rather they are different in every possible way—from goals, to measurements, from employees to culture.[7]

---

7   Steve Blank, "Steve Blank a Startup Is Not a Smaller Version of a Large Company," Steve Blank, June 6, 2021, https://hdd.works/3bZpDj5.

Figure 1-3: The Business Model Canvas

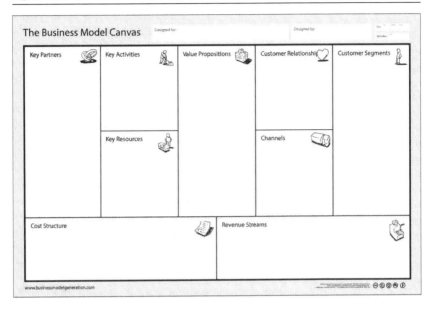

The idea of product/market fit offers a fulcrum between learning and scaling. Essentially, the idea is that once a company has product/market fit for a given product, that's something it can scale. One popular way to describe product/market fit is in the context of a 'business model design', described by Alex Osterwalder's Business Model Canvas, which you can see in Figure 1-3.

Specifically, the Canvas describes product/market fit as a set of relationships between Customer Segments and Value Propositions. Also popular with more mature companies, the Canvas offers a specific but highly visible point of view on a company or line business' focal points. Rather than an elaborate business plan, it offers something any team can visualize and discuss in a few minutes.

To further round out the job of communicating company-wide priorities and how they cascade to individual teams, OKR's (objectives and key results) have proven themselves a robust yet flexible tool for innovation-centric companies like Google.[8] The essential idea is that objectives establish a direction and key results provide a way of defining

---

8 Google, "Google's OKR Playbook: Learn More about Goal Setting and Okrs.," What Matters: OKR Google playbook (Google, September 9, 2020), https://hdd.works/3yAfUY9.

and assessing progress in that direction. Generally, objectives are set on an annual cadence and key results are reviewed and set quarterly. The senior management teams sets OKR's and then managers, areas, and teams cascade those down to their particular work.

While many of these ideas were pioneered by startups, they've also proven useful for the startups of yesteryear that have matured into the durable franchises we have today, for example the FAANG companies: Facebook/now Meta, Amazon, Apple, Netflix, and Google. Product/market fit doesn't come with a warranty—it's always either expanding or contracting. Focus and a disciplined execution still matter for everyone in tech and really anyone with an innovation-centric business model. Plenty of startups who achieve product/market fit and scale to become larger firms struggle when their focus becomes diffuse. Evernote is a relatively recent example of this[9]. Books like 'The End of Competitive Advantage'[10] offer the idea that a sustainable, long term competitive advantage is no longer possible—and yet, assets like data custody and social networks have proven to be a durable source of advantage for many large tech companies.

Whether you call it strategy or not, an intentional approach that cascades down to individual teams is critical for making innovation work at scale, and it's the anchor point for applying Hypothesis-Driven Development. Such a focus allows teams practicing HDD to cascade a testable approach to every substantial decision they make, from the platform they use to run a given app, to what tool chains they use, to which user behaviors they observe in hypothesis testing.

I mentioned earlier that one major thing digital has changed is what a single, 7–12 person team can achieve. Crucial to successful innovation is providing an actionable focus for these teams that keeps their work aligned with the company focus, but affords them the autonomy to pursue their objectives using their own judgment. Even within the team, self-organization is considered by most the paragon of practice. You've probably heard of agile, which is a nearly ubiquitous approach among teams at such ventures to organize their work. In this next section, we'll briefly cover agile and how it fits in with a practice of Hypothesis-Driven Development.

---

9 'Erin Griffith, "A Unicorn Lost in the Valley, Evernote Blows up the 'Fail Fast' Gospel," The New York Times (The New York Times, June 28, 2019), https://hdd.works/3Pnq0Cp.
10 Rita Gunther McGrath, *The End of Competitive Advantage: How to Keep Your Strategy Moving as Fast as Your Business* (Boston, MA: Harvard Business Review Press, 2013).

Agile & HDD

Hypothesis-Driven Development is *a* way for an agile team to operate a product pipeline. Most of how we'll talk about its application has to do with the work of interdisciplinary 'agile' teams of 7–12 colleagues. If that's not what you're doing right now, that's all right. You'll be learning the foundation skills to make teams more productive, however they're working.

What is agile, exactly? A group of software developers created the "Manifesto for Agile Software Development" (Agile Manifesto) in 2001.[11] While it is only 68 words long, it has revolutionized software and product development, and arguably all project management, in groundbreaking ways and is the de facto approach to just about any digital innovation project in business.

The Agile Manifesto essentially says the following:

Individuals and interactions	over	processes and tools
Working software	over	comprehensive documentation (requirements)
Customer collaboration	over	contract negotiation
Responding to change	over	following a plan

The Agile Manifesto is probably the only single thing that everyone would agree is, without a doubt, 'agile'. Agile is more a set of outcomes and circumstances that an individual team is seeking to realize than it is a specific practice or set of practices. That said, while teams will and should adaptively tune their own particular practice of agile, there are a few practices that are nearly universal and worth understanding if you're new to agile and coming to understand it—if you do agile, these are probably familiar to you and you might want to skip ahead to the next section.

While there are several fixed, 'pre-packaged' methodologies for practicing agile, many teams end up with a set of practices they pick and choose based on their experience. Three practices are particularly common across teams:

---

11 Kent Beck et al., "Manifesto for Agile Software Development," Manifesto for Agile Software Development, accessed July 13, 2022, https://hdd.works/3c8yEXe.

1. Sprints or iterations
2. Daily stand-ups (and a few other formal meetings)
3. User Stories and emergent design

'Sprints' or fixed-time iterations are how most agile teams create focal points for adaptively improving what they're delivering for the customer and how they're working together. Their input is a 'backlog' of work items sorted by priority and their output is working software (work in progress is not considered sprint output). The sprint is preceded by some type of planning where a product lead creates the backlog. That product lead might have the title 'product manager' or the role 'product owner' if the team is using Scrum, one of the agile methodologies. Often, but not always, the items in the backlog are designed in the form of 'user stories'. At these stand ups, each team member answers the following questions:

1. What did I accomplish yesterday?
2. What will I accomplish today?
3. What obstacles are impeding my progress?

Colleagues from outside the team are allowed to attend these meetings but the general practice is that they're not allowed to speak, in order to keep the meeting short and focused. The objective with the stand up is to keep the team informed about how everyone's doing and then, beyond that, remove or at least minimize the need for additional meetings. This is important because designers and developers strongly value 'flow' time where they're able to work without interruption. Sprints close with a retrospective meeting where the team explores what went well, what could have gone better, and, critically, what practices they want to add, remove or change as a result.

Figure 1-4: An Agile Iteration or 'Sprint'

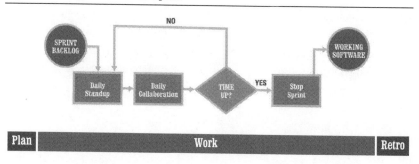

How To Do Agile Well

Broadly speaking, positive signs that agile is working are that a team:

    a. openly discusses issues of substances in retrospectives, and links those to new practices they will test

    b. has a lot of informal communication, particularly between business people and technical people, but few formal meetings

    c. there are relatively few surprises at the end of each sprint

An actionable way to understand and approach agile is with the idea that it's a way to help the team improve its product pipeline, both for end users as well as the team itself.

Using HDD in the Product Pipeline

Figure 1-5: Metrics and the Product Pipeline

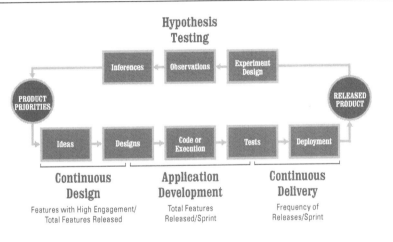

Table 1-1 describes the pipeline's four areas of practice in more detail, including how they relate to various methodologies and practices associated with agile—some of that lingo you may have heard, others maybe not. In either case, they're just there for reference and it's not important to know them.

Table 1-1: Four Primary Practice Areas

Area of Practice	Description	Prevalence	Related Areas and Terms
Continuous Design, where success is improving on the ratio of features released to successful features	This area deals with figuring out what to build. While many agile teams consistently test usability, few run a consistent program for testing across problem diagnosis, demand evaluation, and interface usability. Success in this area means more of the content the team is releasing sees high engagement from customers or high performance from internal users.	Low/ increasing	• Product design • Design thinking • Customer discovery • Customer development • Lean Startup • Lean user experience (UX) • Lean analytics • Design sprints Legacy practices: • Requirements gathering • Acceptance testing
Application Development, where success is improving on the velocity of total features released	This area deals with building software applications and systems. Agile in this area is nearly a de facto standard. Success in this area means the team is improving its "velocity," as measured by the size and amount of features released in a given unit of time.	High/ steady	• Scrum • SAFE • Kanban (loosely) • XP • Pair programming • Test-driven development • Estimating • Story points Legacy practices: • Waterfall

Area of Practice	Description	Prevalence	Related Areas and Terms
Continuous Delivery, where success is improving on the frequency of your releases	This area deals with integrating the jobs of testing and deploying software with the job of building it. Success in this area means the team is releasing more frequently. Continuous delivery means a developer can commit code and automatically (if it passes a series of tests) deploy it to users.	Moderate/ increasing	• DevOps[12] • Continuous integration • Unit testing • Integration testing • System testing • Staging • Release management Legacy practices: • Quality assurance
Hypothesis Testing, where (like Continuous Design) success is improving the ratio of features released to successful features	This area, tightly related to continuous design and continuous delivery, deals with running experiments to drive to an evidence-based definition of "done." Success in this area means that teams assess whether they're "done" with an item based on directly observable user behaviors.	Low/ increasing	• A/B testing • Experimentation

What Gets Measured Gets Managed, in Agile

For each of the four areas above, I've suggested a focal metric teams can use to discuss how things are going and how they might improve them. For example, in Application Development, it's how many features you release per period. With Continuous Design, it's the portion of those features that see engagement from the user at or above your target. With Continuous Delivery, it's how frequently you're able to release new code to end users. Relative to most practices of agile, that's a lot of measurability.

But we're not going to stop there! More measuring by itself isn't better, of course—in fact, it's probably worse, generating more work and blurring the team's focus with overload. However, we're still left with an actual, specific, problem, one I've experienced many times: even with

---

12 Emily Freeman, "DevOps," Amazon (John Wiley & Sons, Inc, 2019), https://hdd.works/3o1awIQ.

metrics for each of the areas, they don't offer a single, specific answer on how performance in these different areas accrues to the success of the team overall.

Let's say it's the end of the week and you're in a meeting where the team is considering how things went in this week's sprint, and what they might want to do differently next week. In agile, they call this a 'retrospective'. They're combining the retrospective with a session where the team decides which features they'll work on next week, sometimes called a 'backlog grooming' session. The site reliability engineer who pays a lot of attention to how efficiently and how frequently they're releasing thinks they need to invest in more automation to test the application, given the number of bugs that have been making it to production. However, the developers generally think the bugs are at a level that's basically all right, and that the team should focus on finishing a new set of features.

These are all reasonable people with good intentions, but other than the area-specific metrics and anecdotes about how they might interact, our current measurability doesn't have a strong point of view on how they relate.

F = The Only Formula You'll Ever Need

For this we'll use the equation you see here. Now, this is not a technical book in the traditional sense. If you've had bad math teachers and don't like equations, that's all right. You don't need to dig into the equation to get what this book has to offer. It's just another way to think about the health of a given team and product pipeline and how to improve it with the application of HDD across disciplines like design, coding, and analytics.

Figure 1-6: Formulation of 'F'

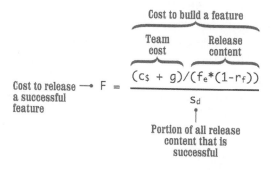

Cost to build a feature

Team cost · Release content

Cost to release a successful feature → $F = \dfrac{(c_\$ + g)/(f_e*(1-r_f))}{s_d}$

Portion of all release content that is successful

'F' is our dependent variable (DV), the thing we want to measure and observe. 'F' measures the cost of a successful feature. When and how might a team use this? Before a given sprint, a team can hypothesize that a certain action will affect one of the terms you see above, improving 'F'. After the sprint, they can see if that was true or not. Fortunately, with agile teams running on modern cadences of a week or so, you don't have to wait long.

How would we arrive at an estimate for 'F'? First, we consider how much it costs the team to release a feature, which is just 'team cost' divided by the amount of content or features they release: '$(c_s + g)/(f_e*(1-r_f))$' in the equation. Let's say that's $5,000.

This cost/content is the term you see on the top of the fraction (the numerator). That cost describes how much it costs the team to create release output. However, output is more important if you're running, say, a sneaker factory, than it is if you're running a digital team. Lots of software ends up in the trash, and a feature can be worth less than zero. If an unused feature encumbers your code, creating technical debt, or, worse still, makes your product more complicated, creating 'UX debt', then this can easily be the case. Given this, we denominate (divide by) the cost/content by the portion of features that are successful, s_d in the equation above. For example, if it costs a team $5,000 to build a feature but only 50% of their features are successful, then their cost to build a *successful* feature is $10,000.

Let's briefly step through the individual terms in the calculation. The top of the equation describes cost/content, the cost to develop a given feature. For that, we first need to know how much the team costs. We can get this by adding the cost of salaries and related items like benefits, 'c_s', and the cost of all equipment and services they need, 'g'. Then, we consider how much output that team produces in a given period of time, shown here as 'f_e'. Then, 'r_f' is the last item we consider in calculating how much it costs the team to develop a feature. The term 'r_f' (release friction) captures how much of the team's time is spent on overhead like manual testing and fixing bugs. This term is optional, but the idea with the equation is to unpack for consideration the various drivers of 'F' and this is often a big one. Even bigger, however, is 's_d', the bottom of the equation, which is the portion of features that are successful, and which we use to denominate how much it costs the team to deliver not just any feature but a successful feature.

The footnote here offers an online guide on how to execute this type of 'innovation accounting'.[13] It is worth noting, though, that whatever figure you arrive at, it's mostly useful for heuristic purposes and as a baseline. Given the wildly different things a given team might be doing and how they might be doing them, I have not found a useful absolute value to target for 'F'.

However, establishing a baseline and then looking at whether it's improving or declining over time is a useful way to consider how the different practices an agile team might try out are performing relative to the team's goals. We started this section with an example of a team getting together for an agile retrospective and backlog grooming session. I can't think of any better hallmark for a high-functioning practice of agile than whether they're having robust, inclusive discussions about what they've learned and how they're going to act on those learnings, both with regard to their practice of agile and the health of their product.

HDD, "Digital Strategy" & Agile IRL

Through the book, I'll use a fictional company called 'HVAC in a Hurry' (HinH) as a way to show specific, inter-related examples of what you'll be learning, along with real examples from practice. HVAC in a Hurry is a large, regional HVAC (heating, ventilation, and air conditioning) service firm that is looking to expand through acquisitions and franchising. I'll follow their new digital applications team, led by intrepid generalist Frangelico DeWitt, as they work to transform the business for growth. These subsections are written from Frangelico's perspective and describe both the company at large and the team he's leading.

HVAC in a Hurry's Market Position

For [facilities managers & business owners] who [need their heating & cooling systems managed and repaired], [HVAC in a Hurry] is a [full service heating and cooling provider] that [allows for easy and responsible management of a business' HVAC systems]. Unlike [smaller firms], our [commitment to best practices and training allows customers to worry less and realize superior total cost of ownership for their HVAC systems].

---

13 Alexander Cowan, "The Interdisciplinarian," Alex Cowan, October 31, 2017, https://hdd.works/3uL1e7H.

HinH's Digital Team And Their Purpose

For [dispatchers and technicians] who [work at HVAC in a Hurry], [H-ify] is an [enterprise software solution] that [improves the HVAC repair and maintenance experience for both internal staff and customers]. Unlike [ad hoc solutions], our product [has been carefully formulated and validated against best practices and also our customer experiences out in the field].

What's Important To This Business? Why? What Does Product/Market Fit Mean For Them? How Do They Deliver On That?

HinH's core market is the Medium Bus. segment. Smaller companies are more expensive to service (relative to revenue) and larger firms have an in-house capability. As we work to sharpen and scale our product/market fit, this is where we currently believe we should focus.

Figure 1-7: Product/Market Fit at HVAC in a Hurry

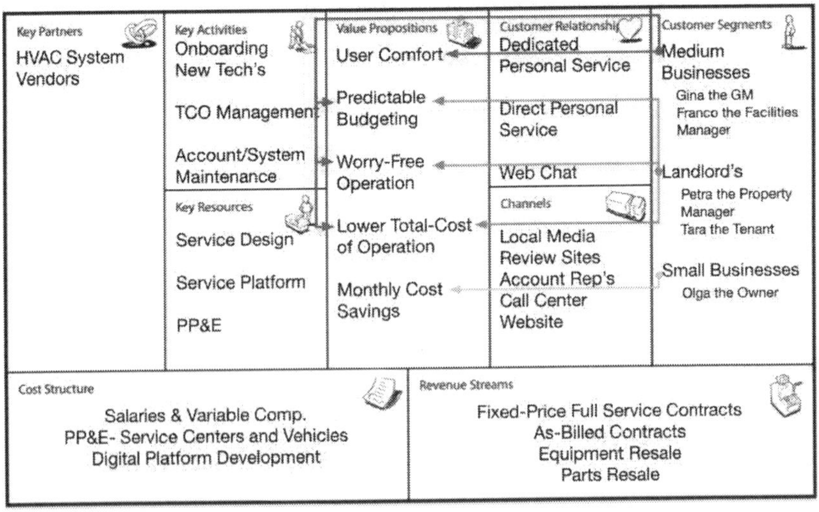

Customers in the Medium Business segment value the ability to outsource their HVAC operation- we're able to help them operate better while saving them money (over the long term) and taking the overhead out of planning and managing their HVAC capability. Our ability to sell and deliver those

Value Propositions is what currently drives profit. Specifically, this is measured by our ability to convert and retain customers in this segment to Fixed-Price Full Service Contracts (vs. As-Billed/ad hoc contracts).

We work with the Landlord segment opportunistically as a way to meet future customers. However, the overhead of interfacing between landlords and tenants as well as their more singular focus on minimizing cost makes it difficult for us to proactively manage these systems, increasing our cost and necessarily our cost to the customer.

The Small Business segment is highly opportunistic and we are considering raising rates or more rigorously screening out these accounts. They generate a disproportionate amount of overhead relative to revenue.

HinH's OKRs

For the business as a whole the headline objective is: **'Become the #1 HVAC service provider in all our regions for the Medium Business segment**.' Key results for the current quarter are:
- KR1: Increase share in the {x} market by 10 points
- KR2: Grow earnings by 8% from same quarter last year
- KR3: Keep customer churn below 5% quarterly

For the digital team, it is: 'Automate and standardize the best of what I've learned to improve user outcomes.' Key results for the coming quarter are:
- KR1: Deploy the parts ordering app in {month 1 of the quarter}
- KR2: Onboard at least 100 users for the test cohort
- KR3: Achieve >80% of parts ordered through the app with the test cohort

Okay, you've seen a comprehensive set of modern fundamentals for operating an innovation-company in 'tech'. Now, let's unpack what you might want to do next.

How To Read This Book

This book will deliver you a foundation understanding of the major topics in tech (within the digital domain). Paired with the kind of directed, high-quality practice the book will help you charter, I'm confident that any techie and any generalist with interest and enthusiasm, can acquire the skills to create fantastic products. As we step through the various topics in the remaining chapters, you'll always learn two fundamental things about them:

1. how to frame the work in terms of testable ideas (hypotheses) which have success criteria directly linked to what drives the company's business model
2. 'technical' fundamentals relative to facilitating work around key economic drivers for each area

The fundamentals will help you formulate and facilitate better ideas. If they're new to you, the fundamentals will give you the creative confidence you need to learn more as you go. If they're already in an area you know, I think they'll help you with new takes on how you might explain the work to your more business-focused collaborators.

My hope is that this book does three things for you:

1. Through a better understanding, it creates even more interest in how and where you want to engage in tech
2. It builds a creative confidence that you can do the work— that while you don't know everything, you know how to know everything
3. It helps you create a prioritized hit list to pair new topics in digital with your work, adapting as you go, and most importantly, enjoying yourself

There's a perception that things change all the time in tech. The reality is that the fundamentals change infrequently, even as particular technologies and products come and go. For this reason, we're going to take a fundamentals-oriented approach, one that's allowed me, my students, and my various collaborators to confidently adapt with the times.

In the chapters that follow, you'll learn to take a hypothesis-driven approach to operating a product pipeline—going from idea to design, design to code, code to deploy, and from release to hypothesis testing. You're going to learn about the economic significance of what drives a product pipeline, the fundamentals of the various practices and technologies, and then see those applied through specific examples. From there, you can create your own applied practice that's relevant to whatever you're doing on the job. One of the hardest parts of applying agile is the proposition that you can't fix command and control with command and control. What do you do, then? One of the easiest wins is to reduce hand-offs and create more fluid collaboration. For this, familiarity with the processes and foundation technology in play across the product pipeline is crucial.

Are we going to cover "all the things"? Not necessarily, but I do think that with these concepts you'll have the foundation skills and creative confidence to pick up whatever new topics you might encounter. If you find you want to engage in some applied practice on these, each chapter offers specific ideas on how you can create relevant opportunities for applied practice on the job. That said, even if some of these topics aren't part of your day to day, I think you'll find it useful to understand their application and how they contribute to making sure a company succeeds with digital innovation and transformation.

What You Will Learn

Is reading this book enough? I think it's an extremely useful start! It will give you a foundation understanding of what I and my students have learned are important for the vast majority of executions in digital. Rather than encountering lots of jargon and concepts on a piecemeal basis, you'll be able to ask and answer questions about the context and significance of these key digital topics so you can make informed decisions about what else (if anything) you need to know about them.

That said, even these 'technical' topics require practice as much as they require a foundational understanding. My intent is that the book allows you to stand on a solid foundation and then, with the help of some of the resources I offer at the end of each chapter, that you'll be able to steadily improve your applied practice of these concepts as they come up on the job and/or in your own personal projects.

I recommend finishing the book before you undertake any of the recommended practice for two reasons. First, as a generalist, it's important that you understand the larger operating context for each sub-topic, and we'll build to that over the course of the book. Second, you shouldn't necessarily dive into them in the order they're presented in the book. Everything else being equal, it's what I would recommend. However, I think in practice it's far more important that you pair them with whatever's on your professional A-list at any given time.

Recommended Practice & Supplemental Resources

As with all the chapters that follow, below are a few areas where you might want to engage in some applied practice.

Describe a Business and its Product/Market fit with the Business Model Canvas

Pick a company that you're familiar with (your employer, your side project, for example) and describe it with the Canvas. Timebox this at 50 minutes but be ready to come back and revise it as you reflect and apply it to focusing product development ideas. This page has notes to get started, including a tutorial, template (Google Slides or PowerPoint), and, if you want more depth, an online course:
> https://hdd.works/3cgjn6N/.

Charter and Focus a Team with OKR's

Pick a company (probably the same one you'd use to practice with the Canvas) and draft a set of OKR's. Particularly if it's where you work, try 'cascading' the company or area OKR's down to your individual team (see resources below for examples). Timebox this at 30 minutes but be ready to revise. This page offers examples and some popular books on the topic:
> https://hdd.works/3oc4XqW.

Practice Agile

I'm going to cover agile as I progress through the chapters, and I think that will be the best next step towards understanding it for most readers. However, if you want more depth on it now, this page offers a primer on the basics and some online courses:
> https://hdd.works/3PExe5n/.

Strategy Meets Digital

If you come from or interface with a strategy group, you may want more depth on 'digital transformation' and generally HDD's relationship to the strategy function. You can find notes on that here:
> https://hdd.works/3aP2UpF/.

Teaching a Degree Program Course or
Workshop with This Material

I maintain my course syllabi, workshop agendas, and cases on this page:
https://hdd.works/3oamJed.

Also, please feel free to get in touch!

2

FROM IDEA TO DESIGN

This may be somewhat anecdotal, but around half of software that's created probably ends up in the trash. This is true across new products, new features on existing products, as well as IT projects.[1] The reason is pretty simple: start with a bad idea, and it doesn't matter how well you design, code, release, or test the software—it's going to fail. The interesting question is how we test ideas, particularly our own, which we're more inclined to regard as positive.

A major driver of these failure rates is the application of more traditional big-batch decision making. Digital affords the opportunity for more adaptive decisions, a practice which reliably improves outcomes and reduces waste. For example, if you're deciding where to build a factory or retail space, it probably makes sense to invest in analysis of historical data and generally groom the decision carefully since it's expensive to reverse. On the other hand, if you're building a new line of business by building or modifying an application, it's extremely inexpensive (relatively speaking) to change course.

---

1 Michael Krigsman, "CRM Failure Rates: 2001-2009," ZDNet, accessed July 13, 2022, https://hdd. works/3ogNWMB; Michael Krigsman et al., "Study: 68 Percent of IT Projects Fail," TechRepublic, December 16, 2008, https://hdd.works/3azAqQT; Martin Fowler, "The XP 2002 Conference," martinfowler.com, accessed July 13, 2022, https://hdd.works/3o04urP; Erin Griffith, "Why Startups Fail, According to Their Founders," Fortune (Fortune, March 2, 2015), https://hdd.works/3PoL37W.

Figure 2-1: Continuous Design & HDD

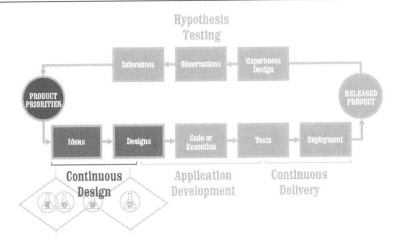

The good news is that in the last decade or so we've learned a lot about what works for innovation as opposed to more traditional business activities. It probably hasn't escaped your notice that for the last few years so many articles are about design and innovation. Given all this attention, why aren't more digital projects successful?

First, doing things well is hard! I have all the information I need to be in perfect physical condition. Am I? No. I'm doing moderately well, and even that's hard because a lot of the habits don't come naturally to me. Second, the best digital practices (product design, design thinking, agile, Lean Startup, for example) are not yet well integrated into how companies operate or even most business education, for that matter.

Hypothesis-Driven Development (HDD) has emerged as a framework for better integrating, focusing, and choosing the right innovation practices for a team, depending on the matter at hand. And in my experience, Continuous Design is where teams are likely to have the most upside.

The Practice of Continuous Design

In Chapter 1, you learned about the four practice areas of HDD, and the first was "Continuous Design":

Table 2-1: The Practice of Continuous Design

Area of Practice	Description	Prevalence	Related Areas and Terms
Continuous Design, where success is improving on your ratio of features released to successful features	This area deals with figuring out what to build. While many agile teams consistently test usability, few run a consistent program for testing across problem diagnosis, demand evaluation, and interface usability. Success in this area means more of the content the team is releasing sees high engagement from customers or high performance from internal users.	Low/ increasing	• Product design • Design thinking • Customer discovery • Customer development • Lean Startup • Lean user experience (UX) • Lean analytics • Design sprints Legacy practices: • Requirements gathering • Acceptance testing

Understanding the portfolio of methods for Continuous Design and how they pair with questions you need to answer about your customer is an important start, and we will be diving into that shortly. However, a lot of what challenges practitioners in this area has as much to do with our emotional dispositions and habits as it does with understanding the methods.

My favorite take on this is from my colleague Jeanne Liedtka. She's worked on how to apply the tools of design to everything from general management in her *The Designing for Growth Field Book* to nonprofits in *Design Thinking for the Greater Good*. She contrasts the dispositions of two fictional protagonists, Geoffrey and George, which you can see in the Figure 2-2.

Figure 2-2 Jeanne Liedtka's George & Geoffrey Mindset Comparison

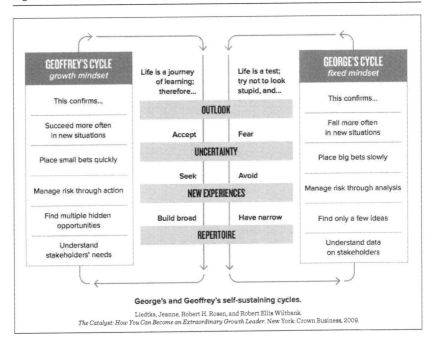

George's and Geoffrey's self-sustaining cycles.

Liedtka, Jeanne, Robert H. Rosen, and Robert Ellis Wiltbank. *The Catalyst: How You Can Become an Extraordinary Growth Leader.* New York: Crown Business, 2009.

Consider your work and your interactions with colleagues—who's more of a Geoffrey and who's more of a George? Why do you think that is? What about you?

Getting to a successful practice of HDD in this area has as much to do with easing your way into a 'growth mindset' as it does anything else. You'll know it's going well if you're excited to try new methods and see what happens. In digital, high functioning teams like Geoffrey's design and test new content that's going to be specifically right or specifically wrong for a certain audience. Low functioning teams like George's work out ideas that are so diffuse that they'll never be specifically *wrong,* per se, but, critically, they'll never be specifically *right* either. Sooner or later their product will start to slide out of its product/market fit.

Continuous Design and HDD

It is HDD's broad applicability across the product pipeline that is its greatest feature, and in the following chapters, we'll focus on its application to development through approaches like test-driven development (TDD), DevOps+continuous delivery, and A/B testing.

For the practice of HDD in Continuous Design, I like to start with the 'double diamond' model of decoupling problem and solution, adapted from the UK Design Council and Donald Norman's seminal book *The Design of Everyday Things*:

Figure 2-3: The Double Diamond Model of Design

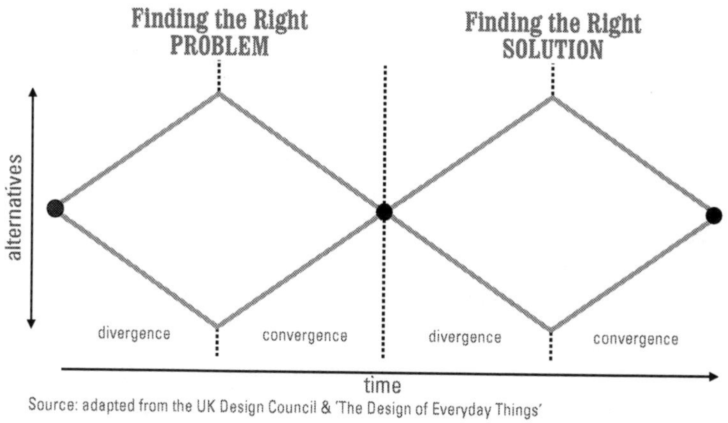

Source: adapted from the UK Design Council & 'The Design of Everyday Things'

The practice of decoupling problem vs. solution is a hallmark of product design, and one of the most noticeable differences between working with a team that's design-literate vs. one that isn't. The practice of diverging your ideas and exploring lots of possibilities before you converge on one (shown on the y-axis) is another.

If it seems relatively simple in theory, it is. However, it's worth noting that for most people the hardest part of executing this way is emotional, as opposed to intellectual. So much of what we're used to doing in business has to do with maximizing efficiency under the assumption that what you're doing is the right answer. In the innovation world, it's finding the right answer that's the hard part since by definition you don't know yet. Many successful repeat innovators like Google even require teams to parallel prototype alternatives and collect results on them before they finalize a feature.

For an HDD-specific approach, we'll unpack the double diamond into the four hypothesis domains you see here in the circles:

Figure 2-4: Double-Diamond & HDD

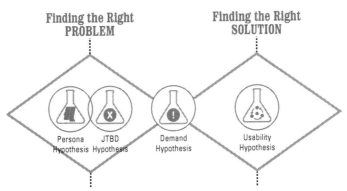

Source: adapted from the UK Design Council & 'The Design of Everyday Things'

In 'Finding the Right Problem', we have two areas of practice: the Persona Hypothesis and the Job-to-be-Done (JTBD) Hypothesis. With JTBD, you're asking, 'Who is this for and what existing job (problem/habit/desire) does it deliver on?' For example, if you're going to build a new dating app, you should probably re-segment that market and focus on a more specific type of user with their own particular approach to dating and the jobs/problems/habits that go with that.

In the Demand Hypothesis, we're working to determine whether anyone wants our dating app. Specifically, for the particular type of user and jobs/habits you identified, how might you test whether anyone wants it with a minimum of time, money, and energy? In digital, this almost always means building some kind of product proxy to test with rather than investing in building out a full blown application. This work is at the heart of Lean Startup[2] and its use of MVP's (minimum viable products).

---

2 "The Lean Startup Methodology," The Lean Startup | Methodology, accessed July 17, 2022, https://hdd. works/3IKRjEM.

Finally, we have the question of usability where we're asking, 'If I assume that I have demand from this particular user to deliver on this particular problem/job, how do I build an interface that makes that as easy and natural as possible?' In the next section, I'll step through how you do the work of finding the right problem.

Finding The Right Problem Or Job-To-Be-Done

How do you do this? You decide what type of user you're going to explore and then ask them a sequence of non-leading questions about your area of interest. Once you feel that you can adequately reach the persona (for engagement, sales, etc.), you know what jobs (or problems/habits/desires) are on their A-list in your area, and you know what alternatives they currently use for those, you're probably best off moving to your Demand Hypothesis and testing your proposition.

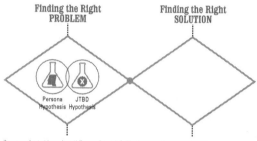

Finding the Right PROBLEM

Finding the Right SOLUTION

Persona Hypothesis   JTBD Hypothesis

Source: adapted from the UK Design Council & 'The Design of Everyday Things'

Hypothesis Formulation & Testing

What do these hypotheses look like and how do you test them? For a given persona, you might interview on the order of 10-25 subjects. Given the sample size and the type of evidence you're collecting, this is not a test that will ever converge to any kind of statistical significance. This does not mean the process can't 'break' or that the evidence isn't actionable.

First and foremost, it is critical to have a screener or your observations are unlikely to ever cohere in a meaningful way. A screener is a small set of factual questions with unambiguous answers whose sole purpose is to determine whether a given human subject is representative of your persona, and therefore the right person to interview. For example, let's say you've decided to explore a dating app for the elderly and you're interviewing for the persona 'Georgia the Golden Years Dater'. You want to understand a day in her life and, critically, if dating is on her A-list.

Screening questions might be:
1. What is your age? [threshold: >=60]
2. Are you single? [threshold: yes]

What you're generally after is a testable foundation for taking your idea to the next step, testing your Demand Hypothesis. However, you can also eliminate ideas here, making space for better ones. For example, Chapter 3's guest editor, Laura Klein, uses the example of a job board for pets—an idea that just doesn't really work on any level.[3] Could you eliminate it by testing your Right Problem Hypotheses? Sure—you could probably just do it by asking pet owners "What are the top 5 hardest things about owning a pet?", find out that no one says 'getting them a job' and move on.

Here's a real life example: I had a student in one of my classes working on a concept which was essentially 'Uber for independent truckers', a marketplace that would help them find cargo at the pickup and delivery points they wanted to travel. What he found was that (at the time) the independent truckers were all older and not inclined to use smart phones, which was key to the concept. There were younger truckers who did use smartphones, but, for various reasons, almost none of the younger generation of truckers was independent. With a good screener and a few interviews, he was able to make space for better ideas.

Let's take a look at the example we discussed in Chapter 1: HVAC in a Hurry (HinH). The team at HinH wants to interview professional HVAC installers. Their screening question might be as simple as, 'How many HVACs did you service last week?' where the threshold is >4.

From there, your job as an interviewer is to ask a sequence of non-leading questions. For example, the worst question you could possibly ask is, 'Wouldn't it be great if I built a system where you could {do something the interviewer thinks is a good idea}? For example, a team at Intuit had a hypothesis that if they could offer a faster set up time for employers on their payroll system, the market would value that. During some usability testing they asked 20 subjects if they'd like to be able to run payroll before the initial set up was entirely complete. They all

3 "Users Know," Users Know, accessed July 19, 2022, https://hdd.works/3OhVMQC.

said no.[4] However, when that same team later ran an A/B test to see if new customers would engage with a 'run payroll first' option as they were setting up their account, 58% of new users picked that option.

Now, the more common finding is actually that subjects will be agreeable to avoid the awkwardness of saying they don't like your idea, but the result is the same: What you can acquire from subject interviews is a hypothesis about a day in the persona's life and what's on their A-list. You can ask about specific examples and learn a lot from that. But if you ask about their hypothetical future behavior, you're likely to get misleading results. You *can* run experiments like the A/B test above that test your Demand Hypotheses, but that is a different Continuous Design facility, which we'll cover in the next section.

Instead, when you're using subject interviews to explore and test your Persona and JTBD Hypotheses, sequence your questions so they go from most general to most specific to avoid leading the subject to a particular answer.

If the team at HVAC in a Hurry is thinking of building an app to standardize and centralize HVAC documentation, evidence that suggests such an app is worth testing would be to find that for the technicians:

a. finding documentation is important and

b. the current alternatives perform poorly for them.

For example, if interviewers asked the question, 'What are the top three most difficult things about completing an HVAC service appointment?' and they consistently heard that finding documentation was among those three, the team has reasonable basis to proceed to testing their Demand Hypothesis.

The following shows an example of what such an interview guide might look like for Trent the Technician.

---

4 Stefan Thomke, "Chapter 2," in *Experimentation Works: The Surprising Power of Business Experiments* (Boston, MA: Harvard Business Review Press, 2020).

Interview Guide: Trent the Technician

SCREENER

How many HVAC repairs did you do last week?
[threshold: >4 repairs]

PERSONA HYPOTHESIS

Tell me about [yourself in the role of the persona]?
Examples for Trent the Technician

- Tell me about being an HVAC technician?
- What do you most, least like about the job?
- What are the hardest, easiest parts of the job?
- I've heard [x]—does that apply to you?

Tell me about [your area of interest]?

- What type of repairs or service do you usually do?
  Would you say you have a speciality?
- Tell me about the last job you did?
- Who else was involved? What was it like?
- What's your definition of success?

Tell me your thoughts about [area]?

- How should it ideally be done?
- How is it actually done? Why?
- Who else was involved? What was it like?
  How should it ideally be done?

What do you see in [area]?

- Where do you learn what's new? What do others do?
- Who do you think is doing it right?
- How did you make your last decision?

What do you feel about [area]?

- Tell me about the last time [something of interest
  from above] happened?

- What motivates you? What parts of it are most rewarding? Why?
- What would it be like in your perfect world?

JTBD HYPOTHESIS

How do you currently [operate in area of interest, if you don't have that yet]? OR Here's what I got on [x]—is that right?
- Can you tell me about your process for heading to a new job?
- What's the first thing that happens? What happens after that?

What's [difficult, annoying] about [area of interest]?
- Can you tell me about your process for heading to a new job?
- What's the first thing that happens? What happens after that?

What are the top [5] hardest things about [area of interest]?
- What are the hardest things about dispatch and preparation?
- About follow-up? About being on site?

Why is/isn't [your specific area of interest on that list]?
- Why isn't {whatever} on your list?

The sub-section below offers an example of what a persona and set of JTBD might look like for Trent the Technician. In and of itself, this material is worthless. The economic significance of testing Persona & JTBD Hypotheses is to minimize waste and thereby maximize the odds of a significant innovation win. Build for a persona that doesn't exist or a job/problem no one cares about, and your team can execute perfectly and end up with an economic zero. For example, let's say the team at HVAC in a Hurry sits together in a conference room and decides it would be great if they build a system that standardizes and centralizes documentation (manuals) for all the HVAC equipment they service. If the vendor documentation is readily available to the technicians and works fine, then this would be a waste of resources and something the techs won't use. In the video you see here, you can see a dramatization of the team learning this.

Figure 2-6: The HinH Team Doing an Interview- A Dramatization![5]

As I mentioned at the beginning of this chapter, the hardest part of doing this work is habitual and emotional. If the team is updating management, a set of prototypes and a project schedule for the HVAC documentation app will show much better than the update that the team feels it needs a week to go and find out what problems actually matter for HVAC technicians— and yet, the first course of action would lead to waste and the second affords the possibility for a win.

5 "Skit: Interviewing Trent the Technician—Getting to Great Agile User Stories," Coursera, accessed July 18, 2022, https://hdd.works/3Psad5w.

Trent the Technician

Screener:
How many HVAC repairs did you complete last week? [threshold: >4]

Trent's been an HVAC technician for 7 years; 4 years of that at HinH. After a couple of years off, Trent enrolled in a 2 year program on the advice of a close friend who was doing the same. Getting his first job wasn't as easy as everyone said—and the money was terrible. But now he's a senior technician at HinH and the money's pretty good.

Figure 2-7:
Trent the Technician

He's always had a knack for fixing things, probably owing to his concentration, curiosity, and tenacity. He's never been much for debating or arguing. He likes figuring things out and even more than that he loves coming through for people. More than his billings on a job, that's what really makes it or breaks it for him—whether the customer is happy and better off or whether they're confused and frustrated.

His day starts as late as it can—he prefers to sleep in but usually has to get to the office early. He prepares for his jobs and then hits the road as quickly as he can to avoid traffic. If he's lucky, he has the parts he needs for the job and doesn't have to deal with the logistics of getting them. If he's not, there's a lot of time on the phone and sometimes back and forth, and not all of it is billable.

He knows dispatch does the best they can, but sometimes he feels like he's zig-zagging all over town and spending most of his time in traffic, which doesn't pay; as a senior technician he's mainly paid on his billable hours. Sometimes that gets pretty frustrating.

He tends to use his own mobile phone at work for email, text, and looking for documents online. The company provides a tablet-based device, but it's kind of hard to use and he just refers to it for dispatch and a few other things.

THINKS:
Trent thinks the dispatch process should be more systematic to avoid jobs that are far away or not consistent with his expertise. Also, he wonders if there isn't a better way to stock and distribute parts—that's a big problem. All this is important because a lot of his time is wasted and he's paid hourly for jobs.

SEES:
Trent sees that a lot of the company's best talent either goes into business for themselves or goes to work at large clients. They often end up with better hours and better pay. Sometimes, though, they end up short on business or having to put in long hours to do their own marketing and admin stuff.

FEELS:
When Trent is sitting in traffic for a job he could have gone to earlier that day in 1/3 the time he feels angry, he feels cheated and like the company doesn't care.

DOES:
Trent works around 45 hours per week. He's regularly on his personal iPhone looking up equipment manuals since it's easier than the company-provided tools.

Table 2-2: Trent the Technician's Jobs-to-be-Done

Jobs-to-be-Done	Current Alternatives	Your Value Proposition
Getting replacement parts to a job site	Call the office and request the part then wait for an update on the phone or through a call-back	If we automate parts lookup and ordering online, then the technicians will use it and it will improve outcomes.
Getting all the necessary information to arrive at a job fully prepared	What the customer tells dispatch isn't always conveyed or consumed by the technician and the customer ends up repeating themselves or the technician ends up with less information than they need. Trent often calls dispatch on his way in and tries to get a quick briefing; he reads the notes on the job if they're available.	If we create a more structured, automated request and dispatch process with better routing and presentation of notes from the customer, then Trent will use these notes and it will reduce his mean time to repair.
CHILD: Customer needs and needs for the job should be discovered and documented for communication to Trent systematically during dispatch calls	Some dispatchers keep a sort of checklist but it's not company-wide.	If we create an adaptive checklist to make it systematic and easy for dispatch to troubleshoot, they'll use the list and it will improve the number of calls that end with the post-mortem 'diagnosed and resolved'.

Cadence & Design Sprints

How do you make time for this kind of persona work and testing? How much is too much and how much is too little? As designer Erika Hall puts it, how do you arrange to do 'just enough research'?[6]

A common but destructive way to treat personas is like the foundation of a building, where once it's 'done' it's 100% ready to have things built on it. Instead, a better way to look at cadence in the context of HDD and Continuous Design is to consider whether a given proposition for something the team might invest in building has an observed and tested persona and JTBD. If not, it's time to do a little research.

---

6 Erika Hall and Kio Stark, *Just Enough Research* (New York, NY: A Book Apart, 2019).

The diagram below shows this approach in action (note: this mentions an addition to the persona called 'Day in the Life', which you can read about in the supplemental resources at the end of the chapter):

Figure 2-8: Testing a Right Problem Hypothesis

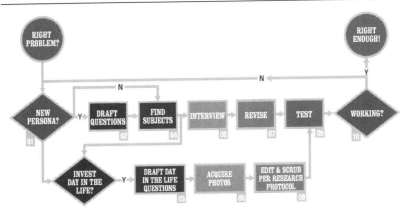

When testing a Right Problem (Persona & JTBD) Hypothesis looks like the right focus for a team, it's important that's where they focus, instead of treating the research as a nice-to-have for when someone has extra time. A popular way to handle this is focusing the team on a one-week 'design sprint' where the team gets in, asks and answers their question, and then makes a crisp decision about what this tells them they should do next, in an agile fashion. A design sprint 'shorts' the product pipeline and you can think of it in the context of the product pipeline as looking something like this:

Figure 2-9: A Design Sprint

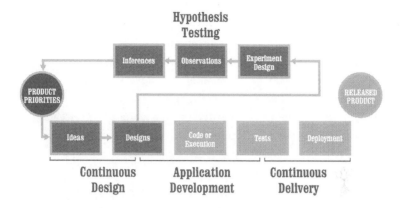

In practice, I see a lot of teams overdo their 'Right Problem' (persona & JTBD) research at the start of a new program and underdo it later on when they actually have better, more pressing questions. For example, if your marketing isn't performing well, and you need better intuition about where and how to connect with new demand, such a design sprint can be an excellent use of time. As a team moves from an early market to a larger, mainstream market, those new customers will likely be different enough where it's a win for the team to update and expand their personas and JTBD. Finally, after they start learning more about what user habits they're able to create around their product and want to better tune their analytics and growth strategies, getting back to the foundation of who the user is and what's on their A-list is an excellent way to avoid getting stuck by trying to solve problems or do jobs that aren't actually important to the user.

The final section of the chapter offers ideas on practice and resources.

Antipatterns & Failure Modes

While there is certainly no single right way to do this work, there are some common anti-patterns and failure modes.

1. *Focusing on Output over Outcomes*

   This work does not show well to management that lacks experience with hands-on, applied innovation. It's much easier to focus on work that looks and feels more tangible, like prototypes and project plans. The article 'Why Great PM's Don't Work on Solutions' at the end of the chapter is an excellent discussion of this.

2. *Outsourcing the 'Market Research'*

   A legacy take on this work is that it is 'market research' and amenable to outsourcing.[7] However, for an innovation team, this *is* the work and outsourcing it usually leads to low fidelity results and a lack of integration into the team's iterative/agile processes.

3. *Big Design Up Front*

   Often tied to outsourcing, this approach involves large, up-front design work where the outputs are not well linked to related downstream processes (like testing the Demand Hypothesis, let alone development) and conducted too infrequently.

4. *Design Theater*

   If a group of 30-somethings sit in a room, draft the 'Georgia the Golden Years Dater', and then do no actual subject interviews, this would be design theater. Strong design has everything to do with curiosity and engagement with real users.

5. *Partial Attention*

   If this is something that one person on the team does if they can while the team proceeds to do the 'real' work of building software on an uncertain foundation of demand, this will yield poor results.

---

7 By this I mean outsourcing the work entirely. Working with consultants/trainers to practice the work can be a good way to get started and enhance the teams' skills faster.

6. *Not Being Specifically Right or Wrong*
   This is the most subtle but difficult failure mode. It's easy
   to build a product that some people say they like and that
   looks 'fine' and then have it encounter an echoing silence.
   A digitally literate general manager instead takes big ideas,
   sequences them into testable pieces, and tests them as
   efficiently as possible to a definitive, actionable result to
   minimize waste.

How do you test demand with a minimum of waste?

The right way to test demand is simple: You decide what evidence would
demonstrate demand and test for it. The wrong way would be to a) build
out the whole product and then see if anyone wants it or b) ask potential
customers 'Would you buy this?' Path 'a' is bad because there are usually
options for testing that don't require you to build out the full product, and
'b' is bad (though common) because a subject will almost always tell you
'yes' to avoid being sold to and also avoid the general awkwardness of
telling another person 'no'.

Figure 2-10: Double Diamond and the Demand Hypothesis

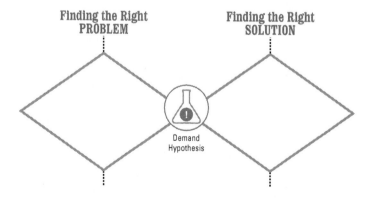

It would be nice if you could just ask subjects if they'll buy or use your solution, but the story of a focus group Phillips ran for their yellow boombox does a great job of showing why this doesn't work. Phillips, the Dutch consumer electronics giant, was rolling out a yellow boombox and held a focus group to see what the public thought. They held a focus group asking about colors, and most of the participants (teens) chose yellow.[8] Here's the surprising part—they were also offered a boombox on the way out, most chose *black*. As weird as this sounds, if you've done design research and seen it through to testing with the customer, this story probably doesn't surprise you. Focus

group participants, even interview subjects, are mostly motivated to finish. It's not their job to make sure your test results are valid; instead, they'll probably just supply you a false positive (an arbitrary "yes") so they can get on with the rest of their lives.

Hypothesis Formulation & Testing

The good news is that there is a body of work around Lean Startup and the use of MVPs (minimum viable products), that works well for testing a Demand Hypotheses. While often mistaken for a 1.0 of your actual product, the idea with an MVP is to instead create a customer experience that's as minimal as possible for testing your Demand Hypothesis. The diagram below summarizes the process:

---

8 R Cross and A Dixit, *Customer-Centric Pricing: The Surprising Secret of Profitability*, (Business Horizons 48, 2005), 483-491.

Figure 2-11: The Demand Hypothesis: From Idea to Decision

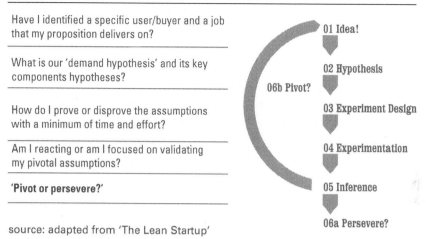

Have I identified a specific user/buyer and a job that my proposition delivers on?	01 Idea!
What is our 'demand hypothesis' and its key components hypotheses?	02 Hypothesis
	06b Pivot?
How do I prove or disprove the assumptions with a minimum of time and effort?	03 Experiment Design
Am I reacting or am I focused on validating my pivotal assumptions?	04 Experimentation
'Pivot or persevere?'	05 Inference
source: adapted from 'The Lean Startup'	06a Persevere?

In step 01, you want to make sure you have a strong idea that's worth testing. Ask any practicing scientist about how to get a good experimental result and you're likely to hear that the best way is to bring in a strong, well explored hypothesis. This was the role of our prior hypotheses (persona and JTBD) for 'Finding the Right Problem'. Specifically, make sure the JTBD you observed substantially exists on the part of your persona, you understand the current alternative, and have a testable view of why you think the persona would prefer your alternative, your Value Proposition. Here is an example from HVAC in a Hurry.

Jobs-to-be-Done	Current Alternatives	Your Value Proposition
Getting replacement parts to a job site	Call the office and request the part then wait for an update on the phone or through a call-back	If we automate parts lookup and ordering online, then the technicians will use it and it will improve outcomes.

In step 02 of the hypothesis chart, you frame your idea as a testable proposition, a Demand Hypothesis. You can see an example in the last column of the example here from HVAC in a Hurry. For, say, a dating app focused on the elderly, it might be something like: 'If I offer a dating app to Georgia the Golden Years Dater, she'll download it, try it, and subscribe to the service'. As simple and obvious as these initial Demand Hypotheses might seem, get your team into a room, ask them to create one for your product, and you're likely to find a lot of variation.

In step 03, you design experiments to test your Demand Hypothesis. The body of work around Lean Startup has produced a lot of useful comparables and lessons learned. The general idea is to create the MVP that most efficiently (most 'minimally') delivers you an answer on your demand hypothesis.

A classic is the 'Smoke Test MVP' where, for example, you run Google AdWord (or Facebook, or Instagram) ad campaigns that bring the visitor to a sign-up page where they can opt-in to learn more. Key to doing good work in the area is framing your dependent variable (DV), the variable you're going to observe and making sure you have a clear 'pass/fail' or, in Lean Startup terms, 'pivot or persevere' threshold for these. For example, this might simply mean deciding that a click-through rate (CTR) on your add <3% means you need to rethink the concept.

Depending on where you are in testing your Demand Hypotheses, the body of work on Lean Startup has evolved a portfolio of MVP archetypes: Concierge, Wizard of Oz and Smoke Test. The table below describes these in more detail.

Table 2-3: MVP Archetypes

MVP Archetype	Description	Outputs
Concierge	Hand create the experience of interest for the persona of interest, usually without a digital UI, and observe how it goes.	A general understanding of how the focal persona relates to your reimagined version of the experience.
Wizard of Oz	Present a digital UI to the customer, but have a human operator behind the scenes (the 'wizard') executing the underlying UX.	A general understanding of how the focal persona relates to your take (including the UI) of the reimagined experience.
Smoke Test	Create an exchange of value where the customer would need to exhibit some type of buying behavior, even if it's preliminary—clicking through on an ad, for instance.	A definitive pass/fail based on your target threshold for the behavior in question: click-through, purchase, or sign-up, for example.

The team at startup Aardvark used a portfolio of MVPs to test a backlog of B2C concepts and then iteratively test their way to what became the social search engine, Aardvark. They started out with a set of ideas as wide-ranging as a phone-based concierge to help you do things online to a web automation tool for consumers. Through 'smoke testing', they eliminated five ideas with low demonstrated interest from prospective customers and settled on a 'social search'. Their observation was that while Google was great at answering factual questions like 'What day of the week does Christmas fall on this year?', it was not great at answering contextual questions of opinion like 'What's the best renter's insurance?'

Their solution design had users add friends through their social networks after which they would ask and answer questions for each other. While these two-sided transactions are a durable asset at scale, they present the challenge of testing how to get to that scale. For this, they used a series of Wizard of Oz Archetype MVPs where, for example, human operators would manually route questions to a given user's social network to observe and learn what worked and make sure the 'asker' had a good experience.

This team could have easily invested years of their lives and millions of dollars into a concept they were able to test and discard after just a few weeks. Even after that, they could have lost momentum or invested in the wrong take on the final solution, which they avoided by careful stepwise testing of the solution with Wizard of Oz MVPs. The team acquired quite a few happy users, and Google acquired them in February of 2010 for $50M.

My last company, Leonid Systems, built enterprise software for communications companies—cable, phone, and mobile operators, for instance. Out of a total of four products, we built three using Concierge MVPs and one just because I was sure it was a great idea. Guess which one out of the three didn't sell well? Yes, that's right, the one I built based on my inspiration.

Another great feature of the Concierge MVP for us was our ability to deliver value through it with consulting. For example, we had several consulting engagements helping clients standardize and streamline their provisioning process–the creation of new user accounts. After a few, I identified a few JTBD that were begging for automation. Our first software product Loki Provisioning, was sold before we wrote a line of code and continually improved on the basis of what was working for customers. In 2015, the company was acquired by BroadSoft (which was later acquired by Cisco), and I'm proud of the work we did there–except that one product I had us build without evidence. I'm less proud about that one part!

The only bad experiment is one that's inconclusive. This is sometimes the case with a team that's new to the approach, but with a little practice, this is an excellent investment in getting to more valuable outcomes with a hypothesis-driven approach. The next section shows a more fully articulated experiment design to test our 'dating app for the elderly' example, and the resources at the end of this chapter offer a few ideas on active practice, if you're interested.

Here you can see an example of what a 'Smoke Test MVP' might look like.

Table 2-4: Summary Experiment Design (Dating App for the Elderly)

Component	Notes
What Demand Hypothesis will this test?	If I offer a dating app to Georgia the Golden Years Dater, she'll download it, try it, and subscribe to the service
How?	I'll run a set of Google AdWords campaigns to test acquisition
What is/are the pivotal metric(s)? What is the threshold for true (validated) vs. false (invalidated)?	absolute click-through-rate; I'd like to see >=3% on the top campaign
What will you do next if the result is true? False?	True (along with previous): Build a simple 1.0 False (top CTR's <3%): Revise customer creation plan & test an alternate topic assessment strategy

Does every concept the team is thinking of developing need to go through this type of testing? Not necessarily, but once teams have the experience of avoiding a few bad decisions and racking up a few wins this way, they tend to carefully consider testing demand/interest before they invest substantial resources. Also, as a product and customer base mature, some of these experiments become more simple and routine. For example, new features are sometimes tested with a 'fake feature test' where a small subset of users are presented with a button or menu item to engage with the hypothetical feature that leads to stub (or error) as a way to measure interest.

Antipatterns & Failure Modes

1. *An MVP is just a 1.0 with Less Features*

   Frequently, companies use these terms interchangeably. Words are faulty instruments and what matters is practice, but these two items have different objectives that rarely overlap in strong practice. In our framing of Continuous Design, the goal with an MVP is to test your Demand Hypothesis with a minimum of waste—ideally not writing any software at all. The scope for a 1.0 is whatever you feel is the right next vehicle to experiment with *given that* you feel you've validated your Demand Hypothesis.

   Now, I'm certainly not the Lean Startup police and practice will vary, but, in general, the downside of conflating these two is that for the same amount of time and money, you get fewer shots at a really great outcome.

2. *Diffuse Targets Delivering Noisy Results*

   The intention of moving from Persona and JTBD Hypotheses to Demand Hypotheses is that teams are much more likely to connect with demand since they've narrowed with the Persona and JTBD hypotheses to a specific, screenable target for testing with MVP's. On the other hand, if you start with an interesting Demand Hypothesis and test it with whoever shows up, your results may look poor even if with a more specific population it would perform well.

3. *Validating vs. Testing*

   As much as it's all our natural inclination to want to be right, the whole idea with testing is to be curious about whether you're right or wrong, and about what might be next. This is pretty crucial to a successful practice of HDD.

How do you take an evidence-driven approach to usability?

The single most common issue with Continuous Design and usability is where the team confuses usability with more fundamental questions you've learned about—finding the right problem or testing demand. For example, this is not the place to ask a subject, 'By the way, would you want this feature?' They will always give you a yes, and for an actionable test of demand, the team is best served by using the methods from Lean Startup.

Instead, you want to prompt the user to try to do something with a version of your interface (even just a clickable prototype), and then you see if they can do it, and how smoothly, how efficiently, they completed a given task with the UI.

In this testing, we are over in the second diamond, 'Finding the Right Solution', so if you haven't validated your Right Problem hypotheses and your Demand Hypothesis then you may be designing something no one wants, even if it's highly usable.

Figure 2-12: The Usability Hypothesis

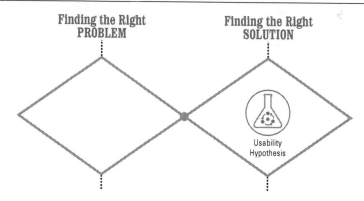

Finding the Right
PROBLEM

Finding the Right
SOLUTION

Usability
Hypothesis

User Stories & Hypothesis Formulation & Testing

Long a central feature of agile development, the agile user story does an excellent job of serving as a working usability hypothesis while fitting in well with the work of a digital team. These have the format you see in the user story diagram.[9]

Figure 2-13: Agile User Story

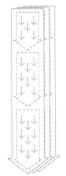

"As a [persona],
I want to [do something]
so that I can [realize some testable reward]"

Figure 2-14: Usability Hypothesis, Expanded

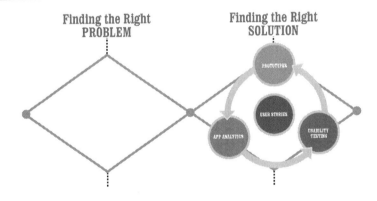

---

9 Like so many things in agile there is no absolute or even universally accepted format for user stories, but the one you see here is common and helps keep each atomic user story testable.

For example, if HVAC in a Hurry is designing a feature to help technicians look up the pricing and availability of HVAC replacement parts, they might start with a user story like: '

> As Trent the HVAC technician, I want to know the pricing and availability of a part that needs replacing so I can decide my next steps.'

The most important, most neglected, part of these user stories is the testable reward. Of course, this is the part that makes them compatible with a hypothesis-driven approach. It is the anchor point for both single subject usability testing and for thoughtful work on descriptive analytics once a version of the story's released. However, time and time again, when I'm coaching someone on user stories, the easiest way to improve them is through making sure there's a relevant, testable reward. It creates clarity around who the user is, their goals, and whether the story is arbitrary and prescriptive (ex: 'I want to push the buy button...').

If you and your collaborators are having trouble coming up with that third clause, the testable reward, that's a *good sign* in the sense that you're asking each other the right questions. For example, one of the main startups I work on right now, Jedburgh Technologies, offers a VR language learning app for advanced learners in places like the US Department of Defense. One of our focal personas is Airman Allie, who's in an intensive language learning program. We were working out a new live practice feature and had this seemingly obvious user story: *As Airmen Allie, I want to practice live with a peer, so I can ...*

What? We had ideas, but we weren't sure. Would this live practice be a mandatory part of the student's classes? Would it count toward a general bucket of language lab hours? Would it be just a voluntary activity they could undertake to improve their scores? It turned out we had a little (not a lot but a little) work to do to refine our JTBD Hypothesis before we could really dial in the specifics on this user story and connect it in a relevant way to the rest of what the student was doing on the application.

Once you get into the details on UX and writing stories, you'll actually find there's a lot of smaller stories within the stories, and good stories are relatively small. One thing I like to do when I'm decomposing one of these broader (often called 'epics') user stories to smaller stories is sketch a storyboard, and you can see an example of this transition from epic to testable 'child' stories in the examples below.

The excellent part about doing this work from the standpoint of HDD is that these user stories are ready to go as test items, and you can see an example of them working that way in the section that follows. Anyone on the team (with a little practice) can then draft a usability test plan to prompt the user to action and observe the results and draft an interactive prototype in a tool like Balsamiq to do the testing. You can see an example of such a prototype in the next section and an example of such testing in the video linked here.

Figure 2-15: Usability Testing—A Dramatization![10]

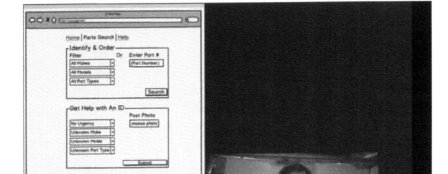

The most crucial part of creating good prompts for the subject is figuring out how to avoid leading them. For example, if your user interface (UI) has a red button that says 'Buy' on it and you ask the subject something like, 'Can you show me how you would click on the red buy button?', it's unlikely they'll fail. But that doesn't tell you much. Instead, align your prompts with the underlying intention of the user story. For example, 'Would you show me how you'd complete the purchase?' would be a better prompt in this example.

---

10 "Running a Usability Design Sprint Skit," Coursera, accessed July 21, 2022, https://hdd.works/3z19Isi.

The examples that follow unpack this epic with child stories, related testing prompts, and an early prototype: *As Trent the HVAC technician, I want to know the pricing and availability of a part that needs replacing so I can decide my next steps.*

Figure 2-16: Storyboarding an Epic User Story

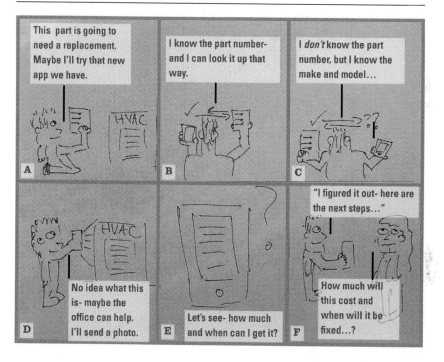

Table 2-5: Child Stories as Usability Test Items

#	Research Objective	Notes
1	How am I doing on this user story: I know the part number and I want to find it on the system so I can find out its price and availability.	**MODERATOR GUIDE** Hand the user the applicable prop (HVAC part with a part number visible) and ask them how they'd look it up on the system. Ask them to use the paper cheater to enter the part number. Then (on success), progress to the next page and ask them to ID the part and its pricing and availability **OUTPUT** Did the subject find the correct field for the part number and click the right button to advance? Did they ID the pricing and availability of the applicable part on the following page?.
2	How am I doing on this user story: I don't know the part number and I want to try to identify it online so I can find out its price and availability.	**MODERATOR GUIDE** Hand the user the applicable prop where the make and type is clearly visible and ask them how they'd look it up on the system. **OUTPUT** Did the subject find the correct fields and click the right button to advance? Did they ID the pricing and availability of the applicable part on the following page?
3	How am I doing on this user story: I don't know the part number and I can't determine it and I want help so I can find out its price and availability.	**MODERATOR GUIDE** Prompt the user that they aren't able to ID this part and want help. **OUTPUT** Did the subject find the correct fields and upload a photo? Do they understand what's going to happen next?

Figure 2-17: Clickable Prototype Example (tool: Balsamiq)

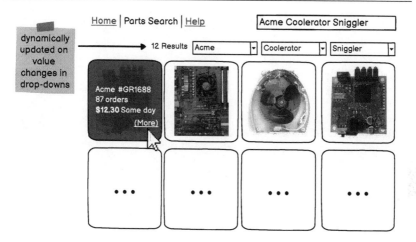

Designing towards a Clickable Prototype

How does the team arrive at this prototype? Generally, a team will start with user stories and then ask, 'What kind of interface elements might the user be expecting for this user story based on similar things they've done in the past?'

The team then answers that question by considering comparable UI's and user interface patterns. These need not be from your particular domain, in fact, you have much better odds of arriving at good answers if you push yourself to diverge and look at more alternatives. For example, given that the user stories at HinH have to do with finding a particular item among several similar items, looking at certain details about it, and then ordering it, they might take a look at online shopping sites as a relevant comparable.

Figure 2-18: Online Shopping Comparables

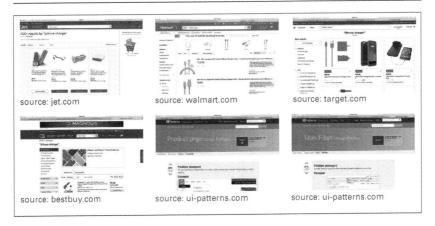

source: jet.com   source: walmart.com   source: target.com

source: bestbuy.com   source: ui-patterns.com   source: ui-patterns.com

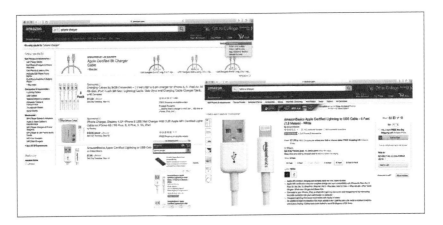

While good, these sites deal with a more varied set of items. How might the patterns be different for a site with a set of more similar items, since the HVAC parts are fairly similar? The team might also take a look at used car sites.

Figure 2-19: Used Car Comparables

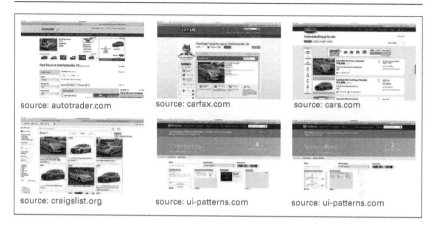

source: autotrader.com

source: carfax.com

source: cars.com

source: craigslist.org

source: ui-patterns.com

source: ui-patterns.com

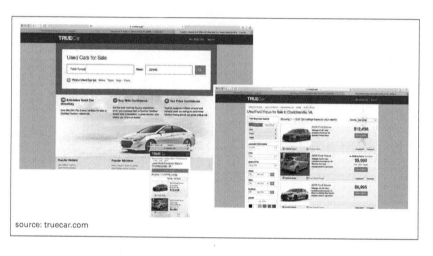

source: truecar.com

Someone on the team also suggests looking at photo search sites, since much of the searches are visual. For easier contrast, the team decides to capture these comparables with photos of cars.

Figure 2-20: Photo Site Comparables

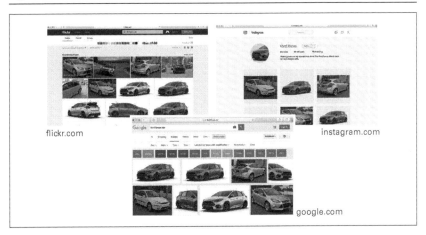

flickr.com

instagram.com

google.com

From the comps, the team makes notes on what they see as the good, the bad, and the interesting of the various application components and interface patterns. From there, the team develops parallel prototypes, here again pushing themselves to diverge and consider several possibilities.

Figure 2-21: Parallel Prototyping

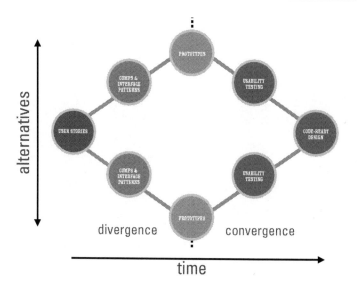

They converge on two takes, both of which they'll test with users.
Concept 1 is more informed by commerce sites where Concept 2 is more
informed by photo search.

Figure 2-22: Parallel Concept 1

CONCEPT 1

Home | Parts Search | Help

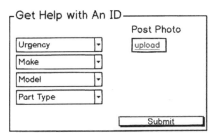

┌─Identify & Order──────────

Filter   Or   Enter Part #

| Make ▼ | (Part Number)

| Model ▼ |

| Part Type ▼ |

Search

┌─Get Help with An ID──────────

Post Photo

| Urgency ▼ | upload

| Make ▼ |

| Model ▼ |

| Part Type ▼ |

Submit

A) 'I know the part and I want to order it so I can figure out next steps on the repair.'

B) 'I don't know the part and I want to try to identify it online so I can move the job forward.'

C) 'I don't know the part and I can't determine it and I want help so I can move the job forward.'

Figure 2-23: Parallel Concept 2

CONCEPT 2

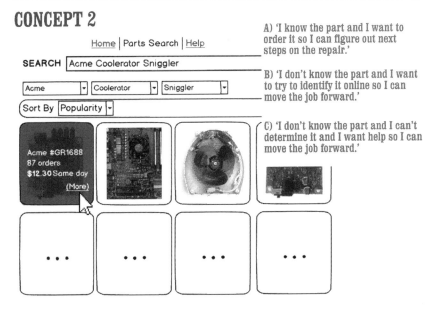

Home | Parts Search | Help

SEARCH   Acme Coolerator Sniggler

| Acme ▼ | Coolerator ▼ | Sniggler ▼ |

Sort By Popularity ▼

Acme #GR1688
87 orders
$12.30 Same day
(More)

• • •   • • •   • • •   • • •

A) 'I know the part and I want to order it so I can figure out next steps on the repair.'

B) 'I don't know the part and I want to try to identify it online so I can move the job forward.'

C) 'I don't know the part and I can't determine it and I want help so I can move the job forward.'

It's always a lot more convenient to sit in your office and build another prototype or update the code, rather than dealing with the messy business of recruiting test subjects and seeing what they actually do. But there's no substitute for taking a hypothesis-driven approach and doing it in small batches. The alternative is to generate waste, depriving you and your team of time and energy to pursue another idea or item that will deliver the results you want.

Working in small, agile iterations with testable hypotheses specifically helps avoid overcorrection. For example, I worked with some collaborators on a mood board product called Brand Lattice. It involved a drag and drop affordance which wasn't something users were particularly accustomed to doing on the web–where many didn't have a 'mental 'model' of how it would work. We knew this was a risk and tested our UIs early and often.

The first take (see left image below) tested pretty poor with 70% of users getting stuck. We had an increasingly heavy-handed set of fixes, a video pop-up for instance, but when you're asking for the user's attention and energy for a given task, less is always more. Given how often we were testing, however, we were comfortable starting with the very minor update you see on the right—a tiny annotation. When we retested, it turns out this did the trick, with all the subjects getting through the task.

Figure 2-24: Evidence-Based Iteration at Brand Lattice

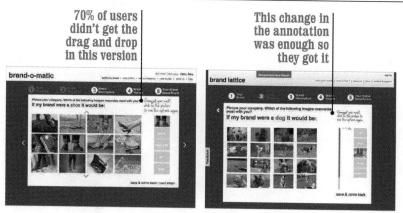

Cadence

For any material interface update or code investment, it's hard to see the case for investing in detailed design let alone development if the team hasn't done early exploratory testing of usability. Once the team is in the habit of doing this, the drafting and discussion of user stories and exploratory testing that goes with it map readily into typical agile cadences and processes and help avoid waste while improving collaboration among the team.

Thinking about testability will help you provide better, more thought-out inputs to your design and dev collaborators. Over time, it gives a team perspective and lessons they can apply to making crisper decisions. By contrast, in the case of products with less intentional design programs, if you try to find out why something was built a certain way, all you may find are rumors and hearsay. That may sound like a minor nuisance, but over time many good products transition to bad products because the team or teams don't have the confidence to remove outdated features and UI elements. This results in a progressive accumulation of 'UX debt' that can lead to a product that's bloated and difficult to use.

Anti-patterns & Failure Modes

1. *Trying to Test Demand (or Right Problem) with Usability*
   This is deeply problematic for two reasons. First, putting a user in front of a prototype and asking them if they would buy it does not deliver reliable indicators of demand. Second, a team that hasn't done the work to make sure they're building something their user wants is likely to push for validation of their idea (vs. objective testing).

2. *User Stories with no 3rd/Testable Clause*
   The format for user stories we've explored is:
   > 'As a [persona],
   > I want to [do something]
   > so that I can [realize some testable reward].'

   This is what makes this central, everyday design artifact so compatible with a hypothesis-driven approach. A user story without the testable reward clause is not readily testable and, in my experience, is very likely not that well thought out. I have never seen a user story that didn't improve with refactoring it to have a testable reward.

3. *Only Doing Late-Stage Validation Testing*

Many teams will do heavy validation testing before they release. In part a holdover from times when companies were doing infrequent releases (and shipping physical media like CD's), teams rarely have the time or motivation to make substantial changes at this point, and if they do, they've de facto generated a lot of waste.

What success in Continuous Design Looks Like

How do you know if you're on the right track?

The real answer is that you never do exactly, and that rather than stepping through the Continuous Design process you've learned about here once and hoping everything's 'done', it's probably more important in practice to be able to diagnose what's going on with your users' relationship to the application and pair that with just enough testing to be reasonably sure you're on the right track. The table here summarizes how we've applied hypothesis-driven development to the Continuous Design process:

Table 2-6: Continuous Design & HDD

Type	Questions	Experiment Design(s)	Answers
Persona Hypothesis	Do we know enough about our user? Do we know where their latent and overt needs lie? Do we know how to reach them? Do we understand a day in their life, and where our product fits in?	Factual Screener to Recruit the Right Subjects Single-Subject Discovery Interviews with Non-Leading Questions (Ex: What are the top five hardest things about completing an HVAC repair?)	Convergent (but not identical) answers for your focal points Other outputs: • Photos • Day in the Life • Personas with Think-See-Feel-Do • Pairings with Existing Data on Users

Type	Questions	Experiment Design(s)	Answers
JTBD Hypothesis	Do we know what's on our user's A-list? By Segment? Do we know what alternatives they use now? Do we understand the trigger events and cadence for our target JTBD?	(same as persona hypothesis)	Prioritized List of JTBD & Alternatives Notes on Triggers & Cadence
Demand Hypothesis	Do we understand how our user engages with our JTBD of interest, step by step? Do we know that our user is looking for a new alternative for our target JTBD (problem/market fit)? Do we know if users would buy (use) our alternative, buy into our VP (product/proposition fit)?	Demand Tests with MVP's: • Concierge Test • Smoke Test • Wizard of Oz Test	Notes on Customer Experience (Concierge Test) Pass/Fail by Channel and Proposition (Smoke Test) Proposition (Smoke Test) User Behavior with Target UX (Wizard of Oz Test)
Usability Hypothesis	Have we reached a reasonable level of usability for {a given feature}?	Single Subject Usability Tests (Exploratory & Assessment Testing) User Analytics (Validation Testing)	Recordings and Iteration on Prototypes Pass/Fail on Thresholds for Target Dependent Variables on User Behavior

How do you make such a diagnosis? For my money, the top three are focus, consistency, and a sincere interest in your user. Designer and author Donald Norman introduced the framework you see here to sequence, understand, and observe (and test) user interactions.

Figure 2-25: Donald Norman's 7 Steps of User Cognition

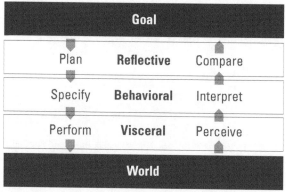

source: adapted from 'The Design of Everyday Things'

In summary, the user starts a Goal, decides on a way to achieve that Goal, interacts with something (World), and then decides whether or not they've achieved what they wanted with regard to the Goal.

Figure 2-26: Donald Norman's 7 Steps of User Cognition (Numbered)

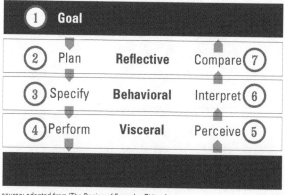

source: adapted from 'The Design of Everyday Things'

Let's take a closer look at the user story from above:
'As Trent the HVAC technician, I want to know the pricing and availability of a part that needs replacing so I can decide my next steps.'
and apply this framework across its seven steps.

Table 2-7: Donald Norman's 7 Steps Example

#	Step	Example	Definition & Testing
1	Goal: What do I want to accomplish?	JTBD: Getting Replacement Parts to a Job Site	For describing this step, I've been using the idea of a 'job-to-be-done' as equivalent to a Goal. What's critical in defining these is to make sure you're understanding it as the user does: not with regard to your particular proposition. For example, I frame the Goal as you see in the example and not with regard to our user story or as 'Ordering a Part on the Parts Ordering Application'.
			For understanding what Goals or JTBD exist on the part of your Persona ask a sequence of non-leading questions about how they operate in your general area of interest (see section above on Right Problem Hypotheses).
2	Plan: What are my alternatives?	Current Alternative: The HVAC technician calls dispatch for pricing and availability. New Alternative (our 'Value Proposition): Have the tech instead use a self-service application for obtaining pricing and availability.	I've been describing these in terms of 'trios' of JTBD, current alternatives, and new alternatives or 'Value Propositions'. For finding out about the prevailing alternatives for a given JTBD, you can use the same discovery interviews that will help you understand the Goal or JTBD itself—simply ask the subject for an example of how they last engaged on a JTBD.
			However, ask the subject whether they'd prefer your alternative/VP and you'll almost always get a 'yes' since they want to avoid the awkwardness of a 'no'. Here, you'll hit the limits of what you can substantially learn in subject interviews- and, instead, you need to design experiments against your 'Demand Hypothesis' with an MVP and a material exchange of value (see section above 'How do you test demand with a minimum of waste?').

#	Step	Example	Definition & Testing
3	Specify: What can I do?	Working prototype, and test plan for this user story: *'As Trent the HVAC technician, I want to know the pricing and availability of a part that needs replacing so I can decide my next steps.'*	Here you describe with user stories what you assume to be the user's intent to engage with your VP and then put in front of them an interface that maps as naturally as possible to how they're used to doing such things. For example, if they'll need to search or filter a set of items, consider what interface patterns they're used to using for this.
4	Perform: How do I do it?		Then, test whether or not you're right, not by seeing if they want to engage with your VP, but simply whether they can use your interface to make progress on their assumed Goal/JTBD. For example, HinH would ask an HVAC technician to find a given part with their prototype and observe how easy (or hard!) it is for them to do this.
5	Perceive: What happened?		You should also test whether your test subject understands the feedback they've gotten. In the HinH example, you can observe this indirectly by whether the subject is able to find the part and tell you its pricing and availability. However, if you were building an interface that, say, sends a request through on a form, you would close this loop by asking (after they click 'Submit', etc.) 'What just happened? What do you think is going to happen next?'
6	Interpret: What does it mean?		These items are more applicable to steps of the Reflective layer, steps #3 and #6. Steps #4 and #5 deal with a lower, more basic layer of user cognition—how the user is *subconsciously* reacting to the interface. You're often assessing this indirectly, but the easiest way to do well here (other than or in addition to working with a trained visual designer) is to carefully implement visual consistency with a style guide, and there are resources at the end of the chapter on this.
7	Compare: Is this okay?	JTBD: Getting Replacement Parts to a Job Site	Here, you observe whether or not your alternative for the JTBD is in fact preferred by the user relative to alternatives. Here, you're looking for repeat usage and continued engagement. In the HVAC in a Hurry example, they'd be looking at analytics to see if users who ordered at least one part with the application came back and ordered more, and, ultimately, whether or not they make a habit of or standardize on the team's new alternative. For example, have they ordered most (>80%) of their replacement parts through the application?

While you'll soon be learning how to apply quantitative data to your practice of HDD, that's for seeing if you're right, not finding the next big win. The valuable ideas generally come from the 'small data' you acquire from Continuous Design. For example, former Procter & Gamble CEO A.G. Lafley famously visited households to see what they were up to.[11] When the Tide (detergent) team was unsure about the wisdom of investing in R&D to make the detergent a small percentage more effective, they decided to go 'outside the building' and visit some households. When they did, they kept seeing flathead screwdrivers on top of washing machines. What they found was that customers needed these to open the metal spout on the cardboard boxes which packaged the product. The team started focusing on the process of using the product itself, leading to innovations like more liquid detergent and detergent pods.

Anti-Patterns & Failure Modes

1. *Building Prematurely*

   Many successful managers have a bias toward action, and to them, particularly if they don't have a background in product design, it may mean simply starting to code a solution. The problem with this is that to one degree or another we all hate the idea of being wrong and are all susceptible to the sunk cost fallacy.[12] In practice, what this means is that as soon as a team starts investing in building against a certain solution concept, it's very hard to change course and teams will tend to avoid evidence that proves them wrong.

2. *Hedging vs. Testing and Adapting*

   Big batches require excessive hedging—since you won't be able to try a change for a long time. These days that's anything beyond a month. If you're using big batches, you'll have to make more complex and probably questionable assumptions. Instead, executing in small batches provides better opportunities for adaptive design and designing against evidence.

---

11 "P&G Chief's Turnaround Recipe: Find out What Women Want," Gazette, June 1, 2005, https://hdd.works/3Phv4J8.

12 "Sunk Cost Fallacy," BehavioralEconomics.com | The BE Hub, October 14, 2020, https://hdd.works/3PgyN9o.

3. *Keeping Expensive Tech Talent Busy*

This is a hard one, but whether you're creating a new team as an 'intrapreneur' or building a new company as an entrepreneur, the last thing you want is a bunch of expensive talent you have to keep busy with inputs that aren't ready. Plenty of teams get locked into bad ideas because they got started on something and weren't willing to discard it. Working in smaller batches helps with this, but you still fundamentally have to have an investable, testable basis for creating a specific solution. This is one reason why many team leads are OK, for example, taking their dev colleagues on design sprints—rather than just building code that doesn't know what problem it's solving, they gain perspective that will help them engage better with their work on the product pipeline.

The Definition of Done in Continuous Design

Are you ever done in HDD & Continuous Design? Unfortunately, it's usually *not* after your first take on building a good product or feature. In fact, particularly with an existing product, this is more a matter of deciding what to prioritize as opposed to arriving at a singular definition of done. All that said, 'a great product is never done' is not a practical way to charter or run a digital program.

The single most important habit for general managers in Hypothesis-Driven Development is to pair the team's solution concepts (in the form of user stories) with relevant analytical questions and metrics. Since this 'Finding the Right Solution' step is the last phase in the Continuous Design process, this allows the team to exit the current iteration with a specific point of view on what constitutes 'done' as they move into the next iteration. Critically, such questions are based on what users *do* not what they *say*, which is a major flaw with 'acceptance testing', a popular practice where teams ask users (who are busy with their day jobs) whether a new delivery is acceptable. In the table below, you'll find an example of how this might look for the individual stories I've considered at HVAC in a Hurry.

Table 2-8: An Outcome-Based Definition of Done

#	User Story	Analytical Questions, Metrics and Experiments
1	I know the part number and I want to find it on the system so I can find out its price and availability.	How well does this search type work relative to the alternatives? How often is this search used per transaction relative to the alternatives? Metrics: • Searches of this type relative to others • Sequence of this search relative to other search types • Conversion to order from this type of search (%) Candidates for A/B testing: • Add/remove UI for user story #3 and see how it affects click-through to subsequent screens.
2	I don't know the part number and I want to try to identify it online so I can find out its price and availability.	(see above)
3	I don't know the part number and I can't determine it and I want help so I can find out its price and availability.	(see above)
4	I want to see the pricing and availability of the part so I can decide on next steps and get agreement from the customer.	How often does this lead to a part order? How will techs that do this perform relative to others? Metrics: • Conversion rate to order • Customer satisfaction per job of techs in a cohort that use the tool vs. baseline (mean customer satisfaction per job) • Billable hours for techs in this cohort vs. baseline (billable hours per week) Candidates for A/B testing: • Variations in UI and how they affect conversion to order

What We Learned

An iterative, hypothesis-driven approach to going from idea to design offers a specific body of practice that teams have been using to deliver successful outcomes. After this chapter, you can now:

1. Explain the concept of product/market fit in economic terms
2. Analyze the work of a business or product lead in terms of a sequence of testable hypotheses that minimize waste and maximize wins
3. Do the work to make sure your team is focused on a job/problem/need/desire that actually exists for a certain identifiable buyer or user.
4. Avoid false positives and minimize waste by applying Lean Startup to testing whether your proposition is competitive with the prevailing alternatives
5. Make a habit of designing for and testing usability early and often so you minimize friction for the user
6. Identify the analytics necessary to make crisp decisions for an iterative, emergent design with an outcome-focused definition of done.

These take practice and focus. But they also take a willingness to be wrong and more importantly a curiosity about the user and how you and your team can operate better. A big part of starting, continuing, and arriving at successful practice also requires an interest and willingness to more fundamentally adapt your mindset and behaviors, acting more like a Geoffrey vs. a George.

Recommended Practice & Supplemental Resources

Build Your Personal Innovation Portfolio

Just about every week I observe a paradox in how companies find the talent to execute on what we just covered. Senior managers can't hire enough product managers (or digitally literate consultants, etc.) and MBAs have trouble landing their first product management job. The answer for companies is to create a more purposeful onboarding process for new product managers, but that doesn't help you if you're in this position. My advice to anyone in this situation is to create the experience you want to have and don't wait for someone else to give it to you. Everyone has ideas—just pick one of them, start working on it, and start creating what I call a personal innovation portfolio. Regardless of where you end up on a given product, if you follow a disciplined process like the one you learned about here, the worst thing that can happen is that you learn the skills employers want and have a place to showcase them. The link here has examples and templates of portfolio entries you can use to get started:
https://hdd.works/3PDbqqv.

Focus and Test a Right Problem (Persona & JTBD) Hypothesis with Subject Interviews

Pick a specific persona (buyer and/or user) and a specific area and go do some customer discovery on a day in the life for them and what's on their A-list in your area of interest. This link has tutorials, templates, and, if you want, online courses:
https://hdd.works/3coH3Gg.

Focus And Test A Demand Hypothesis With Lean Startup

Take an idea you have and think about how you could drive to a conclusion about whether there's demand there in one week. This link has tutorials, templates, and, if you want, online courses:
https://hdd.works/3ATBA4o.

Focus and Test a Usability Hypothesis with User Stories

Pick a set of features you're thinking of building and draft user stories, followed by a usability test plan and clickable prototypes you can test with real subjects. This link has tutorials, templates, and, if you want, online courses:

https://hdd.works/3zeBBOU.

Define and Apply Visual Consistency

Create a style guide and a design system which you can update as part of your process of Continuous Design:

https://hdd.works/3RE8c89.

Learn More about the General Practice of Design

If you're interested in more depth on practice, this page offers articles and books from designers and designer educators like Don Norman and this chapter's guest editor, Jeann Liedtka:

https://hdd.works/3aPgNEA.

Guest Editor: Jeanne Liedtka

I met Jeanne when I first started teaching at Darden. She was an established superstar, if not *the* established superstar, and, frankly, I was nervous. All I got was a lot of help and a wonderful friend who my wife and kids also adore.

A year or so later, I remember the first event we did together. I remember thinking "I have a lot to learn, a long way to go, but this is where I'd like to arrive." One thing I've learned at Darden is that teaching is a job. Jeanne's pioneering interest in design thinking, engagement with industry, and practice of teaching has delivered what I think is the best set of material available on learning the actual practice of design thinking. If you want to learn more, check out her book *Experiencing Design: The Innovator's Journey* or her online course *Experiencing Design: Deepening Your Design Thinking Practice*, which you can find on Coursera.[13]

Three questions with Jeanne

Where did you first see design thinking at work and what interested you about it?

I was trained first as an accountant (my BA) and then as a business strategist (my MBA) so the underlying concept of design was really foreign to my training. But I knew that we were in sore need of new tools to help managers grow their businesses organically, because almost all of our strategy tools are evaluative, using data from the past. Clearly they were not going to cut it when our goal was creating new futures. My original interest in design was grounded in architecture, reading about how people like Frank Gehry worked. They had a goal, a strategic intent, and a set of values. With these as a guide, they iterated their way to shaping spaces. I thought that was a great metaphor—the

---

13 Jeanne Liedtka, Karen Hold, and Jessica Eldridge, *Experiencing Design the Innovator's Journey* (New York: Columbia Business School Publishing, 2021); Jeanne Liedtka, "Experiencing Design: Deepening Your Design Thinking Practice," Coursera, accessed July 17, 2022, https://hdd. works/3zbFrID.

idea of designing a purpose-driven space—for the work I wanted to do in strategy. Of course, metaphors are cool, but they are not tools. But then along came design thinking and the toolkit and methodology it brought. Its behaviors were very different from what we were teaching MBAs—but I noticed they mapped almost exactly onto the intuitive approaches of the natural growth leaders I studied. So I started to believe that if we taught them to the Georges of the world, they could begin to imitate Geoff's' innovation success. Not by becoming Geoff, but by expanding their toolkit to do what Geoff did intuitively. A decade later, I believe that my hypothesis has been proven true.

What do you think we've learned about design thinking in the last 15 years that we either didn't know or weren't sure about?
Since I knew nothing at all about design thinking 15 years ago, everything I have learned is new! Even after all this study and teaching though, I still find myself (with my old accountant and strategist training) bumping up against the very different set of beliefs that underlie DT. My false sense of efficiency—that getting to "the" answer quickly is best, even though I know now that there is no single "right" answer—still rears it ugly head. Worries about "small n" still trouble me—even though I know that the front-end of DT uses data to *inspire* rather than to *prove*, so sample size is less relevant. And the old consultant in me still winces when students show their client stuff that looks like a kindergartener produced it—but I'm getting there!

What do you think will be the big differences between the MBA of 2030 and the MBA of today?
The MBAs I see today are already quite different from the ones I taught ten years ago. In many ways, the difference is more about their mindsets than their skill sets—today's young are much more willing to be skeptical about big business, to be committed to issues like environmental sustainability, to make their way without the same worries about the career ladder and the like that have always been characteristic of business school students. A lifetime of playing video games has left them much more comfortable with the idea of losing or dying in this round, with the intention of learning by trial and error

to do better in the next one. I contrast it to those of us who grew up reading the rules to each other on the lid of the Monopoly box, and I see a lot that is a good change. I worry though that, as educators, the skills we are teaching them haven't yet caught up to these shifts in mindset. Design thinking, agile and Lean Start-Up, and this new generation's interest in these new methods is helping, but I still think we have a long way to go. We are still turning out analyzers rather than experimenters. That shift is an extremely difficult one, both in terms of mindsets and skills, and I don't think we educators have yet got the teaching tools we need to help students navigate the change. But I am pleased to see books like this one from Alex, that will help us get there.

3

FROM DESIGN TO CODE

Figure 3-1: Application Development and HDD

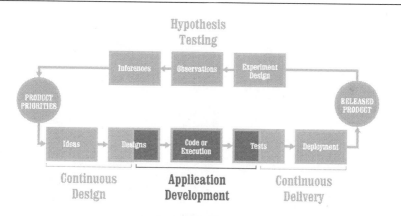

If you've ever seen a movie where a hacker has to do something under intense pressure, you probably saw them furiously type something, press a key, and then have everything magically work, saving the day. This is almost never how coding works in real life. Given this, it's no wonder anyone who hasn't coded before is confused about what the work actually entails and how they make themselves a better collaborator to the coders that do it.

Metaphors to explain code development are notoriously fraught. Construction metaphors are easy to understand, but fall down in a number of places, particularly in how code needs to be amenable to change. You could just as accurately say that coding is like writing a screenplay that has to be very tightly executed.

For the last five years, I've taught a class called 'Software Development' for MBA students at UVA Darden.[1] Believe me, it's even stranger than it sounds. It's not a 'coding bootcamp'—these students aren't looking to do a career pivot into being a software developer. It's also not an intro-level computer science course, since they're not looking to major in CS. These students are specifically looking to get better at working with collaborators, going from design to code. They do it by coding, and by the end of the week, they're all writing fully functional applications in HTML, CSS, and JS.

But the coding is very much a means to an end. The important learnings for them have to do with how the quality of a design, in particular its testability, helps or hinders the process of going from design to code.

Do you need to learn how to code?

In a word, yes. It's rare to find a high-functioning manager in tech who sees themselves as completely apart from the work of their 'technical' collaborators. In an innovation-intensive environment, small, inter-disciplinary teams with fluid boundaries and interfaces are more likely to be successful than siloed teams with larger, less frequent hand-offs.

Do you need to be as informed and experienced as your collaborators in development? In a word, no. Also, of course not—that's not your job. Mainly, your technical collaborators want you to bring them high-quality inputs, inputs that help them think through how to create a durable infrastructure for the target UX. Sometimes you'll need to understand the details of what's going on with the code, sometimes you won't. On the whole, acquiring an intuition about how software is generally built and then staying inquisitive will take you a long way in your practice of HDD.

---

1 The syllabus is available here: https://hdd.works/3nX8SrI, and an online version of the class is here: https://hdd.works/3yDwLJR.

The Model-View-Controller (MVC) Framework

The MVC is extremely useful as a first-order framework for understanding or explaining a software application. The basic idea is to decompose the software in terms of the MVC's components. Basically, the Model is where the data lives, the View is what the user sees, and the Controller is the set of logic, including the specific instructions coded into the software, that tells the application how it should respond to inputs from the user. The components interact in that the user passes inputs to the View, which then consults the Controller, which usually needs to retrieve data from the Model, do something else, and then return the updated data to display in the View.

Figure 3-2: The Model View Controller Framework

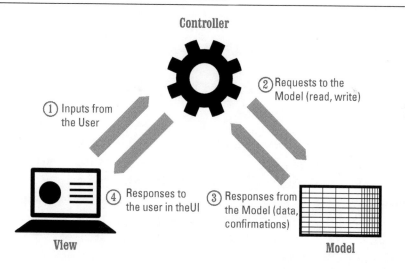

Let's start with the example of logging into Facebook.[2] A user visits the site (or opens the app) and sees a View something like what you see here. They type their email and password into the View you see, and then they press the 'Log In' button. Now, the View passes those inputs to the Controller and it executes a series of steps something like this:

1. Check if the username exists by looking it up in the Model (where all this data lives)
    a. if it does, proceed
    b. if not, return an error to the View letting the user know
2. Check if the password is correct by checking it with the Model
    a. if it is, log the user in, fetch their feed and show that to them in the View
    b. if it is not, return and send an error to the View letting the user know

You may see or hear about more particular takes on the MVC, particularly as it's implemented in various development frameworks, but if you just explain that by *Model* you mean where the data is, *View* what the user sees, and *Controller* the application logic, I think you'll find this a useful way to initially unpack and understand a software application or system with its developers. In fact, you could even explain it in a sentence or two to someone that's not familiar with the MVC using an example, and that's a great way to test and practice your understanding.

There's nothing inherently 'right' about the MVC. It's only useful to the extent it helps collaborators arrive at a productive, shared understanding of their work together. 'User Interface' or 'UI' is another term you'll likely hear for what the MVC calls the View. While it does less well at describing the diversity of approaches we have today, you may also hear about 'front end' vs. 'back end' development.

---

2 Yes, I know it's for old people now.

The idea with this front end vs. back end distinction is that there's code that handles user interaction and then code that deals with the rest of the application or system. In this case, the 'front end' code will have a View, of course, and also its own logic, sometimes called 'front Controllers'. While it may have some of its own data, more likely it is interacting with an interface on the 'back end' that gives it access to the relevant Model. The 'back end' code will have a data Model and Controllers, but what about a View? Interestingly, the back end's API (application programming interface) that the front end code uses to communicate with is often referred to as a 'View', even though it's a view for other developers vs. end users.

Implementing Design into Code

The single most important thing is to know what you want to have happen and be able to work from there to a good implementation. This is important for two reasons. First, as a generalist collaborating with technical talent, your single most important job is to give the inputs to build something valuable to the user.

Second, as you build creative confidence around coding, you need a focal point to avoid getting lost. Before I started teaching the Software Development[3] class at UVA Darden (and Coding for Designers, Managers, and Entrepreneurs[4] online), I would talk with MBAs who had just finished an online coding tutorial like Codecademy, but then found they didn't know what to do next, forgot the material quickly, and weren't sure if they 'really' knew how to code. In order to discuss code in this way, let alone develop it, the best way to acquire durable learning is to actively pursue a design goal you understand and have some investment in realizing.

This brings us to the three core activities we'll focus on in this chapter. I've seen this work for MBAs and other generalists across everything from building a 1.0 application in HTML, CSS, and Javascript to coding convolutional neural networks in Python for testing hypotheses with data science. They are:

3 "Software Development Class (Syllabus)," Alex Cowan, September 3, 2019, https://hdd. works/3cmgzF3/.
4 Alex Cowan, "Coding for Designers, Managers, and Entrepreneurs," Coursera, accessed July 17, 2022, https://hdd.works/3yDwLJR.

1. Unpacking Your Design into Code-Ready Steps

As you'll see in the balance of this chapter, going from design to code requires a detailed orientation that's new to most students who don't have prior experience designing or building digital applications. While your ability to see the big picture as a general manager is the foundation of what you do, being able to zero in on specifics and unpacking details is critical to successful collaborations in software development.

Our user stories serve as the input to this, and as long as they have the third clause on the reward ('...so that I can...') and some analytical questions (how you'll measure engagement), then you're starting the process with a strong anchor hypothesis about what you're trying to achieve, code-wise.

2. Effectuating a Viable Solution

Coding is not physics. For any given objective, there are lots of ways to go about it. Should you code it from scratch? Find some sample code to start from? Interface with a third party module or API?[5] Making good choices relative to your team's situation is a skill developers refine over the course of their entire career. However, even a relatively small implementation requires you to weigh alternatives and drive to a workable solution.

Why not an 'optimal' solution? For all intents and purposes, a singular, optimal solution is impossible to identify in advance. While you'll certainly have more context, it's really not even possible to figure out in retrospect since a product of any substance has so many forces determining its success. Really, no such thing as an optimal solution exists. When will the code be rewritten next? How will the user engage with it? What else will you and your team be doing in six months? These would all inform the 'optimal' choice and are unknowable, so even the most experienced developers are forced to make reasonably good choices relative to their assessment of the circumstances.

What kind of choices, specifically? For any given part of your application, you face a kind of build, borrow, or buy choice—even small stuff. Let's say you're putting together your personal blog and you want to add buttons that let your readers share your posts on social—Facebook, Twitter, etc., something like what you see here:

---

5   application programming interface

Figure 3-3: Buttons for Sharing on Social Media

How do you do that? You could just write the code yourself. As you do, you might find what you want to have happen is a little more involved than you thought: Where does the article title come from? What is the default text to describe the post? Maybe it's just the first 100 characters in the body, but then what if on some posts you want to be able to change the default since you've come up with something you think will work better on social? Oh, and what if you find you want to append a code to the end of the URL so you can easily track how many shares you're getting from your analytics system?

You can also borrow, since, thankfully, we live in an age when most coding/dev questions have pretty good (or great) answers available on Q&A sites like Stack Overflow, including sample code. Often, this works well, but these are generally snippets you'll still have to maintain. Also, sometimes those solutions are more broader and somewhat different from what you're after, and you can end up with a chunk of code that's bigger than it needs to be, a little off topic, but still has to be maintained by the team.

Finally, you can buy, even with a small item like this. Depending on how you developed the rest of your code, various third party add-ins or services may be available to take over that job for you at a price that's economical. For example, if you built your blog site on top of the WordPress application, a 'content management system' for building such sites, there's a third party plug-in (add on) called Jetpack that deals with the functionality you'd need for social sharing.

This chapter's guest editor, Laura Klein, recently worked on this with a client for 'product tour' functionality, the overlays you see when you first visit a new app or page that offers to step you through how it works with a button that says "Get Started!" or something similar.

Figure 3-4: Product Tour Wireframe

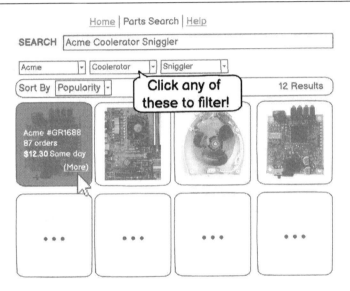

Like most new features, it looked simple at the outset—maybe they should just build it themselves? Well, it turns out it's a bunch of work if you want to allow anyone but a trained developer to be able to edit the content. Also, the product teams that were going to use it wanted to be able to A/B test and otherwise configure tours to work only with certain cohorts and types of users. Pretty soon, they realized the best choice was to use one of several 'product tour' tools that are commercially available from companies like Userpilot, Intercom, and WalkMe.

Is this part of going from design to code hypothesis-driven? Ideally, yes since this is a good way to have better, more explicit discussions about the choices you and the team are making.

3. Analytically Debugging to a Working Version

On the macro scale, week to week, individual dev's might be working on any number of things—building new software, maintaining old code, sorting out issues that made their way to production, or writing automated tests. However, regardless of which one of these they're focused on, at the micro scale devs spend most of their time debugging. To debug is to code. This comes as a surprise to many of my students who start out thinking this is a kind of clean up activity you undertake when things go wrong. In coding, something's always wrong.

The good news is that taking a hypothesis-driven approach to coding/development is the best way of both doing the work confidently and enjoying it. Essentially this means thinking of all the functional parts of your code as hypotheses where you need to specifically identify what isn't working the way you expect, how you'll instrument the right observation to see why this is happening, and from that get to a resolution. I'll show you examples below. I'm not saying I've never fixed my code by accident and blithely moved on without entirely understanding what happened—but that's not considered good practice.

In the next sections, we'll look at the actual work of going from design to code in these areas starting with the View, since it's the most intuitive and since the functionality it affords determines a lot of what needs to happen with the Controller and Model.

Creating Views from User Stories and Wireframes

Many if not most graphical Views are built with HTML & CSS, or something a lot like it.[6] For such a task, you have two foundation jobs, regardless of technology:
1. describe the functional element you want
2. configure its properties (color, how it relates to other elements, etc.)

---

6 HTML stands for 'hypertext markup language" and CSS stands for "cascading style sheets". This is good to know or at least be able to reference but not particularly important in and of itself.

For web applications (applications that run in a web browser), HTML & CSS are the essential components for doing those jobs. HTML does the job of creating the functional elements and CSS does the job of configuring its properties. Just like everything else in engineering, this distinction isn't absolute and there are various counter cases, but in terms of their core intentions, that's how HTML & CSS work.

If you follow something like the Continuous Design process you saw in Chapter 2, you'll start work on your Views with user stories and some explicit design of how you want your View to look, something like this UI prototype from HinH.

Figure 3-5: HinH UI Prototype Sketch

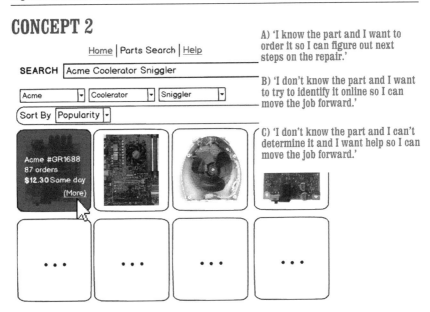

The second image you see here is a rough HTML rendition of that prototype, whose code you can find on a ready-to-use/code platform called JS Fiddle through this footnote.[7] The page is composed of HTML elements that describe the core elements and CSS that helps them look more like the UI we were after in the sketch.

---

7 See Create Views with HTML & CSS at the end of the chapter.

Figure 3-6: HinH UI in HTML

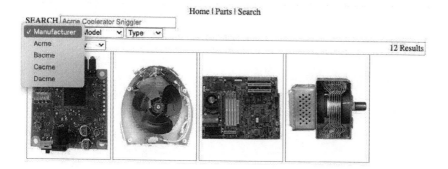

One particular element you'll see a lot of in HTML is the 'div'. This versatile element is kind of like the core rectangular lego in a lego set—you use that one piece a lot and in a number of different ways. Another example is the HTML 'select' element, which creates the drop-downs you see. Check out the 'Specifics, please?' section that follows if you want a more concrete intuition of how these work, and then we'll turn our attention to why it works so well to do the second core job of configuring elements with CSS.

Specifics, please? Laying out Functional Elements with HTML

Let's take a closer look at the drop-down box for filtering the HVAC parts by manufacturer, which is what you see active in the screenshot. If you're not used to engaging with code or equations, please know that they are not required for you to get what the book has to offer— but also that they're there to help you understand and build your creative confidence. If you're up to your elbows in code all the time, what I'll offer is that, likewise, the book is not here to teach coding, per se, but rather to present what I hope will be a vivid and specific view on practicing HDD across disciplines like design, coding, and analytics.

The HTML elements for the drop-down are what you see here. The exterior lego is the HTML element for the drop-down control, called a 'select' element. It starts with an 'opening tag', <select>, and finishes with the same tag, except with a forward slash, '/', which is called a 'closing tag': `</select>`. If you're taking a note somewhere that you need a 'select tag' to make a drop-down in HTML, my advice is: *don't*. There are over a hundred tags in HTML and it's rare for anyone to know them all by heart: rare, because it's not very useful. Instead, what's important to remember is that HTML is composed of various elements that do different jobs, and are designated by their tag names. If you want to create a drop-down in HTML, then you should do a Google search like 'create drop-down in HTML' or 'HTML element for drop-down' (bonus points for giving it a try right now!).

Figure 3-7: HTML Dropdown

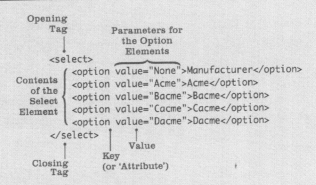

What about all the stuff between the `<select>` tags? Those are another set of HTML elements that do the job of presenting the set of items within a drop-down and they are called `<option>` tags. It's part of the construction of HTML that elements appear inside each other, 'nested'. Notice that inside the opening and closing tags for the options there is text like 'Manufacturer', 'Acme', etc., and that these match what you see in the HTML prototype.

Finally, within the opening tag of each option element, you see an item that says `value={something}`. In this case, those are an optional key (or attribute) that lets you return a different value to code than what the user sees in the drop down.

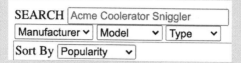

For example, if you write a Controller that says 'tell me the value of the drop-down' and the user has left the drop-down at its default value of 'Manufacturer', the code will actually get a value of 'None' returned to it. Why? Well, in this case it's an interesting difference between what you want for the user experience (UX) vs. the developer experience (DX). For our user, before the drop-down is selected, what they're probably expecting to see is what that drop-down filters for: manufacturer, model, etc. For a developer who picks up the code, if they're trying to figure out what it's doing and look at the logs and see a value like 'Manufacturer', it might be confusing. For this reason, I instead used the 'value' parameter inside the option elements so now a dev who is looking at the logs will see 'None', which I hope is enough of a clue for them, and a user who hasn't filtered yet will see a dropdown that says 'Manufacturer'. If this doesn't quite click for you yet, don't sweat it, you'll see this in action again.

As central as opening and closing tags (ex: <select> and </select>) are to the anatomy of HTML, there are also elements that can use 'self-closing' tags that basically just look like a single closing tag. Why, you might ask? There's a reason: for some HTML elements, like 'image' (</img>), it would create more work and more syntax to type out an opening and closing tag since image elements in HTML just have a set of parameters and no contents. And this is a useful case in point: programming languages are designed for developers by other developers to make it as easy as possible to instruct a computer to do what they want. There's no first principles other than that, at least not like there are in math or physics. Let's take a look at another HTML snippet, one that includes a self-closing tag. This one represents one of the HVAC parts you see on the page above (the one with the fan).

Figure 3-8: HTML Div

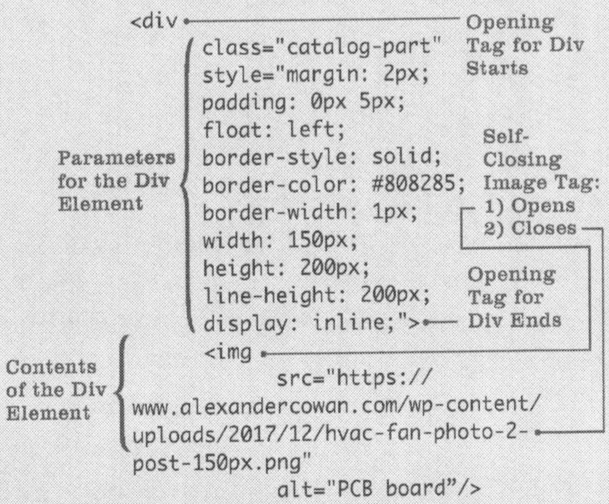

```
                      <div •————————————————— Opening
                      /  class="catalog-part"   Tag for Div
                      |  style="margin: 2px;    Starts
                      |  padding: 0px 5px;
                      |  float: left;           Self-
       Parameters    |  border-style: solid;    Closing
       for the Div  <   border-color: #808285;  Image Tag:
       Element       |  border-width: 1px;   ┌ 1) Opens
                      |  width: 150px;        └ 2) Closes ——
                      |  height: 200px;
                      |  line-height: 200px;     Opening
                      \  display: inline;">•—— Tag for
                                                Div Ends
       Contents    {     <img •——————————————
       of the Div          src="https://
       Element       www.alexandercowan.com/wp-content/
                     uploads/2017/12/hvac-fan-photo-2- •——
                     post-150px.png"
                              alt="PCB board"/>
```

What you're seeing here is an HTML element called a 'div', which is creating the box that you see the fan image sitting inside; the image element is the contents of the div. You can see the image tag open and close within the div (see annotations on the far right). There's a forward slash '/' at the end but you only see one tag for <img/>, which is what's meant by 'self-closing tag'.

Another thing you might notice is that this div has a lot of attributes. Those are doing things like putting the black border around it, establishing its height, stuff like that. Now, if you think about the fact that there are four of these in this sample code and that in real life there would be thousands, then you're talking about typing out a lot of parameters. And what if something changes? This is the problem CSS solves in the dynamic (literally) duo of HTML & CSS.

Code that's human-generated is expensive and prone to error. What this means is that if we have a whole bunch of functional elements that are similar, Div's in HTML for example, and that are created by hand, then that's a lot of extra work and room for error. Just specifying what width of border you want around the HVAC parts is a line of code. Given this, it's probably pretty easy to see why you'd want to somehow automate the process of specifying the border width for a given type of div. It would be a tremendous amount of work to do that by hand for thousands of HVAC parts, and just imagine if we change our mind and want a different border width!

In the case of web applications, this is the motivation behind using HTML to do the job of describing functional components, but then decoupling the job of specifying their properties and implementing it in another related technology, CSS. Essentially, CSS allows you to centralize and reuse your definition of how a given functional element should behave. For example, in the HinH site, there's a single CSS entry that describes how each of the HVAC parts should look and behave, and you just need to reference that CSS entry in the applicable HTML.

Specifics, please? Cascading Style Sheets

CSS allows you to group a set of attributes in a single spot and then reference them as many times as you want in HTML. There are a few ways to create these groupings (entries) in CSS, but two of the most common are by creating an ID or a class. Then, you reference these in your HTML with a single parameter like `class='catalog-part'`, which you can see is the first parameter in the opening tag of the div above. Right now, that class reference isn't doing anything. However, with a CSS entry like this:

```
.catalog-part {
  margin: 2px;
  padding: 0px 5px;
  float: left;
  border-style: solid;
  border-color: #808285;
  border-width: 1px;
  width: 150px;
  height: 200px;
  line-height: 200px;
  display: inline;
}
```

I can simplify our div to this:

```
<div
        class="catalog-part">
        <img
              src="https://www.alexandercowan.com/wp-content/
uploads/2017/12/hvac-fan-photo-2-post-150px.png"
              alt="PCB board"/>
</div>
```

Back in the CSS entry, while you see the same key value pairs, you may notice a couple of differences. First, to declare a class in CSS, you precede the name with a period, like this: .catalog-part. Then you enclose the entry in curly braces, as you see above. What about the ID? How do you declare one of those and reference it in HTML? Don't worry about it now! These are the kind of things you can Google once you have the basic idea.

As long as you understand the following, you're in good shape:
1. HTML & CSS work together to create Views
2. HTML is coded with various element types working together, which can have parameters (like border color) as well as contents (like text or images)
3. CSS is a way to centralize those parameters and reference them from the HTML

WYSIWYG Editors for HTML & CSS

If you've ever used website building products like SquareSpace or Wordpress, you have some experience with 'WYSIWYG' editors as a way to manage HTML and CSS. 'WYSIWYG' stands for 'what you see is what you get' and what these products attempt to do is allow the user to edit HTML & CSS without dealing with the underlying syntax. Some design tools like Figma also allow users to export HTML & CSS.

They approach the jobs of 1) specifying functional elements and 2) configuring their properties with some kind of visual UI. These generally do what they do by creating an abstraction layer that manipulates some underlying programming language. For example, Google maintains a development framework called Flutter, which allows developers to code mobile apps for both iOS and Android. Recently, a startup rolled out an application called Flutterflow which implements a WYSIWYG editor for the Flutter Framework that allows developers to create such apps using a visual editor.

Wordpress, an application that allows users to develop and operate websites implements a WYSIWYG editor that allows you to edit web pages, adding various functional elements as well as text and images.

You can see an example of this below. On the first page, I'm editing the images and text on a page, and on the second, I've opened a pop-up where I can edit the properties of the HVAC part image.

Why code Views by hand when you can use one of these environments? If you want to build something quick without having to deal with the implementation details, it can be a pretty good way to go. However, all of these environments use some simplifications to do what they do for their user. As long as it works for you to 'color inside the lines' the WYSIWYG has, you're OK. But, if you end up needing to do something different or you otherwise want more control over how your View is generated, you'll need to get in there and work with the underlying code.

Generally speaking, should you learn HTML and CSS? If you're going to be working on digital applications, I'd say it's a pretty good bet. First and foremost, if you don't know anything about how to code, it's challenging to participate in the kind of collaborative, interdisciplinary teams that tend to get good outcomes. As you're seeing, everything in the product pipeline depends on everything else and it's hard to do well on 'F' if you're completely at arm's length from that work. To the extent you're coming from a cold start, coding wise, and want to, say, put up a corporate website, you can probably get by just fine with a WYSIWYG environment like Wordpress or Squarespace, another alternative. However, if you're working on a product team, even as a generalist, you don't want to have to tap a dev on the shoulder every time you want to change a few sentences on a web page.

Figure 3-9: Editing a Page in Wordpress

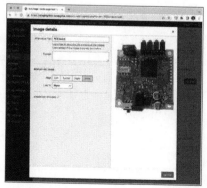

Figure 3-10: Editing an Image in Wordpress

Finally, and maybe most importantly, once you get over the hump, most of my students have found coding pretty enjoyable, even if it's a thing they just tinker with now and again. By way of analogy, why work on a farm if you don't like plants? Why work for a soccer team if you don't like the sport?

At the beginning of this section, I mentioned that most Views are built with HTML & CSS, or something very much like it. Because of this, topically, HTML & CSS is a pretty good bet—just about every company has at least a few web apps running. Also, if you're going to invest in your creative confidence this way, it's still the best bet overall. While there are plenty of them, the rest of the OS-specific tools for building views on smart phones, cars, thermostats, etc. are pretty fragmented. In the next section, we'll take a quick look at what 'very much like them' might look like for the example of building mobile apps.

Native Applications and Their Views

While they might not use HTML & CSS, the various languages and tools that implement OS or device-specific Views are still doing the same basic jobs of 1) specifying UI elements and then 2) configuring their properties. Desktop and mobile apps, for example, are built with similar general foundations but in OS-specific development frameworks (for Windows, Android, OSX, etc.). However, even when an application is written for one of these platforms, many development teams still find it useful to build their views with HTML & CSS. You can imagine how having common HTML & CSS components would be a win for an application like Spotify which runs on the web and then on all the big consumer operating systems: Windows, Mac, Android, and iOS, and, in fact, they use the framework called CEF[8] that allows developers to run HTML, CSS and Javascript inside applications that are built for other operating systems.[9]

If you're interested, the supplemental section below offers an example for the Flutter Framework, a cross-platform app development framework. The idea is that you code once and then can output working applications for both iOS and Android. Somewhat confusingly, this framework uses a special coding language (also maintained by Google) called DART. All that said, I think it's a good example of how tech other

---

8 "Chromium Embedded Framework," GitHub, accessed July 13, 2022, https://hdd.works/3yD1NBA.
9 Gizelle Labay, "How Was Spotify Developed?," Wiredelta, June 1, 2022, https://hdd.works/3o1vWp6.

than HTML & CSS approaches the JTBD of building Views. I chose this particular example since one of their big jobs was to create an abstraction that does a good job of dealing with the plumbing of app dev for both iOS (where apps are written in a language called SWIFT) and Android (where the apps are written in a language called Java).

Specifics, please? Native Views for Smartphones

Let's say your page *or* app needs a simple gray box with some text in it, something like this:

No, it's not super impressive, but the good news is that it's pretty representative of how both HTML & CSS and also Flutter do the jobs of specifying elements and configuring them.

Figure 3-11: A Seemingly Simple Gray Box

Lorem ipsum

The first snippet shows how you'd build this box in HTML & CSS and the second in DART, Flutter's programming language. I haven't covered every single facet, but you can see how generally similar these are in how they approach the jobs of creating the functional element (a box), configuring its size, and giving it the text 'Lorem ipsum':

Figure 3-12: Code Sample for Gray Box (HTML & CSS vs. DART)

```
                          <div class="grey-box"> •————————————————
                          ┤Lorem ipsum
                          </div>

                          .grey-box {
                              background-color: #e0e0e0; /* grey 300 */
                              width: 320px;
   Give it size            height: 240px;
   320px x  ————┐          font: 900 24px Georgia;
   240px       ┤}
                                                                    Make
                                                                    functional
                                                                    element: box

                          DART (Flutter)
                          final container = Container( // grey box •————
                         ┌width: 320,
                         ┤height: 240,
                         └color: Colors.grey[300],
                          child: Text(
   ┌ Give it text  ————   ┌'Lorem ipsum',
   'Lorem                  ┤style: const TextStyle(
   Ipsum'                      fontFamily: 'Georgia',
                               fontSize: 24,
                               fontWeight: FontWeight.bold,
                          ),
                          textAlign: TextAlign.center,
                          ),
                          );
```

If you're curious, you can probably see pretty readily how the two do the job of configuring the typeface, including the font, weight, and sizing.

These samples come from a guide that's called 'Flutter for web developers', which is itself telling: no technology exists in a vacuum and given the ubiquity of HTML & CSS, there's a pretty compelling case to make it highly accessible for devs who are familiar with HTML & CSS.[10] If that sounds excessively conservative, consider the fact that the keyboard layout we use today was designed over 150 years ago and one of the primary design goals was to avoid mechanical failures on typewriters.[11]

---

10 "Flutter for Web Developers," Flutter, accessed July 15, 2022, https://hdd.works/3axllzh.

11 Smithsonian Magazine, "Fact of Fiction? The Legend of the QWERTY Keyboard," Smithsonian. com (Smithsonian Institution, May 3, 2013), https://hdd.works/3PdfoXi.

The Job of Responsive Design

One of the reasons why it's not so easy to completely mask the complexity of HTML & CSS is that it needs to know how to respond when the View's area changes. For example, how should a web page look on a big, horizontal monitor vs. a small phone with a vertical orientation? This isn't a problem that you have to deal with when, for example, you're laying out a design for a more static medium like print. This area of work within creating Views is called 'responsive design'. How do you build Views that respond well when their size and proportions change?

Relative to static mediums, HTML & CSS handle this pretty well. However, much more tuning is required for today's websites. If you did it all from scratch by hand it would be an incredible amount of work, but fortunately there are several great frameworks that layer on top of HTML & CSS to help designers and developers control how their Views respond to different areas. One of these that's increasingly popular (and the one I use in the relevant case at the end of the chapter) is built directly on CSS and it's called 'CSS Grid'. Twitter Bootstrap is another you might hear about, and the community of practice is continually figuring out how to do these jobs even better and coming up with new tools.

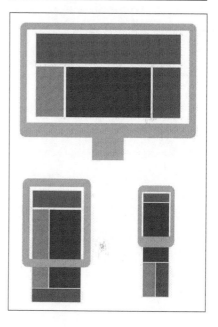

Figure 3-13: Responsive Design Diagram[12]

Hypothesis Formulation & Testing

How do you take a hypothesis-driven approach to building Views? First and foremost, do the work in Continuous Design: make sure you have nice, clear user stories and then iteratively prototype. From there, you still need to code and debug your Views. Sometimes this involves fixing overt issues

---

12 source: public domain via Tomáš Procházk

like something not showing up or being the wrong color–the HVAC part with no border and broken placement in Figure 3-14. Frequently, it also requires interpreting the design. For example, in the HTML debugging case listed at the end of the chapter, you'll see a navigation bar that 'pokes out' too far vertically on the far right, the top note in Figure 3-14, for example). There, the developer (you!) needs to decide whether to make the whole bar a little bigger or that area around the text box a little slimmer.[13]

Figure 3-14: An HTML 'Bug'

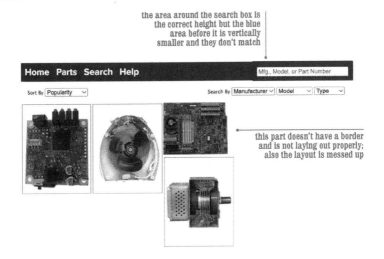

Output

A working View looks something like what you see in the image here. This code is on a site called JSFiddle that allows you to create and save sample code inside a ready-to-use development environment—and this is how you'll encounter it if you want to get your hands dirty with one of the cases at the end of this chapter. In most product teams, however, this code would be stored in a version control system like Github and then deployed to development, test, and production environments. More on how *that* works in our next chapter.

---

13 Some teams have their designers create pixel-perfect designs where this would be specified, but that's not nearly universal or always a good idea given how different the View might look across different responsive situations.

Figure 3-15: HTML & CSS in JSFiddle

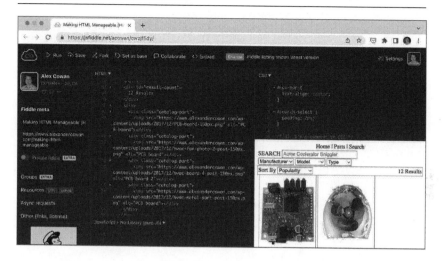

Antipatterns & Failure Modes

1. *Not Anchoring in User Narrative*

Garbage in, garbage out, as the saying goes—to create Views the developer needs to know both what and *why*. Hopefully the examples gave you some sense of the details a dev might need to consider as they go from design to code. As you saw in Chapter 2 on going from Idea to Design, prototypes are important, but it's anchoring them in fully articulated user stories that helps us thoughtfully link work on Continuous Design with the rest of the product pipeline in a hypothesis-driven fashion. In practice, detail matters on the why because of all the little decisions a designer and a developer have to make. So, user stories should be small relative to the amount and complexity of code required to implement them.

2. *Not Pulling Comp's & Novel UI Patterns*

Building novelty isn't just bad design, it's also likely to increase code complexity since those patterns probably aren't as naturally supported by the applicable dev tools and patterns. Instead, for substantial new UI elements, consider comparable UI patterns you think might be relevant to your user for the story in question, and start testing with prototypes from there. That way, once your design's ready to go to code, you're much more likely to be implementing well understood patterns in your Views.

3. *Not Having a Style Guide & Design System*

   As you learned in Chapter 2, just being consistent is a huge design win—it's also a great way to avoid rework and waste as you go from design to code. Instead, find a design system that's easily referenced team-wide for however your various colleagues are working.

4. *Not Building in Responsive Behaviors*

   While you'll get a big tailwind here from avoiding novel UI patterns (#2), it's still important to build in responsive behaviors from the start. It's rare for any web application to have no significant traffic from smaller devices, and having to retrofit these behaviors after the fact will likely generate waste.

5. *Not Testing*

   Good designs are testable designs pretty much by definition— to design is to assign intention to something you're creating and explicit intention is what underlies testability. By making sure your Views are coming from testable designs, you'll both reduce rework and improve fidelity on the why as you take your Views from Design to Code.

6. *Accessibility*

   Accessibility design is focused on making sure those with disabilities can access your application effectively. Like building in responsive behaviors, this is something that's much easier to build in from the start vs. retrofit.

Using Algorithms to Build Controllers

Get ready to have some fun! While many coders see creating Views as tedious, making things happen with code is fun and not as difficult as you might think. The first step is learning to think in algorithms. If you're a coder, this is something you've probably had to introduce to your collaborators in some fashion to get the specific inputs you need to code. If you're not, this is just a more clinical take on how to think through going from design to code.

Thinking in algorithms just means breaking down your intentions for the user experience into discrete steps. Conventionally, you'll probably hear devs refer only to more complex algorithms using the specific term, but the actual definition is just a set of steps to accomplish some kind of goal. In any case, words are faulty instruments, and the reality is that we all sometimes think in algorithms to some degree. That said, going from user story to algorithm requires a little practice for most people.

The idea with these sections is that you get the general idea of what's happening. If and when you want to really get into the details of the code, it's much better to do that with the cases and code samples in a live environment where you can test what the code is doing as you go. These are available for free at the end of the chapter in Recommended Practice. Why? Well, for example, let's say you're perplexed about the placement of a parenthesis or curly brace, as we all are at times. In the live environment (on JSFiddle.net), you can actively see if it's working or not and the IDE (integrated development environment) gives you visual cues about the code's integrity.

We'll start with garbage—actual, literal garbage. Let's say it's my favorite night of the week, trash night. I set a reminder for myself and it reminds me to take out the trash we have if it's either very full or very stinky or both.[14] Another way of saying that is:

```
If the garbage [is stinky] or [is full],
then I'll take it out to the bin.
Otherwise, I won't worry about it.
```

Certainly, these types of if-then statements aren't all there is to coding, but there sure are a lot of them and it's a pretty reasonable start to thinking in algorithms. Very little of this happens automatically, and so as a generalist it's important for you to create inputs or occasions to specify this for your developers or to give them enough intuition about the design where they can make good decisions on these details themselves. In practice, everyone finds some balance of doing some of both. In the supplemental section below, you can see an algorithm coded into a working Controller in the programming language Javascript (JS).

---

14 I'm simplifying: we also have compost, recycling, and green waste. Just so you know.

Specifics, please? From algorithm to Controller in Javascript

Let's say we want an algorithm to tell us if we have enough credits in our class schedule to graduate with an MBA. For the moment, I'll define how many credits our example student has (50 in this example) and then have the algorithm tell us whether I have too few or enough credits to graduate.

Here's how that might look in a programming language called Javascript (JS):[15]

Figure 3-16: If-Then Statements in Javascript

```
Statement 1: creates
a temporary value to
see if the functions
works, sometimes                         These items with
                                         '//' are comments
  |                                      to explain
const credits = 50;                      the code

//in the Alex MBA, you need 55 credits to graduate

if (credits > 54) {
  console.log('you can graduate');
  //code that actually does stuff would go here
} else {
  console.log('you need more credits to graduate');
  //more code that actually does stuff would go here
}
      console statements sends output to the Javascript 'console',
      which you can pull up in any browser for debugging
Statements 2 & 3:
This is an algorithm that sends one message to 'console' if the
credits value indicate you can graduate (#2), and another if you
it indicates you need more classes (#3).
```

Basically, this code has three statements. The first one defines a number of credits as a 'constant', a value that's not meant to change, which is abbreviated in JS as 'const'. This is just a temporary item to see if the code works, sometimes called a 'stub'. In the next iteration, we won't need it. Then there are two statements which send output to the JS console, one if you have too few credits and if you don't have

15 For the working code, see: Alexander Cowan, "MBA Grad Calculator I JS-Fiddle Code Playground," JSFiddle, accessed July 14, 2022, https://hdd.works/3P6Xndh.

too few, then the other that indicates that you can graduate. These are enclosed in what's called a 'control statement', which starts with 'if' and ends with 'else', and, yes, hopefully you guessed it: it just says if (x) is true then do the first thing and if not then do the second. In this case, (x) is the question of whether the example has more than 54 credits.

How does this Controller relate to the View? In this case, it doesn't—at least not to the end user View. Right now, the code itself is a kind of stub that tests our logic by outputting console statements about what it's doing. However, those statements are in some sense a View as they relate to the experience of a developer, and they are crucial to instrumenting observation for the third item in our general purpose design to code process, which is 'Analytically Debugging to Testable Verification'.

Figure 3-17: The Console Debugger in Chrome

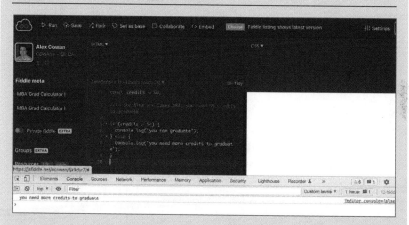

Specifically, given that the number of credits I defined in const credits is only 50 and students need 54 to graduate, when I run it in JS Fiddle, I'm seeing this message from the console that confirms my little Controller is behaving as I expect:[16]

    'you need more classes to graduate'.

---

16 Definitely OK? Not necessarily! But I'll talk about test coverage in chapter 4

Now, obviously, this code isn't ready to play a role in actually doing anything for a user, given that it takes a static value and returns a response to an interface that's only relevant to developers. To make this more realistic, we would turn it into a 'function', which we'll cover next.

If HTML elements are the 'legos' of building Views, functions are the legos of building Controllers. The best way to start thinking about functions is that they have an input, a set of discrete steps they execute (algorithms), and an output. In the case of trash night, I would say the input is my reminder to take out the trash, and the output is my determination on whether I need to take it out or not.

Figure 3-18: Algorithim's Inputs and Outputs

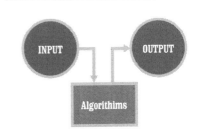

There are exceptions to this— for example, some functions don't have a specific input and sometimes they don't return a discrete output. They might just, say, reset the state of some application.

The general idea, though, is that they have a job to do that fits into a larger set of functions, and their basic purpose is to parcel out the various jobs your Controllers need to do into manageable pieces. In general, this means functions should be small and specific, because this makes changes and debugging easier. If you've seen a drop ceiling, that ubiquitous feature of office life, you've probably noticed that it has lots of small panels. If maintenance needs access to part of the ceiling or needs to replace one of the rectangles, it's easy—at least relative to having huge tiles that are hard to manage or installing a solid surface like drywall. So it goes with functions.

Specifics, please? Creating a Function

If I wanted a function that could do the job of returning whether or not a given student has enough credits to graduate, it might look something like this 'grad credits' function:

```
function grad_credits(credits) {
    //in the Alex MBA, you need 55 credits to graduate
if (credits > 54) {
    return ('you can graduate');
} else {
    return ('you need more credits to graduate');
}
}
```

This is pretty similar to our prior code except for two key things. First, you can now see the 'function declaration' (line 1), which includes the function keyword, the name of the function and an input in parenthesis (which is the number of credits). Second, instead of the console statements I now have statements that say 'return', which is a way of saying 'send this output back to the code that called you'.

I can 'call' the function from elsewhere in my code. For example, I might have a Controller/function that collects inputs (current credits that the user types in, say, or that the code pulls in from somewhere else in the user's account) from the View, passes them to our function, which then returns a response if they're set to graduate or need more credits. A line of code (Javascript) that calls the function would look like this, and since I still haven't connected it to the View to see if it's working, there's a console statement on the third line. I've added line numbers for clarity; these may be present in the program you use to edit your code, but they're not something you add while coding:

```
1  x = grad_credits(50);
2  //to see if it's working since there's no connection to the View
3  console.log(x);
```

The first line's job is to call our function (grad_credits), pass it the value 50 (credits), and then to take that response and store it someplace we can check it with a console statement to see if it's working, which you can see in line 3. The portion to the right of the equality operand (=) is calling our function, the equality operand says 'take the thing on the right and store it in the thing to the left', and, finally, 'x' is what's called a 'variable', which is a place you can temporarily store data in your code so that you can reference it later.

Let's step through those in a little more detail, starting with the function call. It is referencing the function I declared previously, so this function call only works if these two items are in the same file or if the code specifically references (or 'includes') another file where the function 'grad_credits' is written. Next, I have the use of the equality operand (=) to assign a result to a variable (x). In math, you're used to seeing the equality operand denote, well, equality. In a sense it's doing this here but the context is pretty different. Even less immediately intuitive, in most coding languages when you're asking 'are these two things equal?', you actually use a double equality operand ('=='). Finally, I have the use of a variable as a place to store the value I get from 'grad_credits' so I can reference it later. This act of taking a value and putting it some place so you can reference it later is a ubiquitous facility in coding and you'll see many more examples of it as we move along. In closing, what do you think the console statement with 'x' will return? If you guessed 'you need more credits to graduate', you're right. Since the value is less than 54, that's what 'grad_credits' is going to return.

If you want to see a version of this code that has a simple View which collects and returns a response, check out:
https://hdd.works/3ct6HcH

That version does have some additional code which deals with receiving and posting to the View, a pretty typical composition for Javascript.

How do the View and Controller interact? Let's take a look at the HVAC in a Hurry app, specifically this user story: *"I don't know the part number and I want to try to identify it online so I can find out its price and availability."*.

Figure 3-19: HVAC in a Hurry Parts App

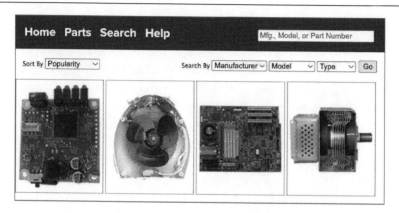

Based on our team's research watching the technicians operate, they arrived at a design where Trent the Technician can filter down the parts he's seeing by picking specific manufacturers and models (of heating, ventilation, and air conditioning equipment). Before I mess around with any code, I need to make sure I'm clear with myself about what I want to have happen. Here's a breakdown of what I think should happen when the user presses the 'Go' button for the filter:

1. Make sure the current view doesn't have any other filters applied
   a. I'll come back to why this is necessary
2. See which drop-downs the user wants to filter by
   a. Which ones are different from their default of 'all'?
3. If a filter is different than the default, then hide all the entries (HVAC parts) that *don't* have the selected attribute
   a. For example, if the user picked the manufacturer 'Acme', hide all the parts (the div's with class 'catalog-part') that don't have the attribute of the manufacturer being 'Acme'.

b. This leaves us with the question of 'clean up' and making sure I'm starting from a baseline state where everything's showing. For example, if the user filters by 'Acme' and then by 'Bacme', if I didn't start from a state where everything was showing, I'd run into a bug. This is why we need step #1 above.

This algorithm requires a couple of 'touch points' with the View. First, we need a way to know when the user clicks the 'Go' button. Second, we need to check the value of each of the drop-downs. For the first thing, a common approach is to use what's called an 'observer' function. This is a type of function that's generally built into your programming language somehow, and what it allows you to do is implement a Controller that can 'listen' for certain events from the View components. In the sample code below, what we tell it is "listen for a click on the Go button". For the second thing, getting the values of the drop-downs, programming languages offer facilities where you can basically say "find this element in the HTML" (or other View technology) and get its value".

Specifics, please? How does the View interact with Controllers?

How do I make this happen in code? First, I need a way to invoke our code when the user pushes the 'Go' button. For this, I'm going to use a coding facility called an 'event listener'. While it's implemented differently across programming languages, as you can imagine, this is a pretty common thing to need to do in digital user interfaces: have your code respond to things the user does.

Here's an implementation that starts by just logging a message to the Console when the user presses the 'Go' button, so we know that's working. It uses 'plain' JS, Javascript without any additional frameworks or libraries.

Figure 3-20: Observer Function

find a thing in the
HTML with id 'go-
btn' and assign it

```
1  const goButton = document.getElementById('go-btn');
2
3  goButton.addEventListener('click', goClick);
4
5  function goClick() {
6      console.log('go!');
7  }
```

listen for clicks on
the button,
goButton, and if it
hears them, calls
function 'goClick'

here's that
function, goClick

Let's take it from the top, starting with line 1. This statement defines a 'constant', abbreviated 'const', which is basically just a variable that's not meant to have its value change. The term you see getting that value is using a native JS facility which is basically saying 'get me the document', which is just all the page's HTML, and then 'go find the HTML element that has the ID 'go-btn'. It then puts this into our constant, 'goButton'.

Next, we reference that variable and chain a function to it from JS called 'addEventListener', to which we pass the type of event we want to listen for (click) and the function that we want to run when that event, the click, happens. Events and event listeners are a big thing in Controllers. They basically let you decouple but integrate the event you're trying to observe and what you might want to have happen based on that event. That allows you to code each one the way you want but then makes it easy to have the two functions interact.

Finally, we define the function that we want to run in response to the user's click, goClick. It just logs "go!" to the console. Not that amazing, but with this observer pattern you can do a lot of stuff. Various libraries like jQuery or extJS offer pre-written code that can (sometimes) help abbreviate or standardize these types of interactions, and some developers prefer those, or are stuck with them regardless since that's a design decision they made back when and it's not yet worth changing. Frameworks, which are basically a more extensive set of helper libraries that extend across the MVC, will also implement these observer patterns differently. Examples of such JS frameworks are React and Angular.

The idea here is absolutely *not* for you to memorize that syntax. In fact, even our little click function could be written a few different ways. For example, this alternative implements a more compact syntax:

```
const ohButton = document.getElementById('oh-btn')

ohButton.onclick = function () {
  console.log('Oh')
}
```

Let's step through that syntax as well to make sure you understand it all. Just kidding! Let's not! The important thing is that you have some specific intuition about how Views and Controllers interact and that if you *wanted* to understand the syntax above, you have enough creative confidence to know that the next step is a Google search like 'what does () mean in js function'. From there, you can figure it all out if and when you want.

In this JSFiddle you can see a few different versions at work and play with them, if you're interested:
https://hdd.works/jsdom

In the Recommend Practice section at the end of the chapter 'Creating View Interactions with Javascript', you can see an observer function working with various other View + Controller interactions. In short, it:
1. See which drop-downs the user wants to filter by
2. Hide all the entries (HVAC parts) that don't have the indicated attribute

Basically, the code does this by getting the value of the select elements in the HTML (the drop-downs) and then using another function that lets us go through each item in a class and checks the attributes of the HVAC part class (manufacturer, model, etc.) against what the user selected in the drop-down. If they don't match, they get hidden.

Let's review what we covered on Controllers and how they interact with Views from the perspective of the three design to code steps at the beginning of the chapter:

1. Unpacking Your Design into Code-Ready Steps
2. Effectuating a Viable Solution
3. Analytically Debugging to a Working Version

In the checking credits example, I wanted to see if a given student is set to graduate based on the credits in their schedule, breaking that down into individual steps. Then, I found a 'control statement', a coding syntax that controls when other code executes, that did what I wanted: the if-else statement in Javascript. Before I even made it a full function, I declared a constant and tested it with console statements to analyze whether it was working (see Supplemental section 'Creating a Function').

With the HinH example, I broke down the steps I wanted the Controller to execute in plain language or, as it's often called in programming, 'pseudocode'. Then I identified the JS facilities you saw as a way to do the job of selecting, reacting to, and manipulating View elements.[17] From there, I implemented and tested, step by step (you saw just one step but you can see them all in the case).

Hypothesis Formulation & Testing

Given the logical and integral nature of Controllers, they're highly testable. As you might imagine or perhaps already know, software testing is its own whole big thing, and a subject in our next chapter on going from code to release. The key thing with software testing is getting it automated vs. having some poor soul test the same thing over and over by hand. For example, you can imagine that we could write test code for the can graduate function we started with that basically says:

1. pass the function the value 54
2. if it returns 'can graduate', the test passes; otherwise, it fails

More generally, getting comfortable with Controllers means being able to unpack into three to four testable layers:

1) what you want to have happen for the user, probably in the form of a user story

---

17 HTML & CSS are often called the HTML 'DOM', data object model

2) the steps you want a Controller to implement for that user story, written in pseudo code or just in your head if you prefer,
3) a working Controller, one or more functions, for example
4) automated tests to test the code—a unit test for example

Finally, it's worth noting that there's a highly test-driven agile practice called 'test-driven development' or 'TDD', and these practitioners reverse items #3 and #4 above.

Output
Here you can see the full version of the working code on JSFiddle, which is here: https://hdd.works/pojcase. For more context, check out the case at the end of this chapter in the Selected Resources section ('Making Stuff Happen with Javascript).

Figure 3-21: HinH Prototype with Javascript

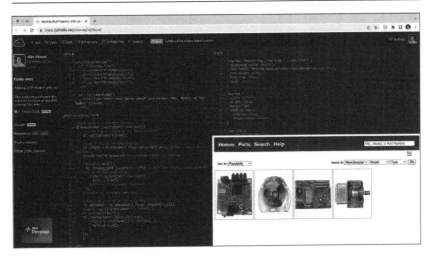

Are most applications created in Javascript? No. Is it every developer's favorite language? Also no. However, it is popular and versatile and so it's a good starting point for learning about going from design to code. As a generalist, getting some practice doing so will give you a huge leg up on acquiring intuition and empathy you can apply to your collaborations.

Antipatterns & Failure Modes

It's worth noting here that computer science is a ... science all to itself and coding well is a lifetime endeavor. Getting a 1.0 out the door is easier than it's ever been, but, particularly at scale, there's plenty that can go wrong, or at least not as well as it could have. That said, a focus that's well understood by the team paired with the hypothesis-driven approaches that you're learning about is a great way for the generalist to improve their collaborations. To that end, the items below are some interdisciplinary 'macro' areas of possible dysfunction.

1. *YAGNI*

   If you've taken an entrepreneurship class in the last 10 years, you were probably advised that writing a business plan is a waste of time and distracting, since you don't know what's going to happen with an early stage venture, there's no point in elaborate planning. YAGNI is that for software engineering. It stands for 'you aren't going to need it' and the idea is that rather than engineering an elaborate system in anticipation of unknowable future needs, it's better to focus on solving the problems, doing the jobs you have now and then to use the dividend of time you get from not over engineering to refactor the code as you learn more about user behavior and system performance. Working to steadily decrease the team's cost to build a successful feature ('F') is a good way to contextualize and manage this.

   Much like Continuous Design, which iteratively gets you to product/market fit, this approach to software engineering gets you to an emergent design that fits better with what you actually need from the software.

2. *Not Building to Test (Automatically)*

   While we haven't covered it here, pairing dev of automated tests with the process of going from design to code is crucial for keeping the pipeline healthy. One working definition of 'legacy code', basically code that's old and hard to work with, is code without automated test coverage. More on this in the next chapter on going from code to deploy!

3. *Too Much Custom Code*

For various reasons, we tend to write too much custom code. Part of this is probably somehow related to how fun it can be to build your own solutions in code. Part of it's probably related to how little most of us want to read someone else's 'manual' or documentation, even if their helper applications or API's are a better choice than custom code. Finally, there's often a bias against spending money for outside solutions, probably related to how much we tend to systematically underestimate the cost of building a feature.

As a generalist, you can help mitigate this with strong, layered design inputs of the type you learned about in the last chapter. These will help give your team better intuition about where the application might go, helping them better consider, for example, how much a given area of code is likely to change and where they might usefully invest in pulling in outside helper applications and services/API's.

4. *Duplication*

This means either that the same code appears in multiple places or that there's different code various places doing the same thing. In general it's a source of waste your team will want to avoid. Some of this is inevitable, and so sometimes excessive duplication is the result of the team not having enough time to refactor their code, meaning to refine it as the codebase grows and evolves. This, in turn, is usually the result of trying to cram too much release content into the pipeline, making it less healthy—something you can help the team with.

Structuring Data Models

Creating data is like adopting a pet—you should make sure you know why you want it and be clear on how to take care of it. While changes to Views and Controllers are relatively easy to make, substantial changes to how you organize your data Model are notoriously fraught.

Given how much I've emphasized the need to make your code amenable to change, this may sound challenging. It is. Rather than trying to perfect your data architecture, though, your best bet is to structure it around your real-world understanding of the entities in question and take it from there. The question a team should be asking themselves here is 'How do we build the best Model?', and good answers depend on high quality explanations of the real world entities you want to model. This is very much the job of the generalist or product person, so let's start with how you do that.

While there are a lot of formal data modeling approaches out there,[18] different teams find different levels of detail work for them in design and planning Models. That said, it minimizes waste and maximizes collaboration when teams have enough shared concepts to talk about data entity relationships in a specific way. *Has-a* and *Is-a* are two starter concepts that can take you a long way with a simple whiteboard session.

Figure 3-22: The MVC

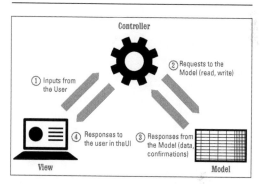

Let's take a look at the HVAC in a Hurry example. The diagram here describes the current has-a and is-a relationships for the HVAC Parts. Essentially, an HVAC part is-a type of part and has various parameters associated with it.

Figure 3-23: Has-A, Is-A

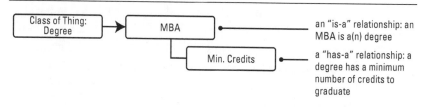

---

18 Entity-Relationship (ER) or UML (Unified Modeling Language), for example

Figure 3-24: Has-A, Is-A Example

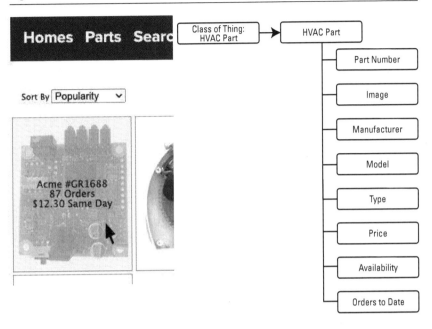

Let's say I add to the View a rollover behavior like the one you see here where, when a user hovers over a part, it shows information about itself. How would that change the data Model you see here? If you answered, not at all, you got it!

Based on the diagram we see here, the Model already has all the data we need. Where does that data live? In the code you've seen, the HinH pages are static/hand-created and so basically the data Model is embedded in the HTML code. This is OK for early, exploratory development, but not something you'd want to do for long. In one of the cases at the end of the chapter (Automating Your Gruntwork with Javascript) we use a Controller to dynamically generate this part of the View from a single table in a spreadsheet, and this is closer to how the MVC disposition might look in production code. However, for something like adding a new View on existing data, as long as you have all the parameters in the Model for your Controller to build that View (and we do), then you don't need to add or duplicate any of those parameters.

Another key part of the Model is thinking about how various entities relate to each other, both naturally and then functionally with regard to your user stories. For example, let's say the team at HinH is planning to add user reviews of the various HVAC parts in their next sprint. Now, we have a couple of other entities in play with this Model: users and reviews. A user probably has a username, password, the usual; a review probably has some kind of discrete scale (stars, for example) and text where the user explains their review.

Now, let's say they have a user story like: *'As Trent the Technician, I want to see all the reviews I've written so I can check whether I've reviewed a given part'*, or *'As Trent the Technician, I want to share my reviews with a colleague who has some questions about them, so I know they're available to that colleague.'* A Controller to post such a page might look something like:

1. get all the reviews created by user {x}
2. for each of the parts they reviewed, get the data for the parts so they can be presented with the review
3. assemble the HTML & CSS for the page

This raises a few questions. First, when I want to specify a particular user in the Model, how do I identify them? If you're familiar with Excel (or Google Sheets), you're probably pretty familiar with VLOOKUP.[19] When I want to do something like 'get all the reviews created by user {x}', I'm doing something like a VLOOKUP, and I need a lot of the same parameters: a search key by which I'll identify or 'index' the user and a spot where the reviews live.

This brings us to a few database concepts that are worth generally understanding: naming, normalization, and keys. The idea with naming is simply that for whoever interacts with the database (developers, database specialists, site reliability engineers that maintain systems, analysts, etc.), the names and comments created for the various components of the database (tables, for example) should be as self-evident as possible. If this sounds familiar, it's entirely consistent with the general idea of self-documenting code you learned about in the Controllers section. How

---

19 "VLOOKUP Function," Microsoft Support, accessed July 19, 2022, https://hdd.works/3RJuOEh.

do you do naming well? Here again, it will be you, the product person, who needs to acquire and explain the real world entities that will go into your Model to help your team.

Next, we have normalization. The idea with normalization is that your data should be stored in components that are conceptually *integral*. Everything that integral means in normalization involves a bunch of database theory, but let's step through a few of the high points. A relational database is made up of a series of tables which are not so different from an Excel file that has multiple sheets. Probably the top two most important focal points on normalization for a generalist are that 1) each table should represent a single conceptual entity (an HVAC part or a user, a review, for example) and 2) columns shouldn't depend on other columns. For example, let's say I have this version of a table for the HVAC Parts:

Table 3-1: Parts Table with Normalization Issue

Part Number	ImageURL	Manufacturer	Distributor	Model	Type	Price	Availability	OrdersT30Days
GR1688	www.alexandercowan.com/wp-content/uploads/2019/12/PCB-board-120pxby150px.png	Acme	Huey	TooCool	Board	$12.30	Same Day	22
BR2048	www.alexandercowan.com/wp-content/uploads/2017/12/hvac-fan-photo-2-post-150px.png	Bacme	Huey	TooHot	Fan	$9.20	Two Day	301
TR0988	www.alexandercowan.com/wp-content/uploads/2017/12/hvac-board-4-post-150px.png	Dacme	Lewy	JustRight	Board	$11.70	Same Day	12

If there's a 1:1 relationship between Manufacturer and Distributor, then instead the way you'd want to normalize this is by removing Distributor from this table and adding it to another that describes the Manufacturers:

Table 3-2: New Parts Table

Part Number	ImageURL	Manufacturer	Model	Type	Price	Availability	OrdersT30Days
GR1688	www.alexandercowan.com/wp-content/uploads/2019/12/PCB-board-120pxby150px.png	Acme	TooCool	Board	$12.30	Same Day	22
BR2048	www.alexandercowan.com/wp-content/uploads/2017/12/hvac-fan-photo-2-post-150px.png	Bacme	TooHot	Fan	$9.20	Two Day	301
TR0988	www.alexandercowan.com/wp-content/uploads/2017/12/hvac-board-4-post-150px.png	Dacme	JustRight	Board	$11.70	Same Day	12
…	…	…	…	…	…	…	…

Table 3-3: New Manufacturers Table

Manufacturer	Distributor
Acme	Huey
Dacme	Lewy
…	…

From there, you would write queries if you need something from the Model that spans multiple tables. Queries are code statements that ask things like 'What are all the reviews user {x} has written?" or "Who is our distributor for Acme?".

Why is normalization so important? Not normalizing well tends to lead to errors or, as they're often called in the database world, 'anomalies'. If that sounds horrible, then, the truth is...yes, it is horrible. Like a lot of things with the Model, this is an area where mistakes and changes are relatively costly.

How do we make those queries? In a relational database, these questions usually get asked with a programming language called SQL (pronounced 'sequel'). Here's an example of a SQL query to get the Distributor for the Manufacturer 'Acme' from the Manufacturers table:

```
SELECT * FROM Mfr2Dist
WHERE Manufacturer='Acme';
```

Conceptually, it's a lot like doing a VLOOKUP or multiple VLOOKUP's in Excel, except that there are a lot more options on how to do it because of the natural variation in what these queries might need to do. This brings us to the last database concept: keys. When you do that VLOOKUP, you're saying something like 'For a given cell (like Manufacturer), go to another range (or table in our case) and find it and then go get (a value from some other column)'. In this case, the Manufacturer is the key. If you're looking up 'all the reviews for a given user', you're doing the same thing except the key is the user ID and the result will be all the records in the Reviews table that have that particular userID. This facility to return more than one result is another difference between SQL queries and VLOOKUP. Each table will have a primary key that uniquely identifies each row (sometimes called a 'record' or 'tuple'). A 'natural key' is something like the part number—as long as it's unique, that's a good option for your key. However, in practice, because these keys must be immutable (can't change) most of the time there's a 'surrogate key' which is an arbitrary value uniquely generated by the database or code.

Where does this data live? As you probably know, the simple answer is 'in a database'. Creating and maintaining databases is, of course, core to any design to code process. Relative to Views and Controllers, generally speaking, changing databases tends to be messier, generating more overhead for a dev. team. Given this and the nature of this leg of the MVC, here are just a few of the questions development teams need to grapple with as they create and maintain the Model in a database or databases:

- How do I design in a way that maximizes what I know but is also amenable to change, given the disruptive nature of database schema changes?
- How do I maintain uptime and availability of the data?
- How do I maximize performance of the database for good UX at a reasonable cost?
- How do I secure the data?
- How do I make the data available to our developers in a way that minimizes overly tight coupling where small changes to the database break a lot of the code?[20]

Does the YAGNI (you aren't going to need it) principle not apply to the Model, then? It still applies, but on the spectrum of investing in design up front vs. designing for change, a reasonable developer might tell you this is a place to err on the side of planning. In your role as product lead or generalist, the best thing you can do is a) make sure you've done your homework to understand the real world entities you're going to design for (HVAC parts, etc.) and then b) sketch your understanding with heuristics like has-a, is-a, so that you enable the rest of the team to think more intuitively about key inter-relationships between the entities so they can make reasonable investments in how they approach implementing the Model.

The two major types of database are relational vs. NoSQL or 'non-relational'. The concept of a relational database is relatively intuitive for spreadsheet users: you have a series of tables that have keys where you can cross index and join the data together as you need with your Controllers. They basically look like the tables you saw above. These have been around a long time and are well supported and understood by developers and database specialists.

---

20 For an excellent take on this, see: Louis Davidson et al., "Ten Common Database Design Mistakes," Simple Talk, August 24, 2021, https://hdd.works/3RySkUr. While this has technical concepts that won't be familiar to you (if you don't have experience with databases) you may find it interesting to skim if this topic is of particular interest to you.

Mainly because of its flexibility, non-relational or 'NoSQL' databases have emerged as a popular alternative. NoSQL is a bit of a misnomer since in a lot of cases you can use SQL, a language for querying (asking questions of) databases, with these. Within the NoSQL family of databases (there are a few types and even more vendors), the Document Database is a popular choice. Here you have Collections which in turn have 'documents'. These are files in a format called JSON, which originally gained popularity as a way to exchange data between applications, for example from your software to a third party service.

Here you can see this in action at HinH with Google Firebase's Firestore database, a JSON-based document database. You can see here two 'collections' of documents, one for users and one for parts. The parts collection is highlighted, and you can see various parts and their fields in the third column over. You can also see that parts have-a relationship to a 'collection' of Reviews, the reviews for that particular part.

Figure 3-25: Google's Doc DB: Cloud Firestore

Just like you, a developer wants to do good work and be part of a team where their work is appreciated and their colleagues' contributions help make the work more impactful. If you already code, I hope this chapter has given you some ideas on how to facilitate better collaboration on going from design to code.

What We Learned

To make the process of going from design to code more transparent to interdisciplinary collaborators taking a hypothesis-driven approach, we looked at a few examples of code. If you were someone who is already up to your elbows in code all day, these would have been easy for you to understand, and I hope they helped you think about new ways to approach collaboration with your non-coding collaborators.

If you are brand new to coding, I think you'll find this was *just enough* code to help you understand the process without overwhelming you with what might be arbitrary specifics that won't matter to you in the longer run. Should you pause your work (or reading this book) and learn to code? My suggestion is not necessarily to do that right at the moment, but to think about how your work around going from design to code is complemented by your understanding of that process. The best way to be a developer's favorite collaborator isn't to show them how much you know—it's showing them how much you care about making the whole team successful.

In the latter part of the chapter, we built on the last chapters' content and approach to help you understand how to apply a hypothesis-driven approach to the process of going from design to code, an approach that will help you improve both the health of your team and the outcomes for your end users.

Recommended Practice

For active practice on going from design to code, I recommend doing the cases below by area (Views, then Controllers, then Data and Models), and interleaving your own project between them. For example, let's say you have a personal or work project that you're using (or plan to use in the future) to apply this material. For that project, draft user stories and wireframes in a tool like Balsamiq.[21] Finish the cases on building Views, then build some Views for your project. Likewise, after that, interleave creating controllers and data.

21 "Balsamiq. Rapid, Effective and Fun Wireframing Software: Balsamiq," . Rapid, Effective and Fun Wireframing Software, accessed July 19, 2022,https://hdd.works/3OeRPw1.

Create a Style Guide to Deliver Consistent Visceral Reactions
If you have a new project/brand, this is a great thing to do right this minute to minimize waste—even if you plan on iterating on your design program later. This page has a tutorial and templates:
> https://hdd.works/3v7Ev5L.

Create Views with HTML & CSS
Ready to give it a try? This page has written tutorials and links to an online course, if you prefer:
> https://hdd.works/3v2rlqQ.

Creating View Interactions with Javascript
Ready to create some Controllers? This page has written tutorials and links to an online course:
> https://hdd.works/3PlEOvQ.

Creating Controllers with Javascript
Ready to create some Controllers? This page has written tutorials and links to an online course:
> https://hdd.works/3cpl161.

Mapping Data to Models and Operationalizing Them
Model time? This page has written tutorials and links to an online course:
> https://hdd.works/3v4K4SG.

Guest Editor: Laura Klein

I first met Laura when I was playing the tambourine, figuratively speaking. It was an evening event for the Lean Startup Circle SF, the community organization supporting the practice of Lean Startup, and I was doing a short opening talk where she was the main event. Her talk on Lean UX was a real eye opener for me. A lot of the time, talks about design are very, well, designer-y. While strong on design, Laura's material offered a practical take on actually working with developers and businesspeople to get better product outcomes.

Years later, there are few collaborations I value as much as my correspondence with Laura. Most of what you've seen in this book has in some form been ruthlessly examined and often revised based on her perspective. If you want to learn more about her work, check out her book *Build Better Products* or her website https://www.usersknow.com.

Three Questions with Laura

You were a coder before you were a designer.
What led you from coding to design?
I moved from coding to design purely by accident. It was the end of the dot com boom, and I was taking some time off to figure out if I wanted to try another startup or do something new or finish the masters program in computer engineering I had started. (Spoiler: I went with "do something new.")

A friend of mine who ran a small interaction design consultancy needed some help with a research report, and since she knew I was a good writer, she asked if I had some time to work on it. After finishing the report, I helped out with other research projects, and I also used my front-end programming skills to build coded prototypes for the company's clients. Since I was helping conduct research and then building prototypes, it was only a matter of time before I learned the bit that comes in the middle—the design part where you figure out how to turn research into usable, useful user interfaces.

It ended up being a sort of apprenticeship program, and after a few years of working alongside very senior designers, I started taking point on projects and became a full fledged designer. I eventually left to go to a startup, where I worked as a sort of combination designer/researcher/engineer, and that's where I learned about quantitative research and metrics. I've spent the rest of my career practicing some combination of all those skills, either in house or as a consultant.

What do you think we've learned about going from design to code in the last 15 years that we either didn't know or weren't sure about?
I'm always a little hesitant to answer any questions about what "we" have learned, since there are things that I learned long after they were well known to others and things I know that somebody new might still need to learn.

One thing that has changed significantly though, is the tools available to us. Many larger orgs now have whole design systems, complete with code components, that make building products much easier. Instead of handing over mockups of design states with red lines showing font sizes and hex colors and margin widths, etc., designers can drop existing design components into their prototypes, and engineers can simply use those same components on the front end. Of course, none of it works quite as smoothly as advertised, but it's about a thousand times better than custom building every element on the page over and over.

Sometimes when I really want to upset a modern front end developer, I'll tell them about using a 1 pixel square, transparent image for spacing. Anyway, things are easier these days.

What advice do you have for someone who wants to be a better product person?
Obviously, the most important thing is to understand the needs of your users and your business and work collaboratively with your team to find solutions that align those goals. In other words, make things better for your business by making things that customers are happy to pay you to use. These days, I'm also making sure to tell people to

please try to consider any societal effects as well, because we live in a society, and I'm tired of tech people making things materially worse for everybody just because it makes them money.

If you want more advice about going from design to code, since that's the point of the chapter, I'd say "know your tools." I don't really care if product people know how to program or use any particular programming language. I do care that they know enough about the technology that they're using to have intelligent conversations with experts and know when to let those experts make the decisions. There can be a lot of pressure as a PM, especially in large orgs, to be the decision maker, but sometimes the best decision is to trust people who know better than you do.

HTML, CSS, and Javascript are great places to start learning, and they're definitely the building blocks of web applications. But larger, more complicated products are made up of a lot more than just those three things. The truth is that most technology you use on a daily basis is a Frankenstein's monster of different platforms, APIs, frameworks, databases, servers, and languages, held together by duct tape, optimism, and occasional infusions of VC money.

One of the most useful things you can do if you're in a position to make any decisions about a product, is to learn which chunks of technology your engineers have inflicted on you and learn the drawbacks, weaknesses, and (if you're lucky) strengths.

4

FROM CODE TO RELEASE

Figure 4-1: Continuous Delivery & HDD

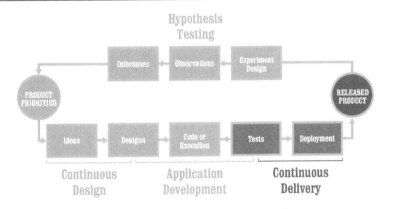

Long considered either a boring specialty domain or a horrible necessity that once in a while couldn't be avoided, the Test and Deploy processes are now one of the most obvious differentiators for high functioning teams. Teams that get good at going from Code to Release, are able to both learn faster and spend less time on demoralizing gruntwork like manual testing, deploying, and fixing emergencies in production systems in the middle of the night.

The tools and practices are out there to make this happen, and they're often referenced under the term 'DevOps'. DevOps is essentially a domain-specific extension of agile. Where agile addressed how the 'businesspeople' and 'technical' people might work better together, DevOps specifically addresses how developers and the folks handling the jobs of test and deploy work together. Like agile, DevOps is a big tent and has more to do with focusing on a set of outcomes vs. a single prescription on how to get there. Like agile, having a loose community of practice with a shared view on outcomes works well since there's so much diversity and variation between different teams and products.

Continuous Delivery is the reward, the outcome you're working toward. We are in a golden age of going from code to release. Just like the original Golden Age, there's a stark contrast between the haves and have-nots. Amazon is a have, deploying code every 11.7 seconds. The 'haves' not only learn faster, putting their hypothesis-driven development on overdrive, but also create less stress for their technical teams because going from code to release is better thought out and instrumented. In fact, studies have shown that companies with a high functioning Code to Release capability actually release more often and have fewer bugs in production.

For years, I was on the receiving end of bad practice here, debugging broken deployments and running ad hoc tests at all the wrong times. Later, as a founder, I helped perpetuate those same dumb practices—until I didn't. As soon as I started learning about the alternatives, I was all in, even though I was not immediately successful.

Getting from a highly manual, infrequent product pipeline to a more continuous one requires making space for those changes, facilitating them, and, to one degree or another, changing how just about everyone works. One example of this you may see on Twitter, etc. is release-savvy engineers lamenting job postings for a DevOps Engineer, not because they don't like DevOps but because they know it takes more than one expert to fix a product pipeline. The good news is that this body of practice is highly consistent with modern takes on agile and Hypothesis-Driven Development.

To understand how this works in practice and what you need to do to support it, we should start with the particulars of what happens in a product pipeline under 'Tests' and 'Deployment'. In a more siloed, high-handoff environment, Dev gets some kind of inputs from 'the business' and implements code against those. They hand off their code to Test to make sure it works. Test does what they can to make sure that new functionality actually works and also that it didn't break (regress) any of the existing functionality. They then hand the software off to Ops. Ops is then responsible for making that new application available to end users through an update to the production systems. And, in the olden days, this was just a matter of distributing media, like a compact disk or a file for download.

Figure 4-2: From Design to Deploy: The Old Way

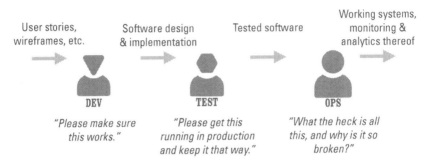

How we Got to Continuous Delivery

How did this golden age of going from code to deploy come about and where is it headed? Ask, and you're likely to hear about everything from the culture of DevOps to applications like Kubernetes (abbreviated as 'K8s') and Docker. However, before we go there, it's useful for managers to understand the more fundamental change catalysts that helped bring all that about, since they continue to drive a lot of successful (and, in the reverse, unsuccessful) practice.

We'll pick up in 2005. At this point, the transition from what we now call 'enterprise' deployments in a customer's facility to 'software-as-a-service' (SaaS) where the application vendor operates the application for you, was still underway. Salesforce, which offered its customer relationship management (CRM) application only as a service online, had gone public a year prior but was still competing heavily with Siebel, the entrenched player in that space, who focused on an 'enterprise' model where companies would run the software on their own machines in their own premises or data centers.[1] What does the history of these two companies have to do with Continuous Delivery? Quite a lot, I would say, and this continues to be the case.

---

1 CNET News.com Alorie Gilbert Staff Writer, "Rivals Vie for Siebel's Customer Spoils," Rivals vie for Siebel's customer spoils | CNET News.com, accessed July 12, 2022, https://hdd.works/siebel

Consider how a dev team relates to their outcomes when they print code to a compact disc or even copy it to a server for someone else to install and operate (ex: Siebel) vs. the dev team that works alongside the teams that operate the software and get the call in the middle of the night when something goes wrong (ex: Salesforce). While I'm not aware of any formal research on the subject, the prevailing observation in tech is that the closer the people that write the software are to the people who operate it, the more continuity and thoughtfulness you get on the transition from code to test to deploy.

What does that process look like on the ground and what's changed about it? In 2005, I worked as a sales engineer for a company called BroadSoft that built voice calling applications for communications operators like Verizon or France Telecom. SaaS was not nearly as common as it is today, and at that time BroadSoft interacted with its customers almost entirely using the enterprise model, where customers installed and ran the software on their own premise. Part of my job was to install our software on servers in a customer's lab for them to use in testing and evaluating our product. It was hard.

Cold and Hungry in the Caribbean, A Personal Tale of Bins and Libs

What is DevOps, why is it such a big deal, and what came before it? Let's start with a specific example: I'm sitting in a freezing cold data center in the Caribbean, starving (no food allowed), really hoping to go back to my hotel and have dinner soon. But the application isn't coming up and working. Is this my fault? Specifically speaking, yes! That said, in all the code to deploy processes leading up to this moment, there were a lot of handoffs, different priorities for each team, and a lot of places where something could go wrong.

First, we have the code itself. There were new releases fairly frequently and each of those had to be tested to make sure that the new features worked properly and the changes didn't break any of the existing features. The test team was pretty sophisticated in terms of automating the testing, so the coverage of tests relative to the functions of the application was good, and given its complexity, the application had relatively few bugs that made their way to production.[2] So far, so good. But in this freezing cold data center, at this point in time, that wasn't even in play because I didn't have the application up and running.

Whoever is installing the application needs some combination of documentation and scripts to complete the install or upgrade. I had both of these, but this was a fairly complex system of multiple applications interacting with each other, and the scripts would often run into errors. How could this happen? Didn't someone test them first? They did, but in this enterprise model there were so many permutations of the baseline configuration an install might encounter, that testing for all those cases was effectively impossible. Let's step through the big differences software might encounter depending on where it's installed, since understanding those is central to understanding the Deploy and Test steps.

Like all applications, the application I was installing ran on an operating system and, in between the application and the operating system, there were a number of crucial 'helper' applications, which you may hear referred to as 'bin's and lib's', short for 'binaries and libraries'. For example, the application I was installing in this freezing cold data center was created in a programming language called Java[3] and ran on a (fairly ubiquitous) operating system called Linux. You may have heard that software is 'just 1's and 0's', and that's true—but it's like saying human beings are just a bunch of water, carbon, and a few other things mixed together—it's not wrong, but it's also not super relevant most of the time.

The way human-readable code makes its way to the 1's and 0's that run on a microchip is something few developers have to contend with day to day: there are a lot of layers between your code and the chip. Those layers are these bins and libs that others have created, so you don't have to. The catch is, yes, you have to get the right bins and libs in the right place for your code to work right. In my case, one of the headliner bin/libs was called 'Tomcat', a component I needed

Figure 4-3: Running an Application, Stacked

Your App
Bins/Libs
Operating System (OS)
Physical Host

---

2 'Production' is the term for an environment where the application is being used by customers.

3 Which, interestingly, is quite different from Javascript, which is what you saw in the last chapter—but that's another story.

for the Java[4] code to run. Tomcat and dozens of other bins/libs needed to be installed in the right way with the right version across four different servers that each ran a different part of the application. Any mistake would cause the application to periodically fail or not operate at all.

Here's another great thing about the enterprise model (not really): I didn't install that OS or those bins/libs. A sysadmin at my customer installed them since it's their server and their system. And guess how concerned they are about whether everything's just the way I need it? Understandably, not as concerned as I was. That customer sysadmin was probably at dinner already with her family; this was no longer her problem.

Worst case, I just have to check everything and make any changes that are needed, right? Sometimes yes, often no. First of all, given what a dangerous jungle the Internet is, a lot of these customers were not OK with me going on the Internet and downloading whatever bins/libs I felt I needed, and they blocked access. Second, the sysadmins who were responsible for these servers themselves had certain standard configurations they preferred to run for consistency of operation—configurations they had tested and knew how to troubleshoot when things went wrong. Often, our engineering team's standard configuration and theirs weren't the same and we had a whole mess to sort out there—enough of a mess where you might miss dinner entirely.

Anyway, once I got these bins/libs running just right (or right enough) on the operating system, was I just about on my way to some grilled prawns and a stiff drink? No. I still had to get our application installed and configured. Installations are usually easier than upgrades since there are fewer variables and so it's easier to define and test the conditions of a fresh/clean install. With an upgrade, different parts of the system might be on different versions and this (reasonably) might cause some of the scripts that help automate the messier parts of my job to break. This was an upgrade.

Once the new version installs successfully, there's the final step of configuring and verifying it. This too would interact with the customer's environment in somewhat unpredictable ways. For example, I mentioned the application was functionally a system of four different applications working together. They needed to communicate through the customer's

---

4   It does a few other things as well—you can read all about it online, of course, if this is current or interesting for you.

network which only allowed certain types of communication, mostly for security reasons. While we sent notes to the customer's sysadmin on how to prepare all this, there were a lot of unique types of communication, and it would be pretty easy to miss something. This too could keep me from finishing my job and getting my dinner.

How would you like to be on a team dealing with all this, quarter after quarter, month after month? What about being a manager where you're seeing this across hundreds of customers and dozens of your staff across development, test, deployment, and sales/customer support? If you're feeling the pain, so were a lot of other people around the same time and this motivated the DevOps movement.

Where we are: DevOps & Continuous Delivery

DevOps is a domain-specific application of agile that's focused on the Test and Deploy steps. If agile initially addressed how 'business' and 'technical' colleagues interacted, DevOps re-segmented the 'technical' folks to more specifically deal with how colleagues from Dev, Test, and Ops interacted.[5] Like agile, it's more a loose but consistent affiliation of ideas and practices vs. a single prescription everyone follows in the same way.

Figure 4-4: From Design to Deploy: The New Way

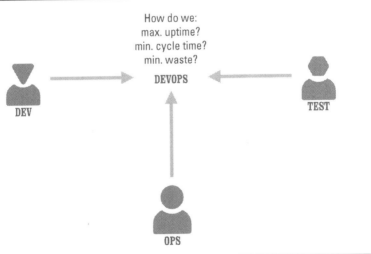

---

5   Other job titles you might hear that fall into this general area are: sysadmin, deployment engineer, and site reliability engineer (SRE)

Back to my delayed dinner in the freezing Caribbean data center, a lot of the momentum for DevOps came from the superior economies software companies could achieve for themselves and their customers by running their application themselves and making it available as a service on the web ('software as a service'—SaaS) vs. installing and maintaining it from scratch in the customer's environment. For example, BroadSoft (now part of Cisco) is now primarily focused on offering its software on a SaaS basis.

Topically, DevOps addresses the processes of Test and Deploy in the product pipeline, including how they interact upstream with Dev. DevOps, like agile, has a couple of general purpose principles. One is a focus on minimizing hand-offs and maximizing self-service through automation. For example, rather than a developer handing over code to a separate team to test by hand, there's a self-service infrastructure that allows developers to write and automatically run their own low-level, code-specific tests.

Moving certain JTBD or at least consideration of them upstream in the product pipeline is something you may hear referred to as 'left-shift', which is prevalent in DevOps as well as its security-specific extension, DevSecOps, which extends DevOps' lessons learned to security. Basically, this is a take on identifying and resolving mistakes or bad practice before they flow downstream and get more complicated and expensive to fix. Another example is the deploy folks building automation for the deploy step that devs can then extend and use in their own work, practicing like they play, rather than writing documentation which may have gaps or lack context.

Continuing to the deploy step, that same self-service infrastructure may also go ahead and deliver the new code to a working environment if it passes all the tests. This may or may not mean actually releasing it to end users in a fully fledged deployment. If the automation extends to that step, that's what's generally referred to as Continuous Delivery.

If the code is instead automatically delivered to a pre-release environment for further testing, but not automatically released to production, this is what's referred to as 'continuous integration'. That might mean that the release step is manual or it might mean that the code is deployed to an internal 'staging' server where internal teams do additional testing.

The second general-purpose principle is infrastructure-as-code, which means treating the platforms that your applications run on as code vs. a set of physical services with particular properties. In practice, this (should) mean being able to add more resources for running a given application with a single commend. Likewise, it should mean that any given server is completely fungible—it catches on fire or otherwise goes kaput and you just need to add a new resource, which is fast and easy. "Cattle not pets" is DevOps lingo for having an infrastructure where no single server is particularly important. In fact, as you'll see, even that process is often automated with orchestration tools like Kubernetes.

For a team, this means focusing on automating their pipeline, rather than writing documentation which then requires manual work. In test, this means coding automated tests vs. writing out test cases and executing them manually. In deployment it means writing code that automates the process of getting the right software running in the right place under the right conditions, as opposed to the kind of documentation I was reading in that data center in the Caribbean. Consistent with the agile manifeso's line on 'Working software over comprehensive documentation', this is essentially a domain-specific application of agile's core points of view.

Boosting 'F' and Devops

The exciting thing about DevOps and achieving a more continuous delivery capability is the finding that teams who get there are able to deploy *more* often while introducing *fewer* bugs into production.[6] Nicole Forsgren & Jez Humble have been observing DevOps practices for several years through their DevOps Research Institute (DORA), now part of Google Cloud. They measure performance across four metrics:

1. Deployment frequency
2. Lead time for changes (from code commit to deploy)
3. Time to restore service (from a a failure)
4. Change failure rate (how often a a change degrades customer experience (CX) and requires a fix)

6 "Announcing Dora 2021 Accelerate State of Devops Report | Google Cloud Blog," Google (Google), accessed July 21, 2022, https://hdd.works/3RRuQtF.

While the details are interesting and you can read about them in the footnote above, the punchline is that organizations who have a high-functioning practice of DevOps have vastly healthier pipelines: Relative to the bottom quartile, their top quartile deploys 973x more frequently, is 6,570x faster from code commit to deploy, has a 3x lower failure rate in production, and when they do break something, they recover 6,570x faster.

In terms of our equation for 'F', that means reducing r_f. Better still, teams that out-experiment their competition tend to outcompete them, something you'll learn about in more depth in the chapter that follows. Given this, teams that make their pipeline more continuous will likely see an improvement in 's_d'. You can observe this by whether your team is excited to release and see what happens vs. dreading the release process. As a manager, you'll probably notice that a shaky release process introduces unnecessary stress in an industry that already moves fast and is notorious for burn out. In short, if you're wondering why tech teams are so excited about DevOps, this is why.

Figure 4-5: 'F' and DevOps

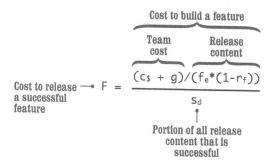

DevOps & Collaborating on Code

A continuous pipeline is an automated pipeline. Specifically, that means the test and deploy steps are automated. How teams get there and the rewards they enjoy is the subject of this chapter. First and foremost, though, this means that the dev, the test, and the deploy functions collaborate readily and relatively seamlessly through version control.

What's version control? Well, if you're as old as I am or if your company still doesn't use Google Docs, you've probably played hot potato with multiple people editing different versions of the same file: CustomerSalesproposal-June-1, CustomerSalesproposal-June-1[Someone's Initials], CustomerSalesproposal-June-1[Someone's Initials]_final, CustomerSalesproposal-June-1[Someone's Initials]_finalFinal, etc. Needless to say, you can't manage code this way and still deploy code every 11.7 seconds (like Amazon does), or even multiple times per week.

The Job of Version Control

'Version control' is the conventional term for the job of having multiple developers, as well as testers and deploy/ops folks, working on a single stream of code. If you deal with version control all day long, you may want to skim this section, and perhaps it will give you some ideas on how to explain its significance to your colleagues that don't use it. There are various software applications teams use to do this, but the one you've mostly likely heard of is GitHub. While they may approach it somewhat differently, these all generally support the same core processes around version control.

Let's walk through a simple example. Sri, Frangelico, and a few other colleagues are collaborating on a single set of code, usually called a 'repository'. They have a single set of versions they update called a 'trunk' which serves as the code stream or 'branch', from which the team will deploy, or at least push to the next step in the pipeline.[7] Let's say that around the same time, they both create their own copy of the trunk to develop on, coding and testing changes. These are called 'branches'.

---

7   You may have heard the term 'Fork'. In fact, it's a command on JSFiddle, the online (mini) IDE where you can find the sample code. This is related to branching but different in that the idea is you are creating an independent copy of the repository. However, this might be for a couple of purposes, which are pretty different. First, you might be forking a repository where you don't have access but intend to submit ideas for changes—this is pretty common for contributors to open source projects. The second reason is functionally similar but intentionally very different—you're intending to take code that has a relatively permissive license and use it to develop your own alternative to the current open source project.

Figure 4-6: Version Control

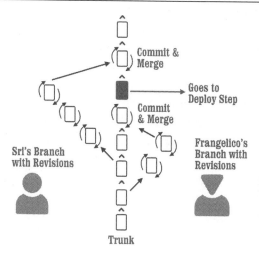

Commit & Merge

Goes to Deploy Step

Commit & Merge

Sri's Branch with Revisions

Frangelico's Branch with Revisions

Trunk

I started the chapter with an analogy about emailing files, and so you might wonder, "Why don't devs just work synchronously on the same branch like I work on a Google Doc[8]?" The main reason is that the changes the two developers will make as they work are likely to interfere with or 'step on' each other. A simple example is that lots of changes will temporarily break part of an application—kind of like replacing the brake pads on a car makes it non-drivable while the repair's underway. This is particularly relevant if the team has some automation in their pipeline and is periodically running a set of automated tests on it.

While branching solves the problem of letting everyone do their thing independently, the tricky part comes when the various devs want to merge their changes in their branches back into the trunk, along with everyone else's. This process is called merging, and merge conflicts are a notorious source of hairballs for developers. Even if Sri and Frangelico are conceptually making changes to different areas of the application, they may end up editing the same code causing a 'hard' merge conflict.

---

8 Google Docs are an online web doc where everyone who has access is editing the same file simultaneously.

While there are a few tools to help automate fixing this,[9] in many cases, the best the version control system can do is show someone who made what change where so they can figure out how to resolve the merge conflicts.

Here's the interesting thing, particularly with regard to teams working on a more continuous release capability and a more agile set of processes: small merges are much easier to manage and much less likely to create merge conflicts, particularly messy, complicated ones. This is relatively intuitive: more changes over a longer duration are just more likely to conflict with the changes someone else is making.

One thing many teams implement is a process around 'pull requests' where rather than merging their own changes, when Frangelico wants to merge code to the trunk, the version control system is configured to notify Sri, who is responsible for reviewing the code and either completing the merge or sending it back to Frangelico for updates. This is a way teams help encourage peer review of code, which not only makes the code better, but is helpful for encouraging everyone to be more aware of what their peers are doing and how the system is evolving.

Making sure that *everything* related to the deploy process is in version control can sometimes challenge teams. For example, it may seem much easier in the moment to just edit a configuration file after the fact vs. deal with automating the process of making sure it gets the right parameters. This is particularly challenging with assets like passwords and tokens that involve authentication and hence security. While there are robust tool chains for these tasks, don't be surprised to hear from someone that deals with delivery infrastructure that they spend a majority of their time managing authentication-related assets.

The Devops Approach to Version Control & the Product Pipeline
The diagram here shows the general relationship between version control and the product pipeline.

---

9   See, for example: "Merge-Strategies Documentation," Git, accessed July 14, 2022, https://hdd.works/3PqB5CJ.

Figure 4-7: From Dev to Deploy

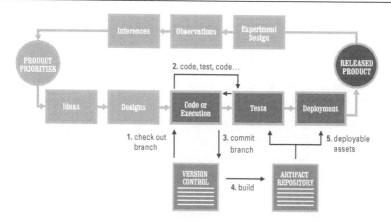

Basically, teams writing code interact with each other and the version control system in the general manner we stepped through above. They check out a branch, code (including manual and automated testing), commit, and then that build proceeds to downstream processes like later stage testing and deploy. Let's take a closer look at the Test step.

The DevOps Approach to Testing Software

Devops testing, and, really DevOps everything, is a lot about investing in automation. In the case of test automation, this *both* lowers r_f (release friction) and improves f_e (feature velocity) in the medium and long run.

That said, it's harder than it probably sounds. The reason is that adding test automation will probably slow things down in the short term vs. speed them up. Why? Because if you're not investing in it, you're effectively spending maintainability and extensibility to buy velocity. This phenomenon is known as incurring 'technical debt'. In fact, one popular definition of 'legacy code', code from an era the team sees as passed, is code that does not have automated test coverage.[10]

---

10 MICHAEL FEATHERS, "Working Effectively with Legacy Code," (PRENTICE HALL, 2020)

What is technical debt?

When developing software, there's often a "quick and dirty" shortcut to get something done and a "right" way to get it done that's more durable. Not surprisingly, when a team is under deadline pressure and a software developer asks—"I can do this quick and dirty, but I'll have to clean it up later. Are you sure you want it the quick way?"—two things usually happen. First, they get a "Yes, just get it done quickly," and second, afterwards it's never quite the right time to go back and clean up that quick-and-dirty implementation and do it the right way.

We all tend to measure our efficiency locally on our own terms, and in the case of technical debt, this leads to discord between managers and developers. The manager sees a schedule whereas the developer sits all day in front of code that is becoming increasingly hard to work with (because of the accumulation of technical debt), while being asked why new features are taking longer and longer to develop. The developer's problem is difficult for the manager to intuitively understand if the manager doesn't have experience as a software developer.

In simplified terms, an increase in technical debt on a codebase is something a team will observe by a decrease in 'f_e', more specifically observable as an increase in how long a given new feature takes to develop. For example—assuming a single feature, X—if a codebase's technical debt is increasing, the investment of effort to develop X will increase over time. The reverse is true if technical debt is decreasing.

Table 4-1: Technical Debt

Time (calendar)	t_1	t_2	...	t_n
Feature	X	X	...	X
Investment of effort*	y_a	y_{a+b}	...	y_{a+b+n}

*In, say, hours or days of engineering time invested.

Those are the particulars. In practice, though, sometimes you'll hear a frustrated developer refer to code or technical decisions they just plain don't like as 'tech debt'. They probably have a reason for that, which in itself will manifest itself as a form of tech debt, but the important thing is to keep a close eye on the particulars of tech debt and facilitate open discussions about where the team should invest to minimize 'F'.

While teams tend to find that it's easy to 'over borrow' on tech debt, it's not inherently bad. The debt metaphor is powerfully accurate in the sense that you are borrowing against the future to capture an opportunity now. If you're operating with little or no Hypothesis Testing on user behavior, it may very well be a great idea. However, in the same way you borrow money and accept that you will have to pay it down over time, if teams or managers never get in the habit of paying down their debt, sooner or later they'll end up in trouble.

It's expensive to build something well, so you want to make sure you're building the right thing. If you have no particular reason to believe anyone will want something, then an engineering concept called YAGNI comes into play: "you aren't going to need it.". What this effectively means is that on the implementation side, don't build something "just in case" something provisional and uncertain *might* happen in the future. This happens a lot, and it's because a lot of engineering training does have to do with building things well. The opposite of YAGNI is *not* just building everything like it might never see the light of day. The opposite (more or less) is 'emergent design'. This is closely related to the idea of paying off tech debt: instead of building out a robust engineering solution, solve the problems you have now and then use that dividend of time to refactor where you need to based on what code turns out to be important. 10–15% is a conventional, though by no means standard, allowance for this refactoring, often called 'slack'.

While the presence of technical debt is a reality for all development teams, it is difficult and rarely practical to measure completely. In practice, test coverage is one of the more consistently practical measures. Unfortunately, test coverage only tells you that you have proven the code does it's job, not that it is maintainable. The best signs of tech debt that you should consider paying down are unpredictable levels of investment for new features or high rates of errors on change. If the team isn't confident that they can safely make changes, it's likely time to pay down some debt.

A rough first order metric for this is the ratio of number of tests to lines of code. Specifically, some teams approximate technical debt by the coverage within the codebase of "unit tests," which is one of several types of tests a team is likely to create. However, even this is problematic because many teams find this leads to an arbitrary focus on unit tests at the expense of a more balanced approach of applying other, complementary types of testing to validating the codebase. In the next section, we'll look at how the quantity, quality, and type of tests drive performance ('F') for teams, starting with the 'test pyramid'.

Prioritizing with the Test Pyramid

You can't test everything, even if 'everything' is a relatively well defined set of user stories. Teams also have to consider the different types of tests available, who might take ownership of creating and maintaining those, and how they'll function in the product pipeline as a whole.

And what are we after with testing, again? Well, certainly to see if the application is broken, meaning, specifically, that it's not working as designed. This is distinct from what you learned about in Chapter 2 where we learned how to look for places where the application is either not doing something the user cares about or the UI is making it harder than it needs to be for them to do what they want.

Once you find what's broken, what then? What we're after with testing is a prioritized list of things that someone needs to fix, and if you've had any coursework on lean you know that unfixed problems get more expensive the further they travel. Attributed to agilist Mike Cohn from his book 'Succeeding with Agile', the basic idea is that given the cost of creating and maintaining automated tests of various types and the optimal use of them by a team, the number of tests you have should look something like a pyramid with unit tests at the bottom, integration tests in the middle, and large tests at the top:

Figure 4-8: The Test Pyramid

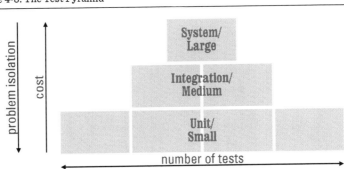

Let's start with the y-axis since that's what's shaping the test pyramid. 'Problem isolation' describes the actionability of a given test result. How specific is the result with regard to the codebase? As you go up the pyramid, the test types increase in abstraction and scope. For example, a 'unit' (or small) test gives the developer a more specific starting point for debugging than a system test.

Second, there's cost, which accrues in two areas. As the tests increase in abstraction, they become more sensitive to small, benign changes causing them to fail in the sense that they give false positives for being broken when really they're fine. For instance, if the team changes the label slightly on a given field, that might cause it to fail when, in fact, the application and the UI are still fine from a UX perspective. Costs accrue as the dev's or testers need to diagnose such failed tests and update them simply so they don't fail and return false positives.

The tests also take longer to run as you go up the stack, and that's the second cost they accrue—loss of developer productivity from more waiting as the tests run. For a developer, it's highly useful to be able to push a button and have all their code tested to make sure it's OK in a few seconds. If a test fails, they can fix the offending code right then and there; if it passes, they can confidently keep on with what they're doing. On the other hand, if the tests take a long time to run, the test infrastructure stops delivering this— the developer has to move on to something else and wait while their tests run. In an extreme case they have to leave the tests to run overnight. In the next section, we'll look more specifically at the different test types.

System or 'Large' Tests

We'll start at the top of the pyramid, just because I think those tests are easier to understand. The naming standards for this part of the test pyramid are somewhat loose; other than 'system' or 'large', you might also hear these called UI tests or end-to-end tests. Terms aside, the basic idea with this test is to test the system as a user would experience it. Sometimes that means writing instructions for an application that tests UI's like Selenium, which simulates input directly to the user interface. Sometimes, it means doing roughly the same thing but through an interface the UI uses to access the rest of the application, often called 'subcutaneous testing'. Rather than isolating and testing a specific function or bit of code, the system tests operate on the larger arcs of user experience.

For example, let's say our team at HVAC in a Hurry is now working on letting technicians create accounts on their new system for looking up and ordering parts. They might then have a user story like this: *'As Trent the Technician, I want to create an account so I can try out the system.'*

Once we get to the point of building a user interface, we can start making more specifically observable statements about how it should work. A popular way to do this is the given-when-then pattern, which you see here for the user story about Trent creating an account.

Figure 4-9: Behavior-Driven Development (BDD)

'As Trent the Technician, I want to create an account so I can try out the system.'

"Given [a circumstance],
When [the user does something]
Then [expected change in state]"

"Given [Trent has an email account at work],
When [he enters his email and a pair of matching passwords]
and [clicks the Register button]
Then [an account is created on the user database]
and [the Log In text transitions to Log Out]

The important thing here is that these statements are readily understandable by anyone and yet specific enough to render into an automated test. In fact, there's a DevOps-friendly body of work called 'behavior-driven development', which focuses on interdisciplinary teams making a habit of creating this kind of syntax and adding it to their test suite as they go. There are even software applications like Cucumber that allow teams to build an infrastructure that automatically generates tests from the given-when-then syntax.

What's great about system tests is that they let you practice like you play, putting yourself in the customer's shoes. For this reason, they're also the easiest to understand. What's not so great about systems tests is that they take a long time to run and they're fragile with regard to minor changes. At my last startup, I learned how to use Selenium's visual interface which simply records your actions and allows you to repeat them. It was so easy that with no prior experience my wife offered to chip in and help write some tests (it was a busy time and we were self-funded). She did great (thanks again, honey!) but then we learned that the smallest changes broke those tests and they all needed a serious update that linked more directly to the underlying structure of the pages, the HTML. And even those tests were only somewhat stable.

At a larger operation, these tests are generally written by someone who's specifically focused on testing: a tester, someone in a QA group, etc. For a small application like the HVAC parts lookup we have here, you might only have 1–2 systems tests. For example, one that deals with new users signing up and logging in and another that looks up and orders a part.

Here, you can see a test script from the Selenium tool. This test handles the process of a user registering and then being signed in to use the application.

Figure 4-10: System Tests with the Selenium IDE

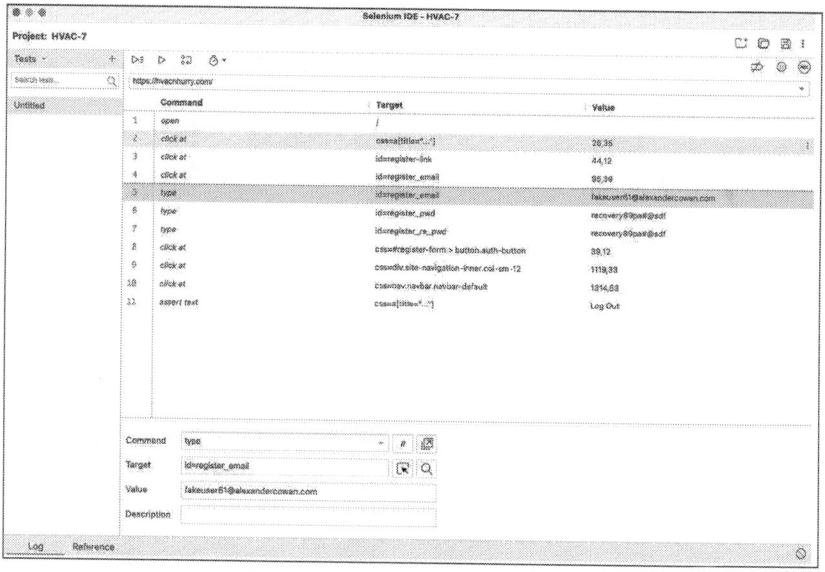

The three columns you see are:
1. Command: the particular command type like 'open' (a URL), 'click' (an element), or 'type' (some text)
2. Target: the item in question, a URL (web address) or the ID of an HTML element, for example
3. Value: the input—the button to click or item to type, for example

The final command is particularly notable: 'assert text'. The idea with assertions is to say 'make sure this is true', returning 'false' is that's not the case. This type of command is generally popular in testing frameworks since it's a readable and compact way of coding tests, regardless of where they sit in the test pyramid. If you want to try one out for yourself, there's a note at the end of the chapter on how to do that.

Medium or 'Integration' Tests

Nestled in the middle of the test pyramid, these test the interaction between two functions. To recap from Chapter 3, these are the 'legos' of the Controller in the larger MVC framework. Generally, Controllers have an input, a set of steps (algorithms) they execute, and an output.

Back to the user story above about the HVAC technicians creating accounts on the system, let's say we want a functional behavior where users can only register if their email is from the company's domain names, let's say hvacnhurry.com and also hvacalot.com, a domain they have left over from an acquisition. Let's say they've written a pair of functions that work together to check this: check_domain which returns a true or false, and which also calls get_domains to get the current list of approved domains:

Figure 4-11: Inputs and Outputs and the Function

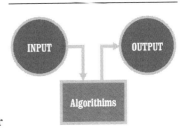

Figure 4-12: Integration Testing

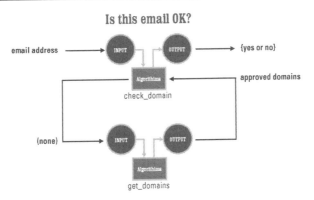

We might write an integration test to make sure that these two functions are working together as intended, supplying them a series of example email addresses and then making sure we get the result we expect, a yes or no/true or false. Generally, a team will have selected a language-specific framework that structures and abbreviates the amount of code a team has to write to get the tests they want. For example, JUnit is a popular option for Java and Jasmine is a popular option for Javascript.

How many integration tests should you have? There's no simple, axiomatic answer, but I consistently hear the same general answer from teams that seem relatively happy with their practice of DevOps: their particular take on test coverage is iterative and retrospective. Whenever a bug makes it further than it should in the product pipeline, the team asks, 'What's the lowest level test that could have caught this?'. If the answer is a unit test, they add one and take note, and likewise for integration and system tests.

Who writes these tests? To me, this has always been a particularly interesting question. In an old school environment, devs don't write tests—they write code and then hand it off to someone else for testing. Predictably, this tends to deliver less involvement on test and more importantly less of a hypothesis-driven take from devs.

On the other hand, particularly in the upper layers of the test pyramid where there's more abstraction and different code from different devs interacting, it can be useful to have a dedicated resource that's looking at application-wide functionality and able to spend the time writing tests accordingly. It's a balance and different fulcrums work for different teams. Generally, developers write unit tests since those are so code-adjacent and relevant to making sure their day to day work coheres.

On the other end of the spectrum, test specialists tend to write system tests since these span so much code and infrastructure, and require a particular perspective to balance coverage with false positives. Integration tests are kind of the ground ball—you have to code to write them, and yet they may somewhat disrupt a developers's flow.

Integration Test Examples

What do integration tests look like in practice? First, let's review a little more Javascript—the code that implements this email checking behavior.[11] As before, if you only get the general idea with this—what these two functions generally do and how they work together—that's fine for our purposes. The code below has the two functions you see in the diagram: check_domain and get_domains. Check_domain takes an email as an input, strips off the user portion of the email address (URI) including the '@' sign, calls get_domains to find out what domains are all right, compares, and then returns a true or a false. Relative to the JS you've seen, the only substantial new item here is an 'array'. These are a data type you'll see across programming languages that do the job of storing a set of related values in a kind of list. The diagram in Figure 4-13 steps through the code in more detail.

---

11 For you coders or emerging coders, you might wonder:

1) Does this handle for someone submitting an email w/ upper case characters? Or someone making a typo of that type in the domains? No, it does not! You can try it in the Jasmine code, which is on the JS Fiddle.

2) If get_domains seems kind of silly as implemented, the idea was just to show two (simple) functions working together. Also, it's something you might put in as a next step to interfacing with a third party system.

3) From a security/standard procedure standpoint, wouldn't you want to have the user validate their email (via email) before you did this? Also, yes! This code doesn't provide for this, but in fact the Google Firebase back-end-as-service that we'll be using already does that.

Figure 4-13: Functions to Check Email Domain

The check_domains function takes an email and returns a true/false

This line calls the get_domains function and puts the result in a variable, 'OKdomains'

```
//Validates email domain
function check_domain(email) {
    OKdomains = get_domains();
    thisdomain = email.substring(email.lastIndexOf("@") +1);
    if(OKdomains.includes(thisdomain)){
        return true;
    } else {
        return false;
    }
}
```

If the email's domain is in the list from get_domains then true, otherwise false

Extracts the domain portion (after the '@') of the mail address

The get_domains function takes no input and returns an array of domains

```
//Gets valid domains
function get_domains() {
    domains = ['hvachurry.com', 'hvacalot.com',
    'corp.hvachurry.com'];
    return(domains);
}
```

Return the variable 'domains' to whatever called get_domains

Puts an array of domains into the variable 'domains'

If you're interested in seeing the code en situ, the above is available at the following JSFiddle, along with the Jasmine testing code that follows: https://hdd.works/3B8bNpd. Again, if you're interested in or substantially curious about something in the code, it's much better to pull it up in the JSFiddle IDE where you can actively play with it and see how it behaves. Note: If you copy this item by hand (vs. use the Fork command to create a copy), be sure to include the Jasmine library, which you can see in the left margin of JSFiddle.

Here you see code in the Jasmine framework (for testing JS) that implements an integration test on the code above:

```
describe("Email domain validator", function() {
    it("validates emails from our domains", function() {
        expect(check_domain('acowan@alexandercowan.com')).
toBe(true);
    });
    it("invalidates emails not from our domains", function() {
        expect(check_domain('alex_cowan@stanfordalumni.org')).toBe(false);
    });
```

```
    it("invalidates badly formatted domains", function() {
            expect(check_domain('alex_cowan@stanfordalumni')).
toBe(false);
        });
    it("validates subdomains from our domains", function() {
            expect(check_domain('acowan@corp.hvachurry.com')).
toBe(true);
        });
});
```

Basically, what you're seeing is a function 'describe' which is part of the Jasmine framework, and then that function's two inputs. The first input is a descriptive name for the test, "Email domain validator" in this case. The second input is a set of functions. These are the four 'it' functions you see. The 'it' function is another function made available by Jasmine. These 'it' functions themselves *also* take a descriptive name and a set of functions, and those are the third level nested functions you see that start with 'expect'.

This is the exciting part, at least as far as integration testing is concerned. The diagram above describes the particulars, and you can find the code in the JS Fiddle above. Essentially, the 'describe' function from Jasmine provides the outer structure and it in turn takes multiple 'it' functions as inputs, each of which in turn have their own inputs nested inside of them (a description and an assertion using the 'expect' function). The View you see here is what the Jasmine library provides:

Figure 4-15: Jasmine Output (Test Success)

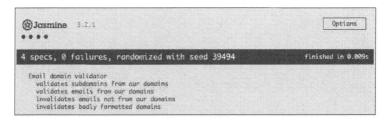

If a test fails, it also does a nice job of telling you about where to look and which of the tests specifically failed and why. For example, in this case, the first test 'validates emails from our domains' failed; it was expected to be false but it turned out to be true.[12]

---

12 Apropos of the previous note, I introduced this failed by adding an upper case character into the domain, which the current code doesn't handle.

Figure 4-16: Jasmine Output (Test Failure)

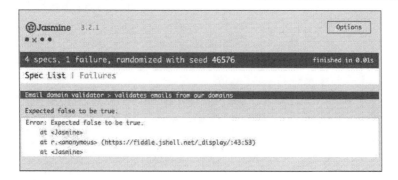

Unit or 'Small' Tests

At the foundation of the test pyramid, we have unit tests. The idea is that each of these tests isolates its testing and its result to a single function. What if the function depends on other functions to work, like the one we just saw? Then we need to simulate that interaction using what's called a 'stub' or 'mock', and this is one of the messier parts of writing these unit tests.

This diagram describes a unit test for the check_domain function where get_domains is mocked: basically, there's code, usually created with the test framework, that basically is instructed to always return a certain static output to the function that calls it, no matter what, in order to isolate the issue to just the function in question.

Figure 4-17: Unit Testing

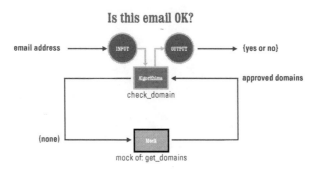

What's so great about this? Why have these *and* integration tests? Well, unit tests run very fast and provide excellent problem isolation. Some developers also practice TDD, test-driven development. This means that they start new development by writing tests, seeing that they fail, and then writing code to make them pass. This practice is closely associated with the XP methodology of getting to agile and a way that some developers find they ensure good test coverage while focusing their work.

What would this look like for a unit test where we want to test check_domains and mock get_domains? It looks the same as the integration test, *except* for this line which 'spies' on the get_domains function and forces it to return a static list of values:

```
beforeEach(function() {
spyOn(window, 'get_domains').and.returnValue(['hvachurry.com',
'alexandercowan.com', 'corp.hvachurry.com']);
    });
```

You can see this in full below and also here live at this URL:
https://hdd.works/3oiPDZB.

```
describe("Email domain validator", function() {
        beforeEach(function() {
        spyOn(window, 'get_domains').and.returnValue(['hvachurry.com',
'alexandercowan.com', 'corp.hvachurry.com']);
  });
    it("validates emails from our domains", function() {
                expect(check_domain('acowan@alexandercowan.com')).
toBe(true);
            });
    it("invalidates emails not from our domains", function() {
                expect(check_domain('alex_cowan@stanfordalumni.org')).
toBe(false);
            });
    it("invalidates badly formatted domains", function() {
                expect(check_domain('alex_cowan@stanfordalumni')).
toBe(false);
            });
    it("validates subdomains from our domains", function() {
                expect(check_domain('acowan@corp.hvachurry.com')).
toBe(true);
            });
});
```

Wait, what are feature flags and do we even need testing?

Feature flags are an increasingly important tool for maximizing velocity & learning while minimizing cost & overhead. Basically, once these are instrumented into code it allows you to selectively enable or disable features by customer segment. They incur a relatively low cost to set up and offer relatively good problem isolation—less granular isolation than a unit test but more than a system test.

Table 4-2: Feature Flag Grid

Features	Customer Segments							
	1	2	3	4	5	6	...	7
1	off	off	off	on	off	on	off	off
2	on	on	on	on	on	on	on	on
3	on	on	on	on	on	on	on	on
4	on	on	on	on	on	on	on	on
5	on	on	on	on	on	on	on	on
6	on	on	on	on	on	on	on	on
7	on	on	on	on	on	on	on	on
...	on	on	on	on	on	on	on	on
N	on	on	on	on	on	on	on	on

Are these feature flags an unqualified win? No. Feature flags require maintenance. They're cheap to put in, but quickly become hard to understand— good for a release cycle, but once you've decided that you're going to make a feature available to all, you need to go clean up all the flagged code (this is now debt) and add appropriate testing to avoid future problems. For example, serial founder and CTO Conor Sibley found that the technical debt from feature flags wasn't worth it at his last company, and instead assigned different customer groups to different 'release pools' on different versions as part of their deploy and release process. This gave them some of the capabilities of feature flags (being able to verify new release content with a subset of the user population) without that particular source of technical debt.

Feature flags can relieve pressure on the jobs that integration and system tests need to do: if the company has adequate observability built into the way they deploy with feature flags, they can roll out new features to small slices of users and roll them back if those changes tank a key metric, like the ratio of visitors to purchases. This allows you to catch errors that escaped your earlier stages of testing from the test pyramid.

Getting to the Right Test Recipe with HDD

What are you after with the jobs of test? How do you know when things are improving vs. degrading? Having users encounter serious bugs is bad, but so is releasing infrequently and spending a fortune on testing. Over time, 'F' will do a pretty good job of answering this question since r_f (release friction) will go up and under-experimenting will depress s_d. That said, the DORA metrics do a better job of unpacking the particulars related to test (and deployment, which we'll cover in the next section) and making them more immediately observable. Those are:

1. Deployment frequency
2. Lead time for changes (from code commit to deploy)
3. Time to restore service (from a a failure)
4. Change failure rate (how often a a change degrade services and requires a fix)

For a team to make fully articulated decisions on how they approach the jobs of testing, one other variable they have to consider is the cost of a bug reaching production. This is substantially different for a blogging platform vs. the software in a self-driving car.

The following table summarizes major test facilities with notes on their pro's and con's relative to minimizing F, the DORA metrics, and consideration of the risk premium on a bug reaching end users.

Table 4-3: Test Facilities

Test Facility	Pro's	Con's
Unit Tests	Developers generally write these against the code they're working, which minimizes overhead, and is an example of left-shift. These tests run fast and provide excellent problem isolation. In addition to reducing the lead time for changes and reducing failure rates, they also make it much easier (and more appealing) for developers to refactor their code. This helps discourage YAGNI and encourage emergent design.	Since they only validate individual functions, these can only ever be part of an overall testing portfolio. Sometimes they're awkward and expensive to write, particularly when the interfaces you have to simulate, the interfaces that your function touches, are complex.[13] Rob, this chapter's guest editor also notes that if a dev is still working out how they want a function or functions to operate, designing unit tests too early can increase the cost of subsequent changes.
Medium Tests	If you need to test code beyond the individual function, these run faster and provide better problem isolation than system tests. If, for example, you find this is the lowest/simplest spot you could have caught a bug that made it to production, it's a good way to go.	These are often written by dedicated testers who code, creating some overhead. They occupy a kind of interdisciplinary gray area—more test abstraction than many developers are inclined to deal with but they require the ability to understand and code in the language in question.
System Tests	Easy to understand and simple (initially) to write, these are a great way to 'practice like you play' since they most directly map to specific user behaviors.	These are extremely brittle and tend to deliver a lot of false failures, especially if they're written in an abstraction layer like the Selenium visual editor. They're also slow to run relative to unit or integration tests and provide worse problem isolation.
Staging Environment	If a team doesn't have a track record automating the processes from test to release, they'll almost certainly want to start here. It offers a way to benefit from automation but keep manual safeguards in place.	Actually simulating production is hard, particularly at scale. You're not dealing with real user behavior and because of privacy, security, and complexity, you're often not dealing with real user data either. Even getting close can be expensive and unreliable with regard to catching issues before release.

13 "TDD Is Dead. Long Live Testing.," TDD is dead. Long live testing. (DHH), accessed July 21, 2022, https://hdd.works/3onXqFL.

Test Facility	Pro's	Con's
Manual Testing	If you don't have automated tests, this is the choice you have to make, unless you want to roll the dice in production. Having a tester who's tuned in to what might go wrong can help uncover bugs that developers might have missed. As our guest editor, Rob Zuber puts it: *Devs like to think they're good at testing, but that's not often the case. Yes they can automate, but they typically test the behavior that follows the assumptions they made (the "happy path" plus a few obvious errors).* *Good manual testers are actually super valuable, because they have fresh eyes and a knack for seeing what the devs didn't. But once they find something you should immediately automate it and let them use their brain power and skills on a different problem. Having them manually test the same cases over and over makes for comically bad ROI.*	If you've ever tested by hand, you have some sense of how time consuming and incredibly dull this is. It's easy for testers to make a mistake due to sheer boredom and given how slow and expensive it is you'll never get in as much testing as you'd like.
Feature Flags	While 'testing in production' used to be a euphemism for sloppy engineering, this is an ascendent means of testing. If you can limit the blast radius of a hypothetical bug and readily observe it, why not?	For some applications, seeing what happens in production is too high risk. Also, these provide relatively poor problem isolation. Without strong observability, automating releases is just playing with fire.

While your team might start out with a general idea of the test investments they want to make, as you hold retrospectives and look at what bugs made it further than they should have in the product pipeline, ask: "What's the simplest test facility that would have caught this?", and adjust your test investments on that basis. While many teams use tools like Coveralls, which report on the ratio of lines of code to unit tests, this is only useful as a first order take on test coverage. Successful teams tend to focus on the messier but more important questions of how their test investments are performing relative to the health of their product pipeline.

While not a universal feature of agile, many teams capture their working point of view on items like test coverage in a working doc called a 'team charter' which describes the current state of their processes. Personally, it's also the place where I like to maintain a working version of the Business Model Canvas and the team's focal JTBD (jobs-to-be-done)—or have a tight linkage to someplace (Google Doc, etc.) where that information resides. There's a tutorial with an example and template in Google Docs or MS Word for this at the end of the chapter.

Part of the beauty of HDD is that it helps draw attention to common practice across business, design, and technical domains. Essentially, think of what you've learned so far on testing as various 'functional hypotheses', which are hypotheses related to the software working as designed (aka not breaking).

You've also learned about the bigger picture of how teams pair work and rewards on where and how they invest in testing. Should a team go whole hog and start practicing test-driven development (TDD)? Not necessarily. Some developers find it isn't worth the work, at least some of the time or until they've learned more about what the code needs to do in practice. Should you not worry about testing and just use feature flags? Here also, probably not. Such a team will likely struggle with bug isolation and analytical debugging.

Ultimately, it's important that a team comes to understand their product's economics with regard to when and how they find bugs, and how they fix them. HDD offers a testable point of view on this and agile provides a strong paradigm for adaptively trying out new practice and iterating to reliable improvements.

Figure 4-19: From Code to Deploy

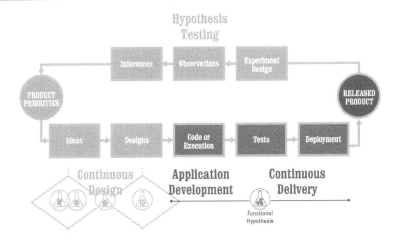

Antipatterns & Failure Modes (Testing)

It's rarely a lack of understanding that by itself causes teams not to implement a DevOps-friendly take on testing. More so, it's just hard to change habits and pair those with tangible rewards—just like getting in shape if you find your blood pressure is too high. You know what to do, that isn't the hard part. Changing your habits is the hard part.

1. *The Ice Cream Cone Test Suite*

   This is essentially an inversion of the test pyramid where there are too many system tests, many of them are failing, and the developers are overwhelmed sorting through all the false positives to see if there's anything they really need to fix. For example, if you hear from a developer that they're 'drowning in system tests', this is probably what they mean.

   Why does this happen? First, system tests are relatively easy to understand and create with tools like Selenium. If a team has testers that want more automation but don't code in the language of the application, this is a pattern you're likely to realize. Also, looking at the test suite solely from a general management and test perspective, it's easy to miss the importance of speed and problem isolation to the developer experience (DX), though this is critical to a productive team.

2. *Not Writing Automated Tests*

Here's a central fact of DevOps and Continuous Delivery that often gets lost in all the excitement: even if your test and deploy infrastructure is great, you can't get to a more continuous pipeline if your development and test (DevOps) teams aren't implementing strong test coverage. Without automated tests, you're still stuck with some kind of a manual process which slams the breaks on Continuous Delivery.

3. *Silo'ing Testing*

Like so much of the work in an agile, innovation-intensive environment, handoffs are a killer here. In a legacy environment, software developers would finish coding and then throw that code over the fence to a separate QA/ test department to test. This created lots of predictable problems: Software developers would often not test as much as they probably should and generally not think as much about testability. QA/test would not know exactly what or how to prioritize in testing, and periodically be idle waiting for new software to test and overwhelmed right before a new release/deploy was scheduled.

As we've discussed, the body of work around DevOps seeks to address this and if you hear the term 'left shift', that's the idea that developers write some of their own core tests (most often unit tests) and generally are involved more in collaborating on the later steps in the pipeline.

How does DevOps approach deploying software?

In deploying applications, the definition of success generally has to do primarily with uptime and how often the team is able to deploy. Agile and DevOps value velocity a lot. Classically, this complicates deployment because every time you update software or otherwise change the system you introduce the risk of downtime. Given this, what DevOps and the community of practice around Continuous Delivery have achieved is pretty fantastic. Some industry research suggests,[14] and it's not an uncommon finding, that with an automated pipeline you can actually deploy more often and have fewer issues in production. Wow.

Deployment Jobs-to-be-Done

Whereas the jobs of testing are tightly coupled to the specific work on an individual team, sprint to sprint, it's more common for all or parts of the Deploy function to be centralized, and terms you might hear for such teams or departments are 'developer experience' (DX), 'developer productivity', or "platform engineering". Their charter is to create an overall infrastructure for the product teams to use on a self-service basis. Whereas these teams used to spend a lot of time physically installing servers, operating systems, supporting packages, and the company's apps, a more modern set up is that they're developing self-service automation for teams to do all this themselves, usually on top of some commercial applications like Kubernetes, Ansible, and Terraform. Some job titles you might see in this area are: ops engineer, site reliability engineer (SRE), and DevOps engineer.

Given all the great technologies and practices out there, let's start with the fundamental jobs that an ops team has, technology aside. Words are faulty instruments and these teams are just as likely to be called a 'platform' or 'infrastructure' team. You can see those in the image here.

Figure 4-20: The Jobs of Deploy

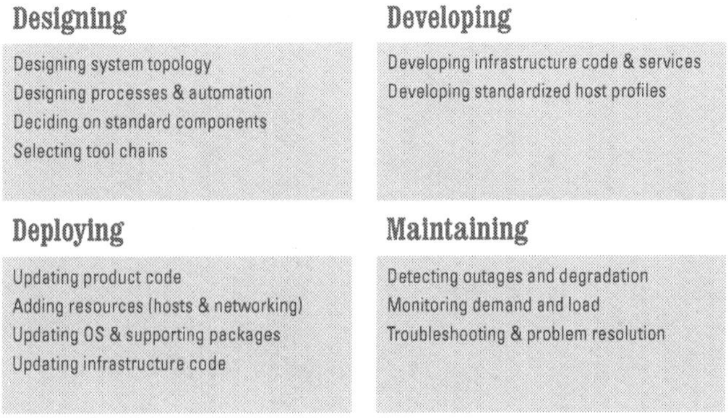

Designing

Designing system topology
Designing processes & automation
Deciding on standard components
Selecting tool chains

Developing

Developing infrastructure code & services
Developing standardized host profiles

Deploying

Updating product code
Adding resources (hosts & networking)
Updating OS & supporting packages
Updating infrastructure code

Maintaining

Detecting outages and degradation
Monitoring demand and load
Troubleshooting & problem resolution

14 "Announcing Dora 2021 Accelerate State of Devops Report | Google Cloud Blog," Google (Google), accessed July 21, 2022, https://hdd.works/3RRuQtF.

Designing

If this looks similar to the jobs-to-be-done that you'd envision for a product team, then you wouldn't be wrong. If they're not embedded with a product team, a team with DevOps-focused engineers often, in effect, does their own product management, building a self-service infrastructure for their customers who are engineers embedded with the product teams. You might hear these teams referred to as a 'platform team', 'platform engineering', 'platform as product', or 'developer experience', to name a few.

First among these jobs of 'Designing', we have the specific job of Designing System Topology. While the particular needs of their customers will vary less than most product teams, there are still a lot of decisions these DevOps engineers need to make. For example, for what services should the company use cloud vs. owned data centers? How do they maximize consistency and standardization while adequately accommodating the development teams working on the end product? What vendor partners and/or open source projects should they depend on? And, like any substantial design task, this is ongoing: certain designs will test out well relative to their original charters and hypotheses, others won't.

Developing

This is where a high-functioning team practicing DevOps spends a big part of its time. This is easier said than done, since if you're a startup there's a push to just get something live, and if you're a gigantic company, change is hard. Companies in the middle deal with relative versions of those same symptoms. Also, it takes a special kind of engineer to do this work because they have to balance making the most out of existing applications and recipes versus just throwing up their hands and building something from scratch. There are two related JTBD here—one having to do with infrastructure code and services and the other with host profiles. The idea with the infrastructure portion is that the team is working on automation to install and configure new hosts and scale up (or down) related resources as needed. The item on host profiles has to do with creating standardized computer configurations where the developer's local machine is configured the same way as the machine her code will run on in production. We'll cover more on the "how" of this in our next section.

Deploying

This is where a team that's still transitioning to DevOps will spend more of their time, since the deploy processes in this case are more manual and require more human intervention. I do not mean to implicitly criticize teams that do this. They're often in a difficult situation where they don't have the headroom for change—and under the heading 'Understand the Managerial Side of How a Team gets to Healthier Pipelines' at the end of the chapter, there are a couple of excellent novelizations of the situation. If you're involved in a digital transformation or similar, I highly recommend them. All that said, this job is radically different if a team is doing these jobs manually versus automating them. I described my freezing cold Caribbean data center story at the beginning of the chapter, and that is something like what the manual process is like.

Maintaining

Finally, we have the job of maintaining. No one *doesn't* have issues in production. The goal of a team is to minimize the blast radius of problems and resolve them as quickly as possible, ideally through automation. Finally a high-functioning team is using the errors that they observe in this JTBD to think about how to improve on their processes and tooling across the work of Deploy.

How does all this happen across everyone's computers?

If you've worked in software development, particularly prior to the last 5 years or so when this was generally much worse, you probably had the issue a lot of the time that someone might say to you: "I can't reproduce your issue. It works fine on my machine." As with most of these kinds of situations, usually no one in particular is at fault. Developers get lots of issues that are red herrings, bad configurations, mistakes, etc. If they sat down and investigated all of them, they'd never get anything done. At the same time, this is also a legitimate issue that occurs frequently: an application assumes a particular configuration and getting the machine that's running it on this configuration isn't well orchestrated.

What do you do? The easiest wins have to do with simplifying and standardizing the baseline configuration, the profile or environment on which your application operates. You may have heard of Docker or the use of 'containers'. The basic idea is to abstract away the operating system (and everything underneath it) from your application. What this allows teams to do is provide standardized containers for everyone to use (product, dev., test, deploy) which allows for identical installs of your application and its supporting 'bins/libs' and removes or at least isolates machine-to-machine differences between the operating system and the underlying hardware. This not only removes the 'it works on my machine' problem, but also simplifies the various automation work crucial to a faster, more continuous product pipeline.

You may also have heard of virtual machines or VM's. These have been around longer and are still popular. They are not mutually exclusive with containers, as you can see in the diagram below there is space to run, say, the Docker engine on top of a virtualized operating system. Virtualizing a server usually happens at a lower level of the host stack, between the physical host and the operating system through a type of application called a 'hypervisor'. This offers tighter isolation between resources or loads running on the physical machine, but has the downside of adding another component to deal with (the hypervisor) and more operating system instances to look after. Note: You may also see hypervisors that run on the OS, particularly for personal computers—these are tools like Parallels and VMWare Fusion.

How does this relate to 'cloud computing'? The classic unit of cloud computing is basically a working OS with the necessary host resources, like storage. For example, in Amazon Web Services (AWS), you may hear reference to an 'AMI' (Amazon Machine Image), which is a standardized configuration/profile/image which companies can add across geographies with the click of a button.

Figure 4-21: Stacks and Stacks

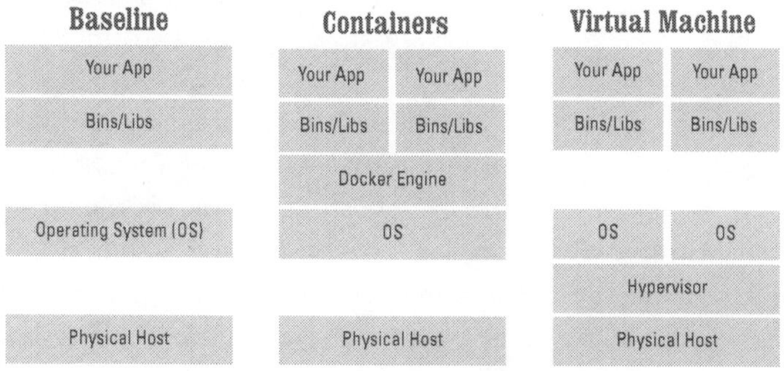

Beyond these, there is 'serverless' computing where the concept of individual server instances are abstracted away completely—teams just interact with an API to add resources.

Automating deployment

Your company or team is operating a large scale application with lots of active users all over the world and a data center where you're operating goes offline. What do you do? Here's another example: You've got 100 servers powered up, networked and ready to (hopefully) serve applications that will make you some money. How do you get your various applications running on all of them in just the right proportions and configurations? Finally, let's say your company has decided to go with a 'hybrid cloud' approach where they're going to use both Amazon Web Services to rent machines around the world as they need them, but also use some machines they own that cost them less money. How do you make that happen without doubling the amount of work your Deploy team has to do?

Figure 4-22: Automating the Deploy Step

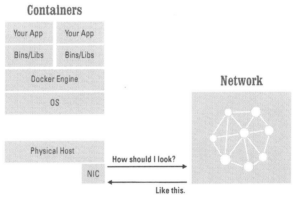

Let's take it from the bottom so to speak: How might a team practicing DevOps automate installation of physical servers? Our input here is a physical server with power and network access, and our minimum output is a server with a working operating system that can announce itself to our subsequent automation services and take orders from there. The old timey recipe is to insert a CD with an OS installer and hope for the best—the same way you (or your parents) might have installed or reinstalled your home computer 10–20 years ago. While there are many options out there now, a common option is to buy servers that are pre-configured to do a 'network boot'[15] where once the server powers on its network interface card (NIC) asks the network how it should look. This uses a protocol called DHCP (dynamic host control protocol) which is the same way your computer gets its network address on, say, Wifi. From there, the system has a working 'image', which is minimally an operating system, but often as well various 'bins/libs' and applications. Even in a simple image, this will ready our server for the next step which is 'configuration management'.

How do we get our server set up to run the applications we want? Our minimum input here is a server with a working operating system and some basic configuration and our output is a server that's (minimally) ready to find out its more specific role in our application infrastructure, and (maximally) ready to get to work serving end users.

Figure 4-23: Automating Configuration Management

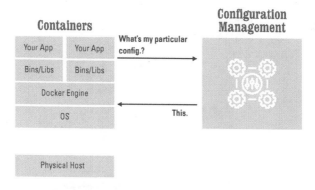

This process or area is generally referred to as 'configuration management'. Tools you might hear about in this area are Ansible, Puppet and Chef. These are built dynamically and more so conform to the infrastructure-as-code concept. Another way of doing this is just to have custom-built OS images that do exactly what you want—this approach is more brittle and changes are messier, but it's certainly better than the alternative of configuring the machines manually.

---

15 A popular standard for Linux servers is PXE which stands for 'Preboot eXecution Environment'

It's worth noting that one thing companies love about using cloud computing providers like Amazon Web Services, Google Cloud Platform, and Azure is that this is their starting point: a fully operational server image—with the cloud, you basically don't have to deal with the 'physical host' part of the process.

Once we have a minimally functioning server with, say, an operating system and a few basic packages (bins/libs), it can ask an application for the most current take on how it should look, all the way up the stack to the particular application version and configuration. Finally, it's worth noting that there's a spectrum or gray area here between our last step of going from bare metal to a working server and configuration management. For example, some teams prefer to do all this work with the image and hand the subsequent particulars to their upper-level orchestration, skipping this type of configuration management altogether.

Figure 4-24: Automated Container Orchestration

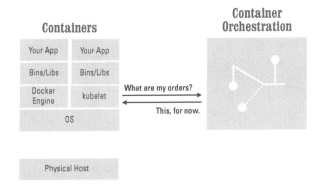

Finally, how do we take a configured application server and use it for maximum benefit? This is a job that server and container orchestration tools are designed to facilitate. You may have heard of Kubernetes, often abbreviated as 'K8s'. These allow a deploy team to declare a desired state for their overall application infrastructure and have all the necessary hosts automatically make themselves available for maximum effect. This might mean rebalancing loads between the same amount of servers or actually reducing the number of instances you're using. Reducing the instances you need is particularly valuable if you're using 3rd party cloud computing services since these generally charge on a variable basis, the number of hours a given type of instance is running, for example.

For example, let's say you do run a lot of your own servers (vs. just a 3rd party cloud service) and the demand for one application, a customer-facing application, peaks during the day but the need for a data post-processing application peaks in off hours or is able to take advantage of available bandwidth. Kubernetes automatically moves the available resources into the desired state. How? Essentially, it maps anticipated consumption or utilization of the overall resource pool and schedules application instances accordingly, rebalancing workloads dynamically to maximize resource utilization.

Mobile & Other Non-Web App Deployments

What if you're deploying to an app store like Apple, Android, Gaming, or a browser extension? In this case, while you may have the steps to deploy automated as far as submitting new versions, you're reliant on the behavior of the host operating system and, in a lot of cases, the user's configuration and choices for if and when they'll install an update. While the trend is toward more apps just updating in the background and not bothering users who just want the thing to work, there's still a fair amount of variation here.

However, it's worth noting that many of these applications also have a server component that the application responds to via requests from these end user apps, and there all the items above would apply in roughly the fashion we stepped through them.

Testing, Deploying, & Security

Security pervades all the jobs we reviewed here. In the jobs of Testing, tests for security may be relevant at all levels and many third parties offer ready-to-use penetration suites (generally at the system level) that automate known attack patterns and report the results. In the Deploy step, it's not uncommon to hear that systems engineers working on automation spend the majority of their time managing the distribution of secure credentials and access to just the right resources to manage security.[16]

---

16 For example, in Amazon Web Services (AWS) this area is referred to as IAM—Identity and Access Management.

Even the dull business of renewing certificates and other credentials can be high stakes—Spotify recently experienced a major outage on their podcast service due to an expired security certificate.[17]

Example: The HinH Team's Deployment Process

Our team at HVAC in a Hurry has a few dev's already familiar with the deploy infrastructure at HinH and they pick a machine image (AMI) on Amazon Web Services so that they can go 'serverless'. While the company has a few areas where they self-host, these tend to be more economical for applications that are running at a larger scale with more predictability.

The AMI includes the Docker Engine and so the team starts with a 'containerized' version of their application from the start—running identical Docker configurations on everyone's machines where that configuration is stored in version control. They use a configuration management tool called Ansible that's standard for the company to build AMI's with any finishing configuration items on the application, and this Ansible code is also stored in version control.

For now, they aren't worried about container orchestration/ Kubernetes since the initial footprint of their rollout will be small. Everything they're doing is 'kubernetes-friendly' in the sense that it is containerized, so if they need more automation for scaling the runway is clear.

Antipatterns & Failure Modes (Deploying)

What a team is after here is that they're able to deploy frequently without surprises (bugs/outages). What this requires is scale-appropriate, team-appropriate investments in standardization and automation.

1. *Separating Development from Deployment/Maintenance*
   When the team that's developing this application isn't substantially involved in and responsible for running it, you get the predictable disconnects you have when any two process areas are tightly interconnected but the teams on either process aren't aware of or invested in the other team's success. As I mentioned at the beginning of the chapter, more companies running on the SaaS model

---

17 Ariel Shapiro, "Massive Podcast Outage Caused by Spotify's Failure to Renew Security Certificate," May 31, 2022, https://hdd.works/3Rw3kSu.

have probably been the biggest organizational/managerial catalyst for the improvements in going from Code to Deploy that so many teams are benefiting from today.

2. *Environments not Standardized*

   For a small team or a new team, this is one of those "stitch in times saves nine" things, but if the team isn't used to working this way, it's easy to lose sight of, even with how easy Docker and containerization make this.

3. *Not Everything in Version Control*

   Making sure code is in version control is pretty standard. But that little configuration parameter someone adds? Those are easy to lose track of and maybe no one wants to make a stink about having to update it as they deploy. However, one of these leads to another and pretty soon it breaks your ability to get to a stable, reliable pipeline.

4. *Issues with Identity and Access Management*

   As I mentioned, this is a challenge for every deploy/ops team I've ever met. It's convenient to loosen up access control; it avoids deploy issues but then opens up security issues. Often, this is followed by an equally disproportionate overreaction where security becomes centralized and arbitrary and difficult for the teams to manage, gradually leading to more exceptions or work arounds and ultimately vulnerabilities. While it's easier said than done, balancing a disciplined, explicit, yet practical (for the interdisciplinary teams) approach to managing this is the only thing I've seen work consistently. In fact, DevOps is increasingly security-focused/inclusive, and there is a whole area of practice called 'DevSecOps' that is working to apply lessons learned from DevOps to security.

CI/CD Automation

You may have assumed that with all this work, the pipeline is now automated. Like so many things with digital, it's not that hard to make it happen, but it doesn't make itself happen, and there is a category of products that deal with Continuous Integration/Continuous Delivery (CI/CD) automation. A few you may have heard of are: Jenkins (open source), CircleCI, Gitlab, and Bamboo (like JIRA, part of the Atlassian suite).

There's a reason this is our last section: while teams new to CI/CD may have a perception to the contrary, these tools don't do much for you if you don't have the underlying processes and automation for your Test and Deploy processes. What these tools do well is help automate and connect those processes. The diagram here shows the major steps in a run of one of these tools where the team has full pipeline automation (CD).

Figure 4-25: Managing a Continuous Deployment Pipeline

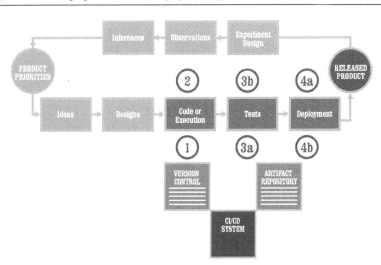

Let's step through how this is likely to work. All these systems do is facilitate and automate the team's process, so different teams will have these configured differently. In the first step (1), a developer commits code to the version control system (their trunk). If the team uses pull requests (PR) there might be an additional step where someone else on the team reviews the code and then commits it. In the second step (2), the CD system will build/configure the code for deployment and automatically deploy it somewhere so that it can proceed to test it in Step 3.

In step 3, the automated test suite runs (generally unit, then integration, then system tests). If any of the tests fail (3a), the developer gets a notice from the CD system about the results of the testing. These

CD systems generally help standardize and make accessible to developers the output of the various tests and the isolation the test suite is able to provide about which code is relevant to the error. If the tests succeed (3b), the system then triggers the Deploy processes, for example, having Ansible update the relevant software to a new version through an automated process the team creates. If it succeeds (4a) then the version is updated to production, and the system is available for end users. If it fails, (4b) then a message goes back to the developer.

For ongoing work, Developers are committing code to version control and that's likely where testers are committing, as well. The Deploy team is maintaining the code and supporting applications (like Ansible and upper layer orchestration systems like Kubernetes) that automate the deploy processes. They are also the most likely candidates to be running the CD system, though sometimes the dev team will do this to a large degree or entirely by themselves.

Getting to Your Best, Most Continuous Pipeline

The first and most important thing a team should do in this area is have an explicit view of how they go from code to deploy—in fact, if they haven't done it already, it's a great idea to step all the way through the team's processes from idea to design to code to deploy. Even if it's not pretty, sketching it out (as a pipeline) on a whiteboard or the virtual equivalent is a critical first step. Don't fall into the trap of describing how everyone or some of the team would like it to be: start with what is.

From there, the team should be holding retrospectives after each agile sprint or iteration where they discuss what worked well, what didn't, and what practices they want to add vs. change vs. drop. In essence, this is the best way I've seen of answering the paradox about implementing agile: How do you fix command and control with command and control? You don't. Within certain broad contours, the individual teams should be adaptively defining their own practice of agile. This way, anyone that's not happy with their state of practice is also responsible for fixing it, which is central to the agile concept of self-organizing teams.

What We Learned

As a manager of some stripe in a tech company, regardless of what team you're on, it's important to understand how the sausage is made in terms of going from code to release since this has become such a crucial part of what makes or unmakes a high-performing team that's crushing 'F'.

You've learned about how teams improve their work on going from idea to design, design to code, and now code to release. Hopefully, you have a sense of how practice for HDD across the pipeline interacts. For example, try to cram too many features into the pipeline and you'll rack up tech debt, which will steadily degrade your time to release. On the other hand, release a few features with more intention while investing in your pipeline and you'll improve 'F' on multiple fronts, both improving your success rate for features as well as your velocity and release 'friction'.

If your team isn't releasing frequently and/or hates releases, I hope you now have a better sense of how important that is and how you might collaborate with them on improvements. When things aren't working the way I think they should, I just want to drop everything and fix them according to my exact plan. This is part of the reason I'm a terrible manager. In practice, steady, incremental changes with testable criteria are the best way to go. Agile retrospectives provide a great format to facilitate a team-wide point of view on priorities and updating practice, even when not everyone agrees about everything, which they generally won't.

Recommended Practice & Supplemental Resources

In this chapter, we've focused on the product pipeline areas of Test and Deploy, transitioning from Code. We've also focused a lot on the continuity of the whole pipeline so far, with a focus on going from priorities to released product. You learned how teams invest in test and deploy infrastructure and some of the big drivers and lessons learned. The practice below, as usual, is ordered (roughly) in the sequence I'd recommend.

1. *Sketch Your Team's Product Pipeline*

   Using the archetypal/general pipeline frameworks you've seen here, whiteboard (analog or digital) the specifics of how your team does this now. Focus on what is, not what everyone would like or should be—for now, just describe what is. There will be many more steps than in the archetypal pipeline you saw here since you'll get into the details.

   It will be messy—that's OK. It's very important for everyone to understand this and then consider and prioritize changes. Otherwise, what will happen is that you'll end up with an imaginary pipeline (from multiple people's imaginations) that doesn't exist. It's not useful for anyone to understand what-is, and it's not clear exactly where and how the team should change it. You can find workshop notes at this link:
   https://hdd.works/3cCJ7dC.

2. *Concept and Prioritize Testable Changes to Your Product Pipeline*

   This follows and depends on sketching your team's product pipeline as it is. From there, work on specific, actionable changes that the team could do in a week. Be sure to describe the conditions under which the team would consider this a failure (i.e. not worth it vs. a success) and something they want to keep. This may be slightly uncomfortable at first because it involves the assumption that not everyone's definitely always right, but it's a good way to diffuse disagreements (let's test it) and encourage reticent and more cynical colleagues to participate.

3. *Draft an Agile Team Charter*

   This is a great way to encapsulate your work and point of view on everything you've done so far. While not universal, it's fundamental to agile that you have an explicit view of what processes you're executing now in a way that's amenable to change. This page has a tutorial with links to a template:
   https://hdd.works/3cwbY3n.

4. *Explain the Fundamentals of DevOps and Continuous Delivery*
I hope you've gotten to a viable starting point on this—and I think you probably have. That said, here are a couple of items where you can acquire more depth if you want it:
https://hdd.works/3vbkQC0.

5. *Learn How to Manage Work with Version Control*
Ready to use version control? If you're asked (or suggested to) by a colleague to put something in version control, do it! It's a great learning opportunity and probably an invitation to get in the game. If you feel ready to go at it, go! If not, here you'll find a written tutorial and, alternatively, some online tutorials on how to get started:
https://hdd.works/3PUo5pr.

6. *Write Some Automated Tests to See How it Works*
While your professional focus is probably not writing automated tests, there's a certain creative confidence that comes with actually trying it out. If you're interested, here are some quick ways to give it a try:
https://hdd.works/3PxwvTl.

7. *Understand the Managerial Side of How a Team gets to Healthier Pipelines*
For this, an interdisciplinary perspective is particularly helpful. On this page you'll find a combination of case studies, stories, and online courses to expand your perspective:
https://hdd.works/3RZ50ZG.

Guest Editor: Rob Zuber

Rob is the CTO of CircleCI, one of the leading providers of CI/CD applications. When he first learned about Continuous Delivery, he thought it was a terrible idea. Releasing was a risky, unpleasant activity that engineering and ops should be subjected to as little as possible. But, his friend and colleague Jim Rose (now CEO of CircleCI) encouraged him to have a look at a few articles about what teams were learning about the process.

They tried it at the small venture they were creating together, and after that, for Rob, there was no going back. In fact, they ended up pivoting and building a CI/CD application for mobile devices (Distiller), which was later acquired by CircleCI. Now, he spends his time learning everything he can about what makes CI/CD work for companies and putting it to work in their product. If you want to know more about what he's finding, check out his Podcast *The Confident Commit*.[18]

Three Questions with Rob

What makes CI/CD work vs. not work for companies?
I often describe this as "push" vs "pull." If CI/CD is just a tool and it's being selected and forced on everyone by their managers, something is missing—and that something is in your culture. I often state that Continuous Deployment is an attitude. When your engineers are coming to work every day and the thing they want to do most is put a functioning product into the hands of users, you'll feel it. You will have no choice but to get them great CI/CD tools because they won't tolerate anything less.

---

18 "The Confident Commit: A Software Delivery Podcast," CircleCI, accessed July 14, 2022, https://hdd.works/3cgOZsP.

What's the best way to get started?

Start small and get feedback as fast as you can. If we've learned anything in the last 25 years of software delivery, it's that we're going to be wrong. Wrong about what the user wants, wrong about where the market is going, wrong about our implementation. So we work in small batch sizes and reduce our risk. The same is true about process and tools. Developers are customers of these systems, so work with them, pick a team that's bought in, try some things and iterate. Soon everyone else will want in because the difference will be so clear.

Where are things headed, CI and CD-wise?

The next step is all about 'testing in production'. That used to be a euphemism for sloppiness, but now we have the tools to do this really well—roll out a small change and know enough about your UX and how it's instrumented so you automatically know whether you're all set or to roll back.

Software delivery is differentiated from many classic engineering disciplines by our ability to deliver incremental changes. When you build a skyscraper or an airplane, it's pretty much going to be that way until you replace it. That's why so many of the practices we've tried to bring over have failed us. So now we're expanding our skills to become experts at validating that our changes are good. And unless every customer for whom you are building is getting the experience you intended, it doesn't matter that your tests passed. Your work is not done.

5

FROM RELEASE TO EXPERIMENTATION

Figure 5-1: Hypothesis Testing & HDD

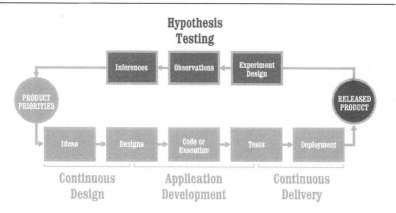

Just as the last couple of decades have seen the ascendance of design and 'design thinking' as a general necessity for product teams, we're now entering an era where experimenting across a customer's whole experience is moving from specialty domain to foundation skill. Better still, as a community of practice, we're getting a lot better at working out how to marry qualitative and quantitative evidence to produce better results. Witness, for example, design firm IDEO's purchase of consultancy Datascope Analytics in 2017 to complement their dominance in design with an analytics practice.[1]

---

1 Datascope Analytics

The glass half full version is that without tight interfaces between Continuous Design and Hypothesis Testing,[2] analytics teams are more prone to making mistakes, sometimes serious ones. 'Machine learning', sometimes aggrandized as 'artificial intelligence' or 'AI', offers powerful tools for making inferences. Relative to much of statistics, they're also relatively easy to use. However, their operation is opaque, a kind of black box where huge amounts of data go in and powerful inferences come out. Sometimes those inferences go wrong, or get wrong after they were right for a while.

For example, a high profile Google project, Google Flu Trends (GFT), was quietly shelved in 2013 after drastically underpredicting that year's flu season due to issues with how they were construing certain Observations on user searches.[3] Part of the problem had to do with what's often called 'ground truth' in data science and statistics, which basically means understanding the source of your Observations–what we'd probably just call 'user discovery' in the design world, and part of what we call Continuous Design in this book's framing of HDD.

Hypothesis-Driven Development offers one of the most promising avenues for creating a durable practice of marrying qualitative and quantitative evidence in service of the actionable, small batch, inferences that supercharge a practice of agile.

Doing experimentation and analytics well has never been easy, and it still isn't. However, much as the cost to release an application has plummeted with the introduction of better infrastructure, tool chains, and practices, so has the execution of experimentation and analytics. Tools like Optimizely, VWO, and Google Optimize have made it easy to design, conduct, and make specific inferences from digital experiments. Today, a lot of the important work lies with generalists who need to help product teams integrate rigorous experimentation into their product pipelines.

What does this look like? Well, for example, travel site Booking.com is generally running over 1,000 concurrent experiments.4 What's great about that isn't so much the sheer number of experiments, but the

---

2 or something like them...

3 David Lazer, "What We Can Learn from the Epic Failure of Google Flu Trends," Wired (Conde Nast, October 1, 2015), https://hdd.works/3RyfRos.

4 Nicola Donovan Click. Magazine Writer et al., "The Role of Experimentation at Booking.com," Booking.com for Partners, July 15, 2020, https://hdd.works/3ceX4yv.

fact that they've created a culture of experimentation and a self-service infrastructure where these experiments are a regular part of product development across teams.

From Output to Outcomes

Beyond just observational studies and analytics, getting fluent in the process of experimentation presents a terrific opportunity for generalists working to supercharge the performance of agile teams. Purposeful iteration vs. just iteration is probably the most important observable feature of a high-functioning digital innovation team. Pairing a high-functioning practice of Hypothesis-Driven Development with a focus on experimentation will help you create a culture of experimentation that shifts the definition of done from output to outcomes.

For example, if you asked someone on your team, "When would we consider {some feature} done?" Are you likely to hear something about output like, "When it's released" or "When it passes acceptance testing"? Or, are you more likely to hear something more focused on outcomes like, "If it moves the needle past our target threshold on {some focal metric}"?.

How would you observe whether a team has achieved this or not? 'The Blue Button Moment' is a simple vignette I like to use for illustrating the answer. Let's say a team is having issues with misconfigured customer orders: most obviously, they should try updating their application with some guard rails so users don't accidentally misconfigure their order. In the output-focused scenario where everyone views their work locally as a list of items to check off, we might have the business lead come with a set of arbitrary requirements they give to the developer who duly, but not enthusiastically, implements them since they don't make much sense to her. Work in the sense of output gets delivered, but the user's problem is not necessarily getting solved, the team's not getting better at working together, and they don't release the fix with a point of view on how they'll test whether it's working or not:

Figure 5-2: Blue Button Moment (Sad Ending)

Over-
prescription
on solution.

Single batch
implementation with no
narrative collaboration.

In an outcome-focused team, the ideas come with specific Observations on user behavior paired with ideas on how an improvement would look in terms of metrics (focal dependent variables). From there, the team can more confidently design, write focused code, and release often knowing that everything's an experiment and the important thing is to see what works. For example, at Booking.com, they even A/B test bug fixes to make sure they're actually working in the way the team intended.[5]

Figure 5-3: Blue Button Moment (Happy Continuation)

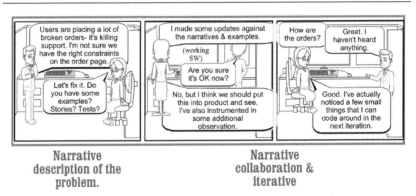

Narrative
description of the
problem.

Narrative
collaboration &
iterative

The product lead is bringing in a clear, specific view of what's happening and generally what they might do, but is also looking to hear from their designers/developers on how they think the team should get to a good

---

5 Lukas Vermeer, "Moving Fast, Breaking Things, and Fixing Them as Quickly as Possible," Medium (Booking.com Development, February 21, 2019), https://hdd.works/3O9r63V.

outcome. They iterate together in small batches on some solutions since they trust each other and enjoy (or at least don't dislike) working together closely.

There is no single formula for creating a culture of experimentation at scale. However, there are some facilities that seem to help. First and foremost is an infrastructure for self-service. For starters, that means having the technology infrastructure in place where teams can easily configure and initiate experiments. Intuit also found that it helped to have a self-service legal infrastructure, meaning that as long as the experiment meets predefined guidelines the team doesn't need manual review from legal.[6]

The table below describes a few consistent traits I've observed of high-functioning teams that iterate purposefully vs. low-functioning teams that focus on output.

Table 5-1: Low Functioning vs. High Functioning Agile Team

Area	Low-Functioning	High-Functioning
How do individuals on the team define their success?	Output related to their specific tasks	Measurable outcomes related to an economically important user behavior
What are the inputs to dev and design?	More formal requirements	Narrative on user experience (JTBD, user stories, storyboards), inferences from previous sprints' experiments, and an experimental design with clear 'pivot or persevere' criteria for the current sprint
How specific is the team's point of view on the user(s) and their JTBD(s)?	General or taken for granted	Extremely specific and evolving based on what they learn. It's common to see photos, day-in-the-life boards and outtakes from customer interviews

---

6   Stefan Thomke, "Chapter 4," in Experimentation Works: The Surprising Power of Business Experiments (Boston, MA: Harvard Business Review Press, 2020).

Area	Low-Functioning	High-Functioning
Generally, how does the team use descriptive analytics?	Analytics are available and some on the team periodically look at them, particularly the topline metrics.	Metrics and the experiments they support are instrumented into everything substantial. These in turn cascade back up to the team and company OKR's.
How does the design process link forward to Hypothesis Testing?	Most analysis is after the fact. The system has a lot of analytics and generally the team assumes it has what it needs, but spends a lot of time piecing together an analysis and what it means, post-release.	The product design is an analysis, iteratively updated based on user behavior. For everything they design and build, the team defines hypotheses and experiments related to observable behaviors. They make sure the relevant Observations are instrumented into the code. Post-release, the link between analytics, inference, and actionability is integral and crisp.
How often does the team discuss the underlying assumption of a given data science model, and possibly needing to verify those with testing or discovery?	It's sometimes discussed, but not a place the team or teams generally invest their time.	The team has frequent discussions about what the team has learned in Continuous Design and how that relates to which Experiment Designs are possible, given the Observations the team has or could acquire. Hypothesis Testing frequently informs priorities for work in Continuous Design and vice versa.
How well are causal explanations designed into the team's experimentation and discussions?	People have their ideas, but if something's working OK, the general sentiment is 'don't mess with it'.	The team leads with well articulated and reasonably observed hypotheses on causality. When the statistics are weird enough, the team goes out and talks to real users. The team questions even promising statistics if there isn't a causal explanation that's both plausible and consistent with the experimental design and results.

Specifically, how do you get there with your team? How do you go from low-functioning to high-functioning? The most reliable approach is to start with small but purposeful experiments, discarding what doesn't work and building on successes. Don't expect it's always going to both a) make the team work better and b) increase customer engagement every time.

It's not easy, but it's worth doing. As we discussed at the beginning of Chapter 2, most software that's built ends up in the trash—lightly used or unused. Let's say you can take the ratio of waste on any new products, new features, or even new IT infrastructure from 50% to 25%; that would be like doubling the amount of engineering talent you have on hand—a pretty big deal. And this is just on the cost side of the enterprise. In a fast-changing, hyper-competitive world with global competition, it's the increased chances at a hit that are most likely to drive profitable outcomes for the enterprise. It will take some work. Microsoft sees positive results from around ⅓ of experiments,[7] Booking.com from around 10%,[8] and Google from less than 4%.[9] Some of that might have to do with how much experimenting the company has done and diminishing returns, some of it might have to do with the size of the experiments, but the point is that experiments aren't about proving you're right and 'validating' your ideas. You have to be ready to be wrong. If you're not, obviously, the experimentation is of limited value and it may leave you worse off, demoralizing a team that thought they were working in an evidence-driven fashion.

How & Why to Frame Your Hypotheses for Testability

Without a clear view of how to unpack and interpret Observations on user behavior, transitioning to an evidence-based approach is impossible. Beyond just understanding, you have to *want* to operate this way. We all love to see graphs with our metrics moving up and to the right, and to check things off our to-do lists. For managers, this often means looking at simple topline or "vanity" metrics instead of asking the hard questions

---

7 "A/B Testing: How to Get It Right," Harvard Business Review, September 16, 2020, https://hdd.works/3PuQQIW.

8 "Building a Culture of Experimentation," Harvard Business Review, June 2, 2021, https://hdd.works/3OguBFN.

9 Kuklovskaia Elizaveta, "DP," Amazon ("Books by Mail" Pub. Co.), chapter 1, accessed July 17, 2022, https://hdd.works/3INeePD.

about what specific customer behaviors drive valuable outcomes for their company. For the analyst or data scientist, this often means optimizing the accuracy of a high-profile prediction instead of working on a more actionable but less sexy problem.

Dependent Variable (DV) vs. Independent Variable (IV)

How do generalists help create focus on the analytics that are really important—the ones that can answer valuable questions and spur significant improvement? For starters, you must be able to frame a dependent variable for actionable focus relative to the matter at hand.

Let's say you run an ice cream shop and you want to predict your revenue over time. The dependent variable would be revenue and the independent variables would be factors that you think are tied to revenue like time of year, temperature, precipitation and holidays, to name a few. You use a model like linear regression to see how well you can predict a DV from a set of IV's.

Figure 5-4: Hypothesis Testing Steps and Items

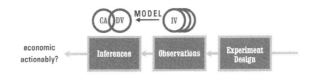

You might think that the IV's and DV are the same as cause and effect. In fact, they're not. When you identify a dependent variable (DV), you're just framing it as the measurement that you want to predict or forecast as a function of the independent variables (the IVs). The relationship between the DV and the IVs might be causal or it might just be correlation.

For example, customers coming into the store might be tightly correlated with the presence of monarch butterflies, but, in fact, these just tend to occur under the actual conditions that bring in people for ice cream, a certain season or weather pattern. If the neighboring county builds a new park for the butterflies, and they disappear to somewhere else, does the ice cream shop actually see a decline in customers? Probably not.

An Experiment Design or model that doesn't answer questions about causality but reliably predicts a DV from a set of IVs may deliver an economically actionable prediction: good enough for you to make a decision, even if it hasn't isolated causation from correlation. However, in practice, a model that doesn't isolate a causal explanation can lead to bad decisions.

First, there's a prevailing sentiment in statistics that if you see a strong effect in your numbers, it's probably wrong–the model may be off or the Observations may be biased in some direction, and you should carefully check that before moving forward. Second, without a causal explanation, there's more opportunity to take actions that won't have the effect you intend.

In 1747, surgeon's mate James Lind ran some of the first controlled experiments on record, testing a set of treatments for a health condition called 'scurvy' with various cohorts of sailors. The cohort prescribed two oranges and one lemon per day did very well, scurvy-wise, which we now know is because of the vitamin C these fruits contain.[10]

However, Lind believed it was the acidity of the remedy that prevented scurvy and went ahead with a boiled concentrate that destroyed the vitamin C, and which also, apparently, wasn't subjected to the same scrutiny. It wasn't until almost 50 years later that the British Navy tried unheated juice that they substantially solved scurvy.

While Lind deserves a lot of credit for advancing the science of controlled experiments, his work on scurvy is a cautionary tale on both isolating causality and continuous testing. Much like the limitations on contemporary understanding of chemistry and human biology created confounders for Lind, the pairing of power and opacity in our current understanding of machine learning does the same.

What if your Experiment Design doesn't even deliver an economically actionable conclusion? What if the results are just plain confusing? In this case, having a strong practice of Continuous Design with a rigorous framework like HDD is useful. Sometimes the data just doesn't make a lot of sense and isn't actionable, and the team needs to make sure they're doing just enough research at just the right time. For example, in the early days of a new product or product update, such a team would feel comfortable questioning their Right Problem hypotheses and organizing a design sprint to do discovery interviews with individual subjects.

---

10 Stefan Thomke, *Experimentation Works: The Surprising Power of Business Experiments* (Boston, MA: Harvard Business Review Press, 2020).

The Importance (and art) of Framing a Dependent Variable

Doing better work on identifying the right DV and ensuring that the related Inferences are actionable will help with analytical clarity and actionability. In the ice cream store example, your first instinct might be to ask for a forecast of sales. The analyst you're working with has probably done this kind of time series forecasting many times and will happily dive into the analysis. You might see some great, colorful charts and graphs showing histories and forecasts of revenue per day over many, many months. For example, Figure 5-5 below shows a time series forecast for the COVID-19 virus by country:

Figure 5-5: Time Series Forecast Example[11]

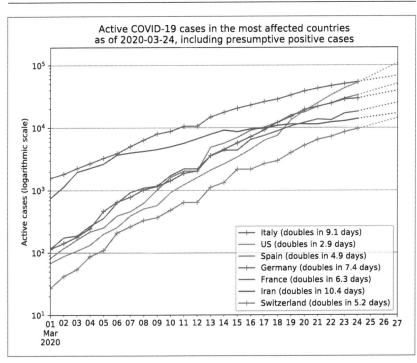

Forecasts like this will take into account IV's or 'features' like seasonality, historical demand, and various other circumstantial items. How helpful are these time series forecasts, in and of themselves?

---

11 Pascal Getreuer, CC BY-SA 4.0 <https://creativecommons.org/licenses/by-sa/4.0>, via Wikimedia Commons

Back to the ice cream shop example, you can easily imagine a forecast that shows predicted sales over time. But, what if the big driver of profitability for your shop is labor, and what if the real point of doing the forecast is to decide how many employees to staff each hour? A great question to ask about actionability is: "What's the intervention? What are we going to do differently based on observing this DV?"

Suppose the intervention is deciding how many employees to schedule for each hour next week. From there, another obvious question is: "Who intervenes?" If, in the ice cream store example, it's a shift manager, then they might not find the charts and graphs your data scientist produces particularly actionable. They might prefer the shorter-term forecast at higher granularity. Or they'd likely just prefer to see the number of employees needed for each shift over the coming week—something that looks like the spreadsheet they already have on their shop computer or the schedule pinned up in the shop's break room.

Beyond the ice cream shop, framing the DV (e.g., sales by day over months or employees by hour over the coming week) can become more nuanced and all the more critical. For example, let's say you work at a retail bank and your charter is to transition in-person customer interactions at the banks to self-service, digital experiences. In a situation like this, I often see teams look at aggregate metrics like monthly active users (MAU), daily active users (DAU) and time on the site. However, if, as a customer, I'm trying to transfer money between accounts, none of those will offer you a useful view of how well things went for me and how satisfied I am. If anything, even though it may be counterintuitive, less time on site may actually be better.

The customer wants a less time-consuming experience. How might we define the DV from their perspective? A DV that measures how easily the customer was able to do what they intended is probably a clearer, more actionable indicator for the relevant team. Furthermore, what we ultimately care about is how much money the customer is banking with us and how long they stay with the bank.

We could frame a DV that considers how many transfers the customer has made historically over a given period of time, and then frame a DV that looks at the 'share' of transfers customer's make online vs. in the branch. But what if we introduce them to online transfers, but our transfer process is worse than our competitors', and once our customers start transfering online, they end up looking for a bank that does it better, leaving for a competitor? This wouldn't mean that the right move is to stop offering online transfers, but it would mean that the team still has work to do and shouldn't move on to something else just yet.

Suppose all this creates controversy within the bank and some say the whole online thing was a mistake? What if we have to be able to prove a causal linkage between onboarding customers to online transfers and customer retention? We could update the transfer feature to make it smoother and then test whether customers that opt-in to it stay at the bank longer.

But what if the customers who manage to find the online transfer functionality are digital 'early adopters' which are generally more likely than the customer base as a whole to switch to a more digital-first bank? This is what's called a 'confounder,' for reasons that are probably obvious. To mitigate this confounder, we could identify a specific control group of 'baseline' customers and then randomly select similar customers to onboard to the online transfer functionality, hopefully isolating the partial effect of introducing online transfers to the customer base as a whole.

While just about all these types of questions about how to frame an actionable DV are answerable, getting to an economically actionable Inference isn't always as simple as it might seem. The good news is that there are processes which will reliably get you there. In the next section, we'll look at the prevailing statistical techniques and what they offer us in terms of Inference. From there, we'll look at how to prioritize what hypothesis to test and how to pair them with an Experiment Designs that will get you what you need with a minimum of time and cost.

Designing Actionable Experiments

Being able to work backwards from the Inference you want to an Experiment Design that will give it to you is another crucial foundation skill for Hypothesis Testing. For a given Experiment Design, it's useful to know:

1. How do you design and run it?
2. What are the Observations (data) you need?
3. What can you infer from the results?
4. How will that inference deliver the economic actionability you need to decide your next steps?
5. What is its relative cost and cost drivers?

Figure 5-6: Hypothesis Testing Steps and Items

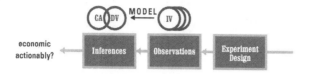

In this section, we'll going to step through three answers to these questions for three prevalent experiment patterns:

a. Retrospective Case-Control (RCC),

b. Prospective Cohort Study (PCS), and

c. Randomized Controlled Experiment (RCE).

The Retrospective Case Control belongs to a broader category of 'observational' patterns, meaning you analyze some existing Observations (data) and see what you can infer from them. The Prospective Cohort Study and Randomized Control Experiment belong to a category of patterns referred to as 'controlled', meaning that you design and conduct a process to collect the Observations the Experiment Design requires.

Most of this work originated in the fields of health sciences and medical statistics, so in order to help you understand the context of these experiment designs, we'll take a break from digital and use another (completely fictional) team that's trying to figure out if shampooing with lemon juice reduces balding in men over 40.

This doesn't mean these patterns don't work for digital—they do. In fact, many of them work *better* in digital. In digital, we already have or we can create massively detailed sets of direct observational data on user behavior with little cost and effort. While I think it's misleading to say 'data is the new oil', most companies do have some real treasure buried in the gigs of logs they have on user behavior.

This is less often the case in health sciences. For most product decisions, you need to run costly controlled experiments to create the Observations you need, which is extremely expensive, or, in the case of hazardous exposures (ex: smoking, asbestos exposure) impossible. Even when you can collect the Observations you need, they're often fraught with bias. Subjects often need to recall their behavior on a questionnaire, so, while the Observations are first hand, they're indirect and much more subject to both error and bias. Recall bias, for example, is when subjects not only don't accurately remember previous events but furthermore systematically over or underreport them because of pre-existing beliefs or their preference to underreport undesirable habits like eating unhealthy foods or smoking.

Instead, most of the Observations we have in digital are direct and objective with regard to the user's behavior. Understanding a portfolio of experiment designs will help you run faster, less expensive, more intentional Hypothesis Testing, testing which will get you to economically valuable Inferences with confidence.

Purposefully integrated into a team's product pipeline, such Hypothesis Testing is an economic powerhouse. It is difficult to overstate the opportunities digital affords for Hypothesis Testing, particularly in contrast to more traditional business decisions. If you work for a retail chain and have to decide on where to construct your next location, detailed sequential planning with Waterfall is likely the right choice. The decision is high stakes and hard to change.

Figure 5-7: Waterfall vs. Agile

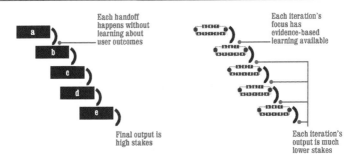

However, all too often managers assume this is how all business is still done, failing to take advantage of the more adaptive decision making digital affords. By taking an evidence-driven approach to the adaptive development agile affords, managers massively advantage themselves relative to competitive alternatives. When former Yahoo! exec Drake Baer reflected on competing with Google, he focused on the velocity of experimentation at the two firms: "They [Google] just outran us. We tried management, all the stuff that management did, but we didn't have that experimentation engine."[12]

Retrospective Case-Control (RCC) Experiment Design

In a Retrospective Case-Control, you're looking at past data to see if a particular DV is associated with a particular IV. Whereas the next two experiment patterns are 'controlled' in the sense that you actively design a particular experience with subjects to get the Observations you want, this pattern is 'observational', meaning that you're just looking at existing data. At most, it shows some association between the DV and the IV or IV's rather than causation, and it is highly susceptible to unknown confounders.

So, why bother? Well, particularly in digital where you have a lot of data on hand, it is a useful complement to your Hypothesis Testing capability since it affords quickly evaluating associations. Don't make the mistake of simply evaluating this experiment pattern against the alternatives. This often amounts to choosing between making a decision based on anecdotal evidence or no analysis at all vs. contextualized data on user behaviors.

Retrospective Case-Controls also serve to help with smarter decisions about where you might want to invest in more expensive controlled experiments. For example, let's say someone at your firm sounds the alarm on churn—it's gone way up and everyone is worried *something* is wrong.

A quick look at the existing data comparing who has churned and who hasn't is a great way to start narrowing the field of possible associations and causes, and making more informed decisions about what to prioritize next. This is also a point where some 'small data' in the form of discovery interviews might be an excellent investment to help you refine your hypothesis and improve your experiment design. For example, if you're investigating churn, you might want to interview, say, three users who churned and three who didn't, equipped with both an interview guide and the quantitative data on how they've interacted with your application.

---

12 S. Cook, interview with Drake Baer, "Why Intuit Founder Scott Cook Wants You to Stop Listening to Your Boss," Fast Company (Fast Company, October 28, 2013), https://hdd.works/3z6wRef.

In our baldness example, we'll frame the DV as whether or not the subject has balding. The IV of interest would be if they regularly used lemon juice on their hair (we'll pretend it's an ingredient in certain shampoo brands).

Figure 5-8: Retrospective Case Control

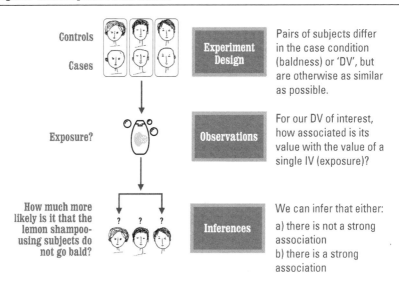

Source: adapted from Reference Manual on Scientific Evidence

Here, I have the 'Control' framed as the haired men and the 'Cases' as the bald men. In the health sciences, the type of subject designated as case vs. control is usually obvious, since they're looking at diseases or adverse health conditions. In a business context, it can go either way.

You might, for example, be looking at which users upgrade to a paid plan and treat them as the 'Cases'. It might also be the exact opposite if you're looking at churn and how to minimize it. There isn't a super strong convention on this, but generally the rarer condition is the 'Case' and the more common the 'Control'.

With balding, particularly with men over 40, the proportions are pretty evenly split and I went with baldness being the Case. Sorry bald guys, and I'm sure I'll be joining you soon enough. The most important things for good experimentation and collaboration are a) to be consistent with your choice and b) not to present the case vs. control choice as anything other than a matter of a convention you'll use to achieve clarity through consistency.

Other than the question of shampoo type, we want to collect Observations on subjects that are otherwise as similar as possible in order to minimize the risk of other factors 'confounding' our result. For example, suppose our experiments show that high blood pressure medication does, in fact, contribute to balding and that lemon juice shampoo is mostly marketed to health enthusiasts who tend to have health habits that lower their blood pressure, and so they're much less likely to be on blood pressure medication. This association is a 'known confounder' and a feature that the experimenters might single out for pairing subjects in their Retrospective Case-Control, making sure they include pairings of bald men and non-bald men who both take blood pressure medication or who both do not take it.

From there, we'll consider how strong the association is between using shampoo with lemon juice and not being bald by asking, 'Given that a subject {is not vs. is} bald, how likely is it that they {were vs. were not} using shampoo with lemon juice?' For example, the table below has a (fictional) set of results.

Table 5-2: Outputs of a Retrospective Case Control

	Use of Shampoo with Lemon Juice			
Item	Never	Sometimes	Always	Total
Non-Bald Subjects ('Controls') n = 500	208 41.6% (=208/500)	100 20.0% (=100/500)	192 38.4% (=192/500)	500 100%
Bald Subjects ('Cases') n = 500	389 77.8% (=398/500)	102 20.4% (=102/500)	9 1.8% (=9/500)	500 100%
Totals	597 59.7% (=597/1,000)	202 20.2% (=202/1,000)	201 20.1% (=201/1,000)	1,000

In Retrospective Case-Controls, you'll often see a table like the one above as a vehicle to help answer the question 'Does the use of lemon juice-based shampoo reduce baldness in men over 40?'. In this case, it does look like if you use it 'always' there may be some association. There might be some as yet unknown confounders, but it improves the investability of an RCE to test for causality.

You might also run a statistical hypothesis test, like the chi-squared test for association. Essentially, what that test would be measuring is the extent to which segmenting the 1,000 subjects into two separate rows by the DV of interest (baldness) changes the distribution of shampoo usage from the totals in a way that suggests those two categories *aren't* essentially the same. In statistical hypothesis testing, you start by defining a 'null hypothesis', a kind of baseline from which your results with the IV of interest would have to differ from enough to say 'this doesn't look like just statistical noise or natural variation–there seems to be some predictable difference from the null when we consider the IV.' Here, if the null was true, then if you just looked at the totals and then, say, looked at the top two rows (the first two in the table above, for example), the percentages of use of shampoo with lemon juice would be the same (statistically speaking) for those top two rows.

The most substantial limitation of Retrospective Case-Controls is the possible presence of unobserved or unknown confounding variables. For example, suppose that:

    a. there is an as yet unknown genetic basis for baldness and that

    b. this basis happens to be strongly associated with a trait that makes citrus smells unpleasant, and

    c. that this attribute (IV) of the subjects is unknown to the researchers.[13]

This would mean that we'll likely see bald men using less products with citrus, that this does not have a causal relationship to baldness, but that, most importantly, citrus shampoo would *look like* it might help you keep your hair.

---

13 This is 100% made up for example purposes.

A mistake like this isn't just a matter of speculation and it's not just a hazard to novices. In the 1950's, R.A. Fisher, considered a founding figure in modern statistics and genetics, went against the grain of emerging medical research of the time, which was beginning to suggest a causal relationship between smoking and lung cancer. Instead, he proposed that lung cancer might be caused by a genetic predisposition that also, it happened, made smoking more appealing.[14]

Ultimately, the key lesson is that a Retrospective Case-Control does not prove causation. At best, it shows an association. That might be economically actionable for your next steps, depending on what they are–how much they cost, how long they take, and whether they're taking you down a course of inquiry that could prove causality. The gold standard way to Infer causality is to control for the possibility of unknown or unobservable confounders, which is a feature of the Randomized Control Experiment (RCE) design, the last experiment pattern we'll cover.

All this said, it's a mistake to eliminate this experiment pattern from your portfolio of options. One of the virtues of this Experiment Design is that if you have access to the data, it is quick and inexpensive to run— you need an analyst to tabulate the results to evaluate associations, but you don't need to acquire your own fresh Observations. At a minimum, the RCC can serve as a useful tool to refine and focus where you want to invest in more robust experiments. While it doesn't prove causality, on the other hand, if you don't see association in a reasonably sized RCC, you're unlikely to see causality in a controlled experiment like an Randomized Control Experiment. Also, sometimes a case condition is just not feasible for prospective studies–for example, anything having to do with user behavior in the face of an adverse event like a privacy breach, billing error, outage, or even a negative support interaction.

Prospective Cohort Study (PCS) Experiment Design

In a Prospective Cohort Study (PCS), you're looking at a population that is otherwise as similar as possible, but differs on their exposure to the IV of interest. You're collecting Observations on how that affects a single DV of interest. Unlike the Retrospective Case-Control, which is observational,

---

14 Ronald A. Fisher, "Cancer and Smoking," Nature News (Nature Publishing Group), accessed July 14, 2022, https://hdd.works/3c2SFOP. He proposed some other things, too, which were at least as implausible.

this is a controlled study, meaning that before they acquire Observations, the experimenters have created an Experimental Design with regard to how the subjects will interact with the IV's of interest. In the case of a PCS, subjects self-select into either the 'treated' cohort or the 'control' cohort.

The cohorts are voluntary, making their own choice. In our shampoo example, one cohort decides to consistently use shampoo with lemon juice and the other uses shampoo without lemon juice. This might be something you arrange, by, say, offering free shampoo subscription of whatever type they prefer, or something that you're able to identify in a population by, for example, sending out a survey.

Figure 5-9: Prospective Cohort Study

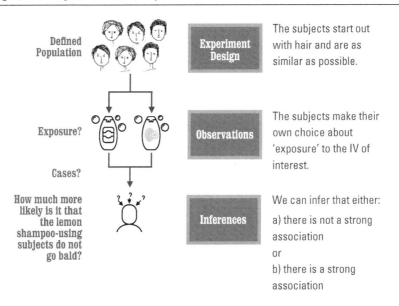

Source: adapted from Reference Manual on Scientific Evidence

From there, you're observing who goes bald and the extent to which that is associated with the IV of interest: in our case asking, 'Given that a subject uses shampoo with lemon juice, how much less likely are they to go bald than the subjects who do not use lemon juice shampoo?' The table here has a set of (also fictional results) for such a study.

Table 5-3: Outputs of a Prospective Cohort Study

| | Subsequent Presentation of Baldness | | | |
Item	Substantial Balding	Some Balding	No Change	Total
Selected Lemon Juice Shampoo	99 19.8% (=99/500)	178 35.6% (=178/500)	223 44.6% (=223/500)	500 100%
Selected Shampoo with No Lemon Juice	329 68.8% (=329/500)	97 19.4% (=97/500)	74 14.8% (=74/500)	500 100%
Totals (Baseline)	428 42.8% (=428/1,000)	275 27.5% (=275/1,000)	297 29.7% (=297/1,000)	1,000

Like the Retrospective Case-Control, while we might run a statistical test for association, this experiment pattern only allows us to infer correlation, or, more generally, association. Confusion between 'correlation' vs. 'association' is likely to crop up as we move forward, so let's take a moment to make sure you're comfortable with the difference.

Correlation refers to how well you can 'fit' a line through a series of data, a line that minimizes the 'residuals' or space between the points and the line. Association is a more general term for any kind of observable relationship between data points. You may have heard the term 'correlation doesn't equal causation'. That's true, and neither does association.

For example, the set of points that form a U in the general association example below have an extremely predictable relationship to each other, but it is not linear and it is not necessarily a causal relationship. This U shape is not uncommon in nature–if you plotted the spectrum of possible human water consumption, say, with mortality on the y-axis and water consumption on the x-axis, you'd get a shape something like this. Drink way too little water, you die; way too much, the same. Association is more of a colloquial term, and probably the best way to think about it is as a candidate for something causal.

Figure 5-10: Correlation vs. Association

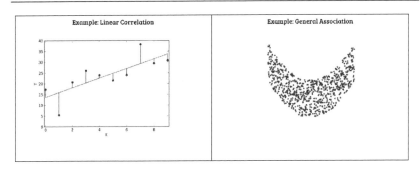

The Prospective Cohort Study is different from a Retrospective Case-Control study in that the experimenters design for the Observations they want, and also that the probability in question is inverted. With the Retrospective Case-Control we're asking, 'Given that the subject is not bald, how much more likely is it that they were using shampoo with lemon juice?' However, with the Prospective Cohort Study, what we're asking is, 'Given that the subject is using shampoo with lemon-juice, how likely are they to keep their hair vs. the non-lemon juice shampoo using cohort?'

Ultimately, the right choice on experiment pattern has everything to do with effectuating your way to valuable action. The PCS gives experimenters more choice about the Observations they collect, including how they might deal with the presence of confounders. Given that the experimenters have a chance to design how they acquire their Observations, and that experimenters are 'there' the whole time and can see if people use lemon juice and if they go bald, PCS gives experimenters more opportunities to design for and understand the ground truth of their Observations. On the other hand, with an RCC we just 'mine the logs' instead of asking fallible humans to remember things. On the other hand, PCS introduces some amount of delay. In a business setting, it's probably not the multiple decades you might need to study an outcome like cancer, but even waiting 6-12 months to understand the effect of a notable IV on churn may be too long.

Understanding and being able to apply these first two experiment patterns offers you a huge advantage over just relying on traditional statistics, data science, and the more expensive 'gold standard' experiment design of Randomized Control Experiment, which you'll learn about next.

Randomized Control Experiment (RCE) Experiment Design

Often referred to as the 'gold standard' of experiments, in a Randomized Control Experiment (RCE) you're observing a population for a DV and changing the focal IV randomly to guard against the effect of confounders, known and unknown. Sometimes, particularly in the health sciences, it's also referred to as a 'Randomized Control Trial'.

Out of the three experiment patterns we've looked at, this is the only way to establish a causal relationship between the DV and the IV because it truly isolates the effect of the IV in question. In our men balding example, this would mean regularly distributing shampoo to the subjects for a period of observation. At random, half of the subjects would always receive shampoo with lemon juice, and the other half would receive shampoo without lemon juice.

Figure 5-11: Randomized Control Experiment

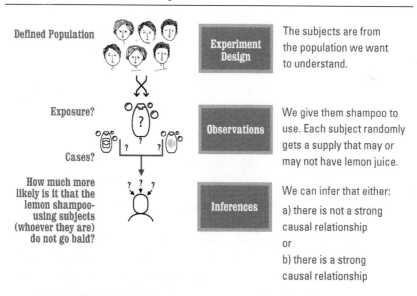

Defined Population — **Experiment Design** — The subjects are from the population we want to understand.

Exposure? / **Cases?** — **Observations** — We give them shampoo to use. Each subject randomly gets a supply that may or may not have lemon juice.

How much more likely is it that the lemon shampoo-using subjects (whoever they are) do not go bald? — **Inferences** — We can infer that either:
a) there is not a strong causal relationship
or
b) there is a strong causal relationship

Source: adapted from Reference Manual on Scientific Evidence

The participants do not need to be paired for similar characteristics or know whether they're getting shampoo with lemon or not. In medical research, the terms single-blind, double-blind and triple-blind are commonly used to describe blinding. These terms describe experiments in which (respectively) one, two, or three parties are blinded to some information. Most often, single-blind studies blind patients to their treatment allocation, double-blind studies blind both patients and researchers to treatment allocations, and triple-blinded studies blind patients, researcher, and some other third party (such as a monitoring committee) to treatment allocations. However, the meaning of these terms can vary from study to study.[15]

While this is the only experiment pattern that allows us to infer a causal relationship between the IV and the DV, that doesn't mean that the other two experiment patterns aren't necessarily the best choice in a given situation. Random Control Experiments (RCEs) are expensive. That is generally less true in digital; site visitors are relatively easy to acquire, and in digital we can readily automate the process of, say, showing a certain version of a page or app to one population and an alternative to another, and A/B test. While not isolated to digital, experimenters will generally have easy access to a choice of mechanisms to randomize their subjects. For example, marketplaces like Uber will often randomize spatially across markets to better control for confounders. Services like YouTube or Gmail will often randomize temporally (by time of day or month).

In Practice: HinH Designs an Actionable Experiment

The HinH team has 3 months of work under their belt, 12 weekly sprints. It hasn't been what they'd characterize as a breakaway success, but in general the process is working and, with a few minor setbacks, they'd certainly say they're making progress with users. Sri, the lead dev, sums it up by saying "I don't feel like we've gotten lucky, but I do feel like we've been making our own luck.".

Going into sprint 14, the team has great Engagement on tech's looking up parts pricing and availability, but they're struggling to Engage the tech's on actually placing orders through the self-service app—only 15% of visits result in an order. After interviewing a few tech's, the HinH team realizes these tech's still don't fully understand the ordering process. The team has an idea to improve the rate of orders/visits—for new users, they could offer a live chat affordance on the app.

---

15 "Blinded Experiment." Wikipedia. Wikimedia Foundation, June 28, 2022. https://hdd.works/3yK5XaV.

How might they execute on this idea? As they design the interface, the team will identify the user behaviors they want to change, frame their designs as experiments they think might change them, run experiments, and then make explicit decisions based on what they observe.

They start with the DV. How do they best frame it for an actionable inference? From both shadowing tech's and their existing analytics, they know the 'ground truth' is that even tech's who do order online will often look up a part a few times before ordering it–to check its specifications, ask the customer if the cost is OK, etc. Given this, the team estimates that an order rate of around 30%-50% would mean that whenever a tech *wants* to order a part they've looked up, they're always placing an order for it.

Might parts ordered/visit be a good DV, then? No. A single large order could throw off this measurement immensely. Since they're specifically interested in how often a tech orders vs. does not order a part, a better DV would be 'visits with >0 parts ordered'/'total visits' with a focus on the cohort or segment that's currently ordering at a rate of <30%. They might refer to this DV as 'order rate'.

Assisted chat would be a good way to go if it works, but who knows. The team wants to either focus on operationalizing it if it looks like it will substantially improve orders, or pivot to something else. The assisted chat does offer some secondary benefits in that the chat transcripts offer more extensive and more specific qualitative Observations about what's impeding the techs' ordering. However, staffing the chat introduces a direct, variable cost to the application. Given the secondary benefit but considering the costs, the team estimates that from their current baseline an increase of 10 percentage points on order rate would make staffing the live chat a break-even proposition in terms of direct costs, which would be fine. A ten point improvement is where the team draws their 'line in the sand', it's their pass/fail threshold for the experiment.

In terms of Experiment Design, the figure here shows the assisted chat signifier in Google Optimize, a tool which provides for self-service experiments, like A/B testing:

Figure 5-12: Creating Tests in Google Optimize

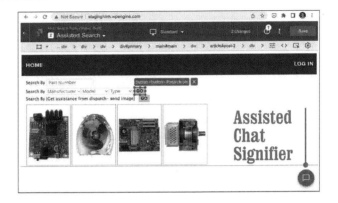

Just about always, an A/B test is a Randomized Control Experiment. The target population is all techs that are ordering at a rate of <30%. This population has a baseline 'order rate' of 10%, five percentage points lower than the 15% you saw earlier, which was measured across the population of all tech's. The 'control' population, or 'A' treatment, will see the existing site with no option for assisted chat. The test population will be exposed to the 'B' experience where there's assisted chat available.

They've designed the test so that technicians who see the chat are treated as a separate 'cohort', meaning that if you are one of the users randomly assigned to see the chat, you always see the chat; otherwise, you're in the current baseline cohort and you never see it. The main reason the team chose this approach is so they can also observe the effect of having their questions answered on the subsequent behavior of the technicians. Specifically, the team wants to understand whether after having a few questions answered, technicians *both* order more through the self-service app and post fewer questions to the chat after they gain experience using the tool. They have one dispatcher 'on loan' to staff the chat. Frangelico wants to make a pivot or persevere decision on this as soon as possible.

How to Make Actionable Inferences

In this section, we'll cover some statistics. If those are new to you or something you haven't particularly enjoyed learning about, that's all right. What I would do is just get a general feel for the technical details and more so focus on the general substance of how this relates to Hypothesis Testing. There are a few key concepts I think you'll find useful, even as the modern tools like Google Optimize mostly take care of the statistical plumbing for you. We're going to look at the Inference question Frangelico is trying to answer and then consider the two most prevalent approaches to making that Inference. You won't need to know the deep statistical plumbing of either, but understanding them will help you focus and discuss your results.

How many Observations does Frangelico need to make a decision on the live chat feature? Say one technician visits and doesn't use the chat—time to scrap the idea? Obviously not, but does the team need 100 Observations to decide? 1,000? 10,000? The most constructive way to answer this question is to work backward from the economic decision at hand. Here, that's the decision whether or not they should expand the assisted chat, adding another full time employee to staff it. From there, the team will make another assessment about how it's going and whether to leave it alone, iterate on it, or scrap it.

How they make that decision gets to the heart of which approaches to Inference you choose, how you tune that approach, and how many Observations you'll need. Now, a common approach among generalists is to completely leave the whole complicated, vexing issue of the stats to the experts. Believe me, you'll need those experts–but they need you, too. While there's a lot of standard practice out there in statistics, many of the accepted conventions are a bad fit for HDD. Selecting and applying better alternatives on Inference has a lot to do with generalists ('businesspeople') better articulating the team's target outcome, development processes, and on that basis facilitating discussions about how to choose the best approach to Inference for their Hypothesis Testing.

For making these Inferences, we'll consider two branches of statistics: 'frequentist' and 'Bayesian'. As much fun as it might be for both of us to make this suspenseful, I know you're busy and also that you might hate stats, so here's the punchline: Bayesian approaches are a much better fit for applying HDD to the kind of product pipelines you've learned about so far. In terms of the innovator archetypes from Chapter 2, George is a frequentist and Geoffrey is a Bayesian. However, so much of current statistical practice is organized around frequentist approaches that without understanding the fundamentals of each approach, you'll probably run into trouble facilitating the discussions you'll need.

We'll start with the frequentist approach. One last time: if you skim this and just get the basic idea, that's still going to help your practice of HDD. You can always dig into the details later, but just understanding the landscape of Inference approaches will help you dig in on the particulars of what matters to whatever you're working on at a given time.

The Frequentist Approach

In frequentist statistics, we take a given set of Observations and try to assess whether or not a given IV substantially changes a DV, or whether the variation we're seeing in our Observations is just random chance. In the HinH example, we want to know how having access to the assisted chat changes the rate of online orders a technician makes.

How do we test for that? Just like any other test, we need to frame this in terms of what we might Infer from our Observations. Generally, you'll see these framed in terms of two mutually exclusive hypotheses: a 'null hypothesis' and an 'alternative hypothesis'. For HinH, they'd look something like this:

1. **Null hypothesis**: There is no relationship between a tech having access to assisted chat and an increase in online orders. The differences in our Observations are just noise, just random chance like flipping a coin and getting a few more heads than tails. In practice, the business is usually hoping that they can reject this hypothesis- that the new UI *does* perform better or the new vaccine *does* work.

2. **Alternative hypothesis**: There is a relationship between a tech having access to assisted chat and an increase in online orders. We're not just observing random chance as you would with an evenly weighted, two sided coin.

Our first step out of the frequentist playbook is probably to run a t-test, a hypothesis test that tells us which of the two mutually exclusive hypotheses is most plausible, the null or the alternative. You'll often hear this expressed as 'rejecting the null hypothesis', and, again, this is usually the hypothesis the business is hoping to reject.

Just to remove some of the abstraction, let's take a look at a sample of the Observations our Experiment Design will deliver. Those might look any number or ways, but the core elements should be:

- Rows of Visits: In our case that's the column 'UID (Visit)', where UID stands for unique ID of a given visit to the HinH self-service application.
- The User's ID: Since our users log in, we have this. If the user's don't authenticate, you might not.
- The Treatment they Saw: Did they get the A or B treatment? In our Experiment Design, this should be the same across visits for a given user.
- Did They Order: This is the DV, the exciting part. In our case, the system marks a '0' for a visit with no order and a '1' for a visit with an order.

Table 5-4: Sample Observations

Observations on App Visits at HinH

UID (Visit)	User	Treatment	Order?
ZSch	jlannister	A	0
rOQz	estark	A	0
SMDI	jsnow	B	0
cgtK	jsnow	B	1
fQGa	btarth	A	0
...	...	...	...

In our case, the specific type of t-test we're going to run is 'two sided' because the effect of the B treatment could be positive (increasing order rate) or negative (decreasing order rate).

At this point, it's not uncommon for teams to just flip the switch and start collecting Observations. They might have a rule of thumb like running the experiment for a week or the number of Observations they end up with might just be happenstance–it might be the number of Observations they happen to have on hand, if the experiment is retrospective, or however many subjects they happen to recruit if it's prospective. Often, in practice, weeks are used to avoid day of week bias–and eliminating bias is good, but you should start with the sample size you need and then figure out how to best do that. Once they have their Observations, they'll do statistics on them and see what they think. They'll probably calculate a p-value, which is a measurement of the chance that they would have gotten the Observations[16] they did if the null hypothesis is *true*. A conventional take on this is that a p-value at .05 is 'statistically significant', meaning that there's a 'reasonable' chance that the IV is changing the DV. Specifically, this would mean there's just a 5% chance we would have gotten these Observations if the null hypothesis was true.

Problems with the Frequentist Approach and How to Solve Them
This approach has problems, problems you should avoid. First, if you don't start your experiments with a specific level of certainty you want in order to make a decision, you won't collect the right amount of Observations. You'll create waste by collecting too many (an 'overpowered' study) or you'll collect too few and fail to reach the level of certainty you want (an 'underpowered' study). Second, if you don't include the minimum effect size you want to Infer, you'll likewise almost certainly collect the wrong number of Observations, since effect size also affects the number of Observations you'll need.

---

16 Or a more extreme set of observations–this may sound fussy but it actually matters a lot to the underlying differences between Frequentist and Bayesian approaches. We'll call this Obs* from here on out.

These problems parallel a lot of the antipatterns you saw earlier in the processes of going from idea to code to deploy. It's a lot like just giving a development team some vague idea and then seeing what happens. You might get lucky, but you're going to generate a lot of unnecessary waste and risk making questionable Inferences.

Fortunately, you can fix these problems with a hypothesis-driven approach in much the same way we did in the earlier chapters. For the generalist, it's mostly about translating their point of view into a more specific intention. Frangelico actually did a pretty good job of thinking this through in his Experiment Design. He wants to see a 10 point improvement in order rate for the subject cohort of 'under-ordering tech's'--from 10% to 20%. He doesn't need to be absolutely certain–if he can be 70% certain, he thinks that's good enough to bring on another support person for the assisted chat and see what happens next.

How many Observations does he actually need for his Experiment Design? And, in his role as the 'businessperson', has he thought through everything he'll need to discuss with a stats-savvy analyst or input to a self-service tool? In general, the more certain he wants to be, the more Observations he's going to need.

The p-value I mentioned earlier is actually an *output* of the t-test and for Hypothesis Testing, its purpose is to compare against a parameter you should define in advance with your Experiment Design called 'alpha ('α'), which is the chance you're ready to take that we're wrong about rejecting the null hypothesis.

Should Frangelico follow convention and set α at 0.05? Not necessarily, no. There's nothing sacred or intrinsically 'right' about this value for the parameter. As one of my colleagues, Sasa Zorc, says "For everyday business decisions, 0.05 is too low [risk averse]; for launching the space shuttle, it's too high [risky]."

Furthermore, back when these conventions like setting α at 0.05 started to take hold, the world was a different place: data was almost always expensive to acquire and most decisions were big batch and high stakes, like whether or not to launch a new product or build a new facility.

By contrast, if you're operating a digital application, data on user behavior is usually somewhere between free and extremely cheap to acquire, but moving quickly is crucial. That said, particularly in mediums like email, you can waste a lot of good will on a bad idea if you overdo your sample size.

An agile approach to development affords adaptive, small batch decisions. Setting α such that you need P-values in the 0.05 range is probably going to introduce excessive delay if the cost of being wrong isn't all that big. All things considered, the goal of being 70% sure (an α of 0.30) that Frangelico defined is probably not unreasonable given the relatively small incremental investment they're considering.

Given how cheap it is to get Observations, does this fussing about setting α and the p-values we get really matter? Probably so, for a couple of reasons. First, you have to set 'α' somewhere if you want to actually take a hypothesis-driven approach to experimenting. Otherwise, you're just discussing numbers and that's likely to lead wherever you were headed anyhow. Second, in practice it likely will matter. If you're small, then even if Observations are cheap, getting the right amount will introduce delay if you don't have a ton of traffic. If you're operating at scale and you do have a ton of traffic, then you will probably have a lot of experiments running and at that scale it's important to set standard so you can run more experiments and have some cohesion across teams about what they're seeing when they see results from Hypothesis Testing.

Finally, there are some operating environments and some decisions where you will want to set α in the range of 0.05, even if it introduces delay or incurs a lot of cost. In the health sciences, this often remains the case. Releasing a vaccine that's ineffective or, worse still, dangerous would be catastrophic for a drug company, perhaps incentivizing them to set α lower than 0.05, which all else equal will require more Observations. That is, a drug company will want to acquire enough Observations to be pretty sure they're not wrong–and yet, recent figures put the cost of one subject for Pfizer's COVID vaccine trial at around $2,000/Observation, just in payments to the subjects themselves.[17]

---

17 Phil Galewitz, "Thousands Volunteer for COVID-19 Vaccine Study," Scientific American (Scientific American, August 7, 2020), https://hdd.works/3PqkIWM.

Now, don't get mad, I didn't invent frequentist statistics, but none of this has actually gotten us too far. Frangelico wants to staff up the assisted chat if the effect is greater than or equal to a ten point increase in order rate. All this t-test has done is tell us whether the effect we saw in our Observations is:

a. probably just random noise

b. probably not just random noise

It has not confirmed for us *anything* else about whether we're seeing that ten point increase. I know... ouch.

The good news is that there is a technique to do this in frequentist statistics–it's called a 'power calculation'. The bad news is that it requires a bit more stats stuff. *But*, the other good news is that these concepts are kind of generally useful for thinking about unpacking and specifying what you mean in a hypothesis-driven environment, and if you're using frequentist statistics this needs to go into your Experiment Design.

Applying Power Calculations

To apply a power calculation, we have to get comfortable with the different kinds of right and wrong we could be about our Inference. To do this, we have to answer two general questions about any given Inference:

1. What's the actual truth? For example, if we were all knowing, is there really an effect from the assisted chat or not?

2. What do we Infer? We're either going to infer there's an effect or there isn't.

Given that each of these is a yes or no question and there are two of them, this gives us 2x2 possible scenarios. You may have seen something like this layed out in a similar fashion in what's called a 'confusion matrix' in statistics. I've reframed that slightly for our purposes here:

Figure 5-13: Confusion Matrix (Modified)

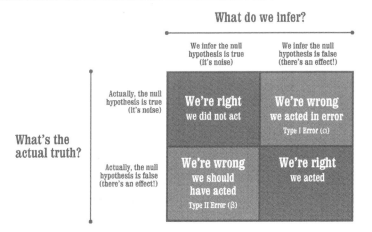

What this shows is that there are two possible kinds of 'right' and two possible kinds of 'wrong'. The first kind of right is that there is actually no effect from using the assisted chat and that's what we Infer (upper left). Good. The second kind of right is that there *is* an effect from using the assisted chat and that's what we infer (bottom right). Also good.

The two kinds of wrong parallel these. In the upper right, we have the case where we Infer that there *is* an effect, but actually there *is not*. This is called a Type 1 Error and in the power calculation we define how willing we are to be this kind of wrong with the parameter 'α'. In drug development, being this kind of wrong will likely lead to a catastrophic decision—for example, releasing a vaccine or cancer therapy that you tell people works, but actually it doesn't. In Frangelico's case, it's not that big of a deal. We persevered when we should have pivoted. He adds another support person, and later, since he's doing HDD and continually resampling and Hypothesis Testing, finds out the assisted chat actually is *not* helping. He then has to repurpose that person. Not a huge deal.

The next type of wrong is where there actually *is* an effect, but we Infer there isn't. This is called a Type II Error and we define how willing we are to be this kind of wrong with the parameter β. Interestingly, the consequences of being this kind of wrong are reversed between drug development and digital innovation. In drug development, this would mean you pass on releasing or continuing to study the effects of a new drug that actually is safe and effective. You might miss a cure for cancer, but, hey, you've got lots of stuff in the pipeline and if you're the CEO you won't get fired for presiding over a catastrophe–Type II errors are often invisible.

In digital innovation, being this kind of wrong is *terrible*: you're in a fast-moving, hyper-competitive environment and you just missed the next big thing. You decided not to try mail order and just made your company the Blockbuster Video to someone else's Netflix. If you're the CEO, you still might not get fired because most corporate boards don't understand innovation very well, but it's still not good.

While α and β are statistical terms, assigning them a value is an economic decision. In the health sciences a typical value for 'α' is 0.05, meaning that you're willing to say a drug is effective when it isn't five percent of the time. A conventional value for β is 0.20, meaning that you're willing to miss the next big thing 20% of the time.

Coming back around (finally–I know; sorry) to the decision in front of Frangelico, what values should he select to make a good decision about the assisted chat? We said initially that being around 70% sure of an effect of 10 points or better was OK. Let's say after unpacking all this, Frangelico still thinks he's OK about being 70% sure about this kind of wrong–staffing another support person when it's not really helping with orders. But what about pivoting too soon or pivoting when there's actually a win to be had with assisted chat? Getting orders up is a pretty big deal for them right now and the team doesn't have a lot of other ideas they particularly like right now, so, after reflecting, he wants to be 85% sure he doesn't miss the boat and sets β at 0.15. This gets us to an answer on the number of Observations they'll need, which is 216, as you can see in this handy online calculator:[18]

18 PharmD Sean P. Kane, "Clincalc," Sample size calculator, accessed July 17, 2022, https://hdd.works/3ciLOB2.

Figure 5-14: Calculating Sample Size

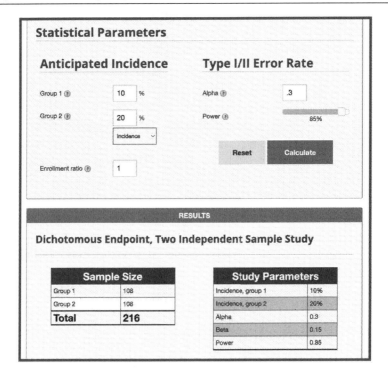

A few quick notes on what you're seeing. First, Incidence is the choice I selected (vs. Increase or Decrease) because we're looking at a binary event: whether or not the techs place an order. The increase or decrease would be the right thing if we were looking at a more continuous DV like purchase total or time on site. As a reminder, the baseline rate of orders in the control population was 10% and we're looking for an increase of ten points, so a 20% order rate, for our test population (Group 2). The final note is that the parameter they show called 'Power' is just the complement of β, just $1-\beta$.

It's worth noting that had this been a feature he thought had the potential to be game changing for HinH, something with end customers for example, he might want a much lower value for β. Eric, this chapter's guest editor, has seen β values for crucial Hypothesis Testing in the 0.01 range, which is often feasible for a site or application with substantial traffic.

To recap, the use of frequentist statistics is conventional for making big, waterfall type decisions in advance, usually with a high aversion to the possibility of being wrong–wrong in the sense of α where you suggest there's an effect when there isn't. Let's call this Type I wrong 'classical wrong'. However, conventional practice is not so averse to the possibility of missing the next big thing, at not least relative to good choices for most teams in digital. This other type of wrong, wrong in the sense of a Type II error where we dismiss the next big thing, we could call 'neo wrong'. Being 'neo wrong' is very bad for digital innovation and practitioners of HDD should consider values of β below the conventional 0.20. Just to underscore how prevalent this thinking still is, even in digital, we (myself and the chapter's guest editor) had to do a bit of searching to find an online calculator that would let us take α up to 0.30 or take β below .05.[19]

Effect size is almost always economically important for HDD in practice, and so if you're going to use a frequentist approach, it's almost universally important to make sure to choose your Observation sizes based on a power calculation. Actually, this is important in science as well, though it's often perilously neglected. For example, a recent project by the Center for Open Science found that out of 193 cancer studies in top journals, only 50 of those could be reproduced, and, of those 50, many had effect size estimates that were on average 15% of the effect originally reported.20 Certainly, part of the reason for this are the incentives to publish original findings vs. test existing findings, but part of it looks like a lack of attention to power calculations and the pernicious effects from a large number of underpowered studies.

In the next section, we'll look at a Bayesian approach to this same Inference, which I think you'll find a much better fit for running your product pipeline.

The Bayesian Approach

Does a Bayesian approach make this easier, given the question we have and the answers we want? What Frangelico wants to know is: 'What is the probability that the assisted search function improves orders by ten or more percentage points?'

---

19 "Sample Size Calculator," Home Page of Evan Miller, accessed July 14, 2022, https://hdd.works/3aGs7Tm.

20 Jocelyn Kaiser, "More than Half of High-Impact Cancer Lab Studies Could Not Be Replicated in Controversial Analysis," Science, accessed July 14, 2022, https://hdd.works/3z6acPb.

To better link useful questions with operational answers, digital experimenters increasingly use Bayesian approaches to statistical reasoning. Digital test infrastructure like Google Optimize does a nice job of helping non-technical, non-stats users ask and answer questions like Frangelico's, and we'll step through the basics you'll need to understand to explain the approach.

In digital, we have lots of cheap data with rich context arriving continuously. For example, rather than measuring the quality of a single batch of barley, we have broad, associated data on who a user is and how they've been behaving. The richness of the data we have is an outstanding asset, and Bayesian approaches are particularly well suited to leveraging prior Observations and Inferences/beliefs and the conditional probabilities they offer.

Figure 5-15: Frequentist vs. Bayesian

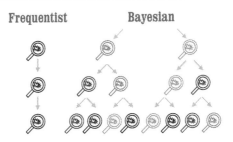

For example, rather than framing a null hypothesis and then doing a separate power calculation, we can use Bayesian Inference to frame and test the following to hypotheses, which get directly at an answer to Frangelico's question:

Hypothesis 1: Offering live chat does not increase orders by at least 10 points

Hypothesis 2: Offering live chat does increase orders by at least 10 points

And, in fact, we can even use it to frame more direct questions, like the one Frangelico wants to ask:

What is the probability that the effect is 10 points or greater?

Frequentist statistics answer the question, "What is the probability we would have seen the Observations we did,[21] if the null hypothesis were true?". In mathematical notation, this is often written as something like P(Observations* | H_0). The 'P' means probability and the pipe character (|) means 'given', so this specifically reads as 'the probability of the Observations in question (*) given the null hypothesis is true'.

The Bayesian approach allows us to reverse these terms for a more natural framing of our question, which is: "What is the probability that the null hypothesis is true given the Observations we have?". In that same notation, this would look something like P(H_0 | Observations) and read as 'probability of the null hypothesis given the Observations in question'.

One key thing the Bayesian approach affords is a natural facility for considering prior data and prior beliefs. For example, let's say we want to know the probability that a given person in New York is walking around with an umbrella, and our Observations look something like this:

Table 5-5: Observations Walking in NYC

Observations on New Yorkers Walking Outside

Date	Observations	Has Umbrella	Weather
Apri 1	400	10	Clear
April 2	378	230	Rainy
April 3	450	12	Clear
...	...	...	...

With a frequentist approach, you'd just say there's, say, a 21% chance because that's what you can Infer from the Observations you have about New Yorkers walking around in general. Obviously, if it's raining outside, the probability is a lot higher. A Bayesian approach makes it easy and natural to consider prior knowledge and beliefs from prior inference so that, assuming we have data on weather as part of those Observations, we could obtain a condition probability of a given person walking with an umbrella given that it's raining. While a version of this is possible

---

21 Or more extreme Observations, denoted Observations*.

with frequentist approaches, Bayesian approaches more naturally frame Inferences against the kind questions you're likely to have because it can readily 'flip' conditional probabilities and easily answer how likely a given hypotheses is given the Observations, $P(H_0 \mid Obs)$. Let's say you're looking out your window—you probably just care about the probability it's raining.

In the case of HVAC in a Hurry and their parts ordering app, this might mean considering other features of our prior Observations to better determine the probability that on any given visit to a parts page, a tech is going to place an order. Let's say that we already know tech's tend to look up a part at least twice before ordering it—once to let the customer know its pricing and availability and then (usually) again later to actually order it. And let's say that's actually something we've been tracking in our Observations, that Observations include a 'new vs. returning' column.

Table 5-6: Sample Observations at HinH

Observations on App Visits at HinH

UID (Visit)	User	Treatment	Lookup History	Order?
ZSch	jlannister	A	new	0
rOQz	estark	A	new	0
SMDI	jsnow	B	new	0
cgtK	jsnow	B	returning	1
fQGa	btarth	A	new	0
...	...	...		...

Bayesian statistics would allow us to frame a relevant conditional probability to answer a question like "What's the probability that a tech will place an order given they've already visited that particular parts page?"

This mechanism of considering the association of your DV with additional IV's allows you to make better inferences in a low traffic environment or take reasonable action in a shorter amount of time—but, in fact, this massively understates the value of Bayesian approaches in digital. I picked this example of 'to staff or not to staff' (assisted chat) at HinH because it's business relevant and a good way to introduce the contrast between what you may have seen or learned about traditional statistics with Bayesian reasoning. However, it actually understates the relatively usefulness of Bayesian approaches because, in fact, so many decisions in digital are dynamic and ongoing, and this is where Bayesian approaches really shine.

Figure 5-16: Hypothesis Testing & Iteration

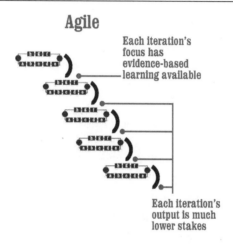

If, for example, you have various alternative user interface (UI) elements for a checkout page and your goal is to maximize ongoing sales, a Bayesian approach elegantly allows you to constantly, dynamically maximize sales with how you present the page every single time. For example, let's say you have two page variations that seem to perform better under different circumstances–where the user lives, the type of device they're using, etc. A Bayesian approach allows you to consider all your prior knowledge up to that very point before you present the page to a given particular user.

In statistics, this is what's called a reinforcement learning problem, specifically a 'multi-armed bandit problem'. Multi-armed bandit is an old timey phrase for a slot machine where, the idea goes, you can pull multiple levers which determine your outcome and the results from those pulls may change substantially over time. The use of 'Thompson Sampling' to select the best option allows you to automate these operational decisions. A Bayesian approach is crucial to this since to answer the right question and automate the right intervention, you need to be able to readily flip and rearrange the conditional probabilities. In practice, many of the tools we discussed, tools like Optimizely and Google Optimize, have these approaches baked into their operation, making all this highly accessible for generalists.

The last big concept here is the explore vs. exploit tradeoff. I'll be honest: you probably *don't* need to understand this to get started. However, it's so generally fascinating that I felt like I'd be short changing you if I didn't mention it. Let's say you're running a dynamic UX based on a Bayesian with sampling–for example, testing multiple, alternative checkout processes for new customers. One thing you need to configure is how much and when you want to try combinations that you currently believe are *less likely* to succeed in order to make sure you're not missing the next big thing.

In math and statistics, this is a tradeoff between 'exploiting' your knowledge of a local maximum vs. venturing out an 'exploring' to make sure there isn't a bigger maximum out there that you haven't found– another, higher peak. And, bear with me, introducing weird variations is central to life on earth as we know it–evolution works by way of the current environment selecting for the most fit. However, if it didn't introduce crazy variations once in a while, all this planet would have is some very, very, evolved plankton. Knowing how to best explore/exploit is not obvious, but a Bayesian approach deploying Thompson Sampling to the multi-armed bandit problem does the balancing for you, for free, in a way that is your best bet to maximize profits.

The end of the chapter offers a few active learning options, and they include references on Frequentist vs. Bayesian reasoning, but the important point for our purposes is that these Bayesian approaches do a much better job at making use of the richness of the Observations we have about user behavior.

The Bradford Hill Criteria for Hypothesis Testing
Originally published in 1965 by Sir Bradford Hill, for public health, the nine Bradford Hill criteria have persisted in importance for the scientific community at large. With the explosive increase that data science and

machine learning have had on digital applications, their influence has expanded there, particularly as the question of quality and causality of analytics has expanded with it.

The nine criteria are:

1. Strength (effect size): A small association does not mean that there is not a causal effect, though the larger the association, the more likely that it is causal.

2. Consistency (reproducibility): Consistent findings observed by different persons in different places with different samples strengthens the likelihood of an effect.

3. Specificity: Causation is likely if there is a very specific population at a specific site and disease with no other likely explanation. The more specific an association between a factor and an effect is, the bigger the probability of a causal relationship.22

4. Temporality: The effect has to occur after the cause (and if there is an expected delay between the cause and expected effect, then the effect must occur after that delay).

5. Biological gradient (dose-response relationship): Greater exposure should generally lead to greater incidence of the effect. However, in some cases, the mere presence of the factor can trigger the effect. In other cases, an inverse proportion is observed: greater exposure leads to lower incidence.

6. Plausibility: A plausible mechanism between cause and effect is helpful (but Hill noted that knowledge of the mechanism is limited by current knowledge).

7. Coherence: Coherence between epidemiological and laboratory findings increases the likelihood of an effect. However, Hill noted that "... lack of such [laboratory] evidence cannot nullify the epidemiological effect on associations".

---

22 Kristen M Fedak et al., "Applying the Bradford Hill Criteria in the 21st Century: How Data Integration Has Changed Causal Inference in Molecular Epidemiology," Emerging themes in epidemiology (BioMed Central, September 30, 2015), https://hdd.works/3cf9uX3.

8. Experiment: "Occasionally it is possible to appeal to experimental evidence".
9. Analogy: The use of analogies or similarities between the observed association and any other associations.

How do we move from association towards causation when we can't run a Randomized Control Experiment? Eric Tassone, one of this chapter's guest editors, spent 12 years as a data scientist at Google, collaborating with and managing dozens of analysts and data scientists, introducing them to the portfolio of approaches he'd seen work. While machine learning (ML) is great at finding associations in giant data sets, it doesn't always help much when we seek to move from association to causation.

One of his favorite questions for data scientists focused exclusively on deep machine learning to uncover associations was: "How would you prove smoking causes lung cancer?" Their first reaction was usually to go deep on a machine learning solution. However, as Eric says, 'Deep learning generally does not get you to causation. What if there are unknown confounders affecting if a subject chose to smoke?" Their next idea was often to run an RCE. This is an option in some settings, but it is typically expensive, and often ethically impossible, such as in the case of smoking, or perhaps too risky for a business.

What are your options in a difficult situation like this? Well, this smoking thing has been going on for awhile and was the catalyst for a lot of the prevailing ideas on how to work toward causality. Sir Austin Bradford Hill used both RCC and PCS to quantify the association between smoking cigarettes and lung cancer since RCEs were not possible due to ethical concerns, a point Fisher made snidely to call into question causal interpretations of the RCCs/PCSs that Bradford Hill and his colleagues used. This is part of what motivated Bradford Hill and company to come up with the thinking described in what we now call the Bradford Hill Criteria for trying to move from association to causation.

Linking Continuous Design forward to Hypothesis Testing

If the results of your experiments aren't actionable, then you just did all this hard stats and science stuff for nothing! In practicing HDD to avoid that, get in the habit of asking and answering two key questions:

1. When you're doing Continuous Design: How do we make sure this design is testable?
2. As you exit one sprint and enter the next: What should we prioritize now, given what we observed?

Figure 5-17: From Continuous Design to Hypothesis Testing (And Back)

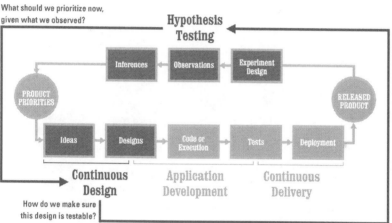

The first few times you do iterate with this kind of rigor, you'll probably find you made mistakes–you'll miss the mark on how to test features; the actionability of your Inferences won't be as crisp as you envisioned. This is fine. Learning from iteration is a foundation element of both agile and particularly of HDD. In this section, the goal is to help you think about how to make this happen.

What should you be learning on this weekly basis, and how does that relate to the more general outcomes you're trying to get with your application? With agile, we're looking to balance giving ourselves the time and focus to do a single thing well with making sure we don't create waste by overdoing a feature that's not going to help with outcomes. Agile does this through discrete sprints, commonly one week in duration. Even without HDD, single weeks tend to generally work well for Hypothesis Testing since it helps you deal with day of week effects. With HDD, we're structuring a more explicit point of view on the inputs, outputs, and processes within that sprint–in this section, that means creating a robust interaction between the team's work on Continuous Design and Hypothesis Testing. For an agile team using HDD, it's useful to think of weekly sprints through the product pipeline towards some 'macro' objective, and then quarterly consideration of those macro objectives.

Figure 5-18: Macro vs. Micro Cadences

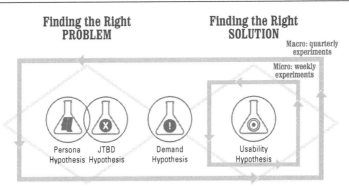

Given that most teams run weekly sprints and have some kind of a quarterly review cycle, with objectives and key results (OKR's) for example, this is a take on experimentation that's compatible with those cadences. For example, in the quarter where we find them, HVAC in a Hurry is working with the field technicians to enable self-service parts orders for the JTBD of getting replacement parts to a job site. On a given week, they might be prepping the infrastructure to test assisted chat or iterating on it based on what they observed. There's nothing universally right about these cadences–other variations might work well for other teams. However, the key is to decide the cadence in advance, stick to it for at least one cycle, and then revise it retrospectively based on how it goes.

Great products are the accumulation of steady, relevant, attention to detail. In the next section, we'll look at the design to test process for 'micro' experimentation with user stories. In the next chapter, we'll look at how to frame the 'macro' customer experience to maximize outcomes. How do we make a habit of experimenting at this 'micro' level of the user story?

How do we make sure we're not just getting the big picture right, but all the small pictures that compose it as well? For a given UI element, do we know if we've delivered something that works great for the user, something that needs revision, or something that should be scrapped altogether?

The Micro View: Improving Your UI with Testable User Stories

The good news is that by approaching Continuous Design the way we have, you will have already done a lot of the hard work by writing fully articulated, testable user stories. These serve directly as your usability hypotheses. In fact, while drafting user stories, I find that an excellent habit is to draft simple, seemingly obvious questions as part of the backlog grooming[23] (sprint preparation) that will help you figure out if in your next iteration of a given story is truly done or needs more attention. You can then pair these questions with ideas on metrics.

Figure 5-19: Unpacking the Usability Hypothesis

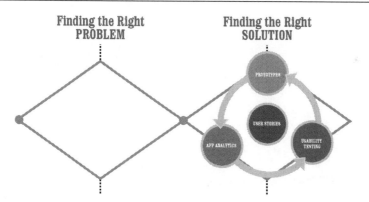

Why not just go straight to drafting the metrics you think you'll use to define done? Aren't the user stories enough? What I've seen time after time, particularly in teams with an active analytics capability, is that they tend to just throw a bunch of metrics at the story—modern tool chains like Google Analytics provide more metrics than you'll ever use. For example, when I ask which metrics with which thresholds they'll use to decide whether a feature is done, the answers are vague and usually amount to,

---

23 This is a general term for whatever an agile team does to prepare for the next sprint. Activities often include a story writing workshop and sometimes early prototyping.

'we'll figure it out later, I guess'. This isn't terrible, but it's easy to do a whole lot better, including avoiding wasteful investments in application development, by investing in making sure you can pair focused questions with your user stories as you draft them.

The table of user stories from the Continuous Product chapter offers a view of how user stories paired with focal analytical questions might look for the 'epic' user story: 'As Trent the HVAC technician, I want to know the pricing and availability of a part that needs replacing so I can decide my next steps.'

Table 5-7: From User Story to Analytical Question

Child Stories, Analytical Questions, and Metrics for Epic: 'As Trent the HVAC technician, I want to know the pricing and availability of a part that needs replacing so I can decide my next steps.'

#	User Story	Analytical Questions, Metrics and Experiments
1	I know the part number and I want to find it on the system so I can find out its price and availability.	**How well does this search type work relative to the alternatives?** **How often is this search used per transaction relative to the alternatives?**
2	I don't know the part number and I want to try to identify it online so I can find out its price and availability.	**(see above)**
3	I don't know the part number and I can't determine it and I want help so I can find out its price and availability.	**(see above)**
4	I want to see the pricing and availability of the part so I decide on next steps and get agreement from the customer.	**Are the tech's finding and accessing these pages?** **How often does this lead to a part order?**

First and foremost, design your user stories with this kind of experiment in mind by simply pairing them with simple questions that would help you make this keep vs. revise vs. scrap decision, as you saw in the table above. The actionability of the DV or DV's for a given user story is this keep vs. revise vs. scrap decision.

From there, draft ideas on IV's you'd use to make those decisions. In the table below, I've added a few of these to the table we stepped through earlier. There's a section for descriptive IV's and then also ideas for A/B testing where we'd look at how user behavior differs between different executions of the UI.

Table 5-8: From User Story to Question to Metrics

Child Stories, Analytical Questions, and Metrics for Epic: 'As Trent the HVAC technician, I want to know the pricing and availability of a part that needs replacing so I can decide my next steps.'

#	User Story	Analytical Questions, Metrics and Experiments
1	I know the part number and I want to find it on the system so I can find out its price and availability.	**How well does this search type work relative to the alternatives?** **How often is this search used per transaction relative to the alternatives?** DV's: Searches of this type relative to others Sequence of this search relative to other search types Conversion to order from this type of search (%) Candidates for A/B testing: Add/remove UI for user story #3 and see how it affects click-through to subsequent screens.
2	I don't know the part number and I want to try to identify it online so I can find out its price and availability.	(see above)
3	I don't know the part number and I can't determine it and I want help so I can find out its price and availability.	(see above)

#	User Story	Analytical Questions, Metrics and Experiments
4	I want to see the pricing and availability of the part so I decide on next steps and get agreement from the customer.	**Are the tech's finding and accessing these pages?** :: How many new users are able to at least try it out? DV: New Users with >0 Parts Lookups/Signups :: Of the users that have tried it, how often do they use it? DV: Lookups/Active User **How often does this lead to a part order?** DV: Conversion rate to order Candidates for A/B testing: Variations in UI and how they affect conversion to order

Since stories #1-#3 all describe different ways the user might find a part, I drafted one set of metrics and test ideas and, in fact, many of them are comparative. Basically, what we want to see is which search type the techs actually use and, in particular, whether there's a difference in a given search type's success in getting the tech to the part they want, which is observable by the tech taking the next steps and not going back and doing more searching.

In the story map, HinH prioritized search story #3 at the bottom since while they heard about a tech's doing this in the field, it wasn't common. The team might reasonably ask: 'Even if we think it might be worth it to put this in, what if it confuses the techs and lowers the success rate of lookups and orders overall?' This is a good candidate for an A/B test where, after establishing a baseline of performance with regard to the DV's,[24] the team compares orders across users that get the baseline site (A) and ones that see a version of the site with user story #3 (email photo for part ID) implemented.

In this fourth user story, our user has found a part and is (we hope) finding its pricing and availability. In single subject/ qualitative usability testing, we can check

Figure 5-20: Parts Detail Page (HinH)

---

24 At least for or ahead of the cohorts in the A/B test

this: we show the user the page and ask them the pricing and availability of the part in question. In the 'wild' with users, we only observe through the Observations the system logs, so we only know if they got to this page and if they later placed an order. Here, when we're looking at quantitative Observations, we want to know how well we were able to move the user to the next steps. For an A/B test, the team might want to try different takes on the parts detail page that you're seeing.

In general, you should make a habit out of pairing these questions, metrics, and experiments with your work on user stories, even if the team doesn't end up instrumenting all of this Observation and running the related experiments. Why? Essentially because it's an easy way to make sure you can measure *the* primary metric in the product pipeline for Continuous Design, Features with High Engagement/Total Features (where feature is ≈ user story). Also, coding, testing, and then deploying gets geometrically more expensive, and you shouldn't build out a story if you don't have time to do this.

User Story Mapping to Maximize Outcomes and Minimize Waste
Wherever possible, designing experiments (qual. or quant.) into one-week sprints most naturally pairs it with the team's decision making about priorities. Where this isn't possible, for example in cases where the Observation interval is longer than a week, the trick is to map those conclusions to similar, existing team 'rituals'. In agile, 'rituals' are any repeating event you do in sequence with your sprints, like weekly retrospectives and backlog grooming. This helps avoid additional overhead which overburdens and eventually loses the team's attention.

Strong practice means everyone's excited to see results vs. arguing/promoting their individual opinions. It also means release content is prioritized for learning vs. administrative convenience or economies in engineering, real or perceived. For example, in the case of HinH, a developer might reasonably and correctly say that it would be more efficient for them to work on all the stories about search (#1-#3) and then move on to showing pricing and availability and after that ordering.

However, efficiently creating software that no one uses or has trouble using and requires rework is not the best way to make progress on the team's stated goals, their OKR's, for example. Instead, the team should focus on implementing a 'horizontal' slice of the user experience from end-to-end to maximize the relevance of the experience for the user and then see how the user behaves. From there, based on what they Infer, they can more intentionally consider additional functionality like alternative search affordances.

Story mapping is a popular approach to managing this within a team. The basic idea is to maintain something like what you see here on a wall or a screen where it's visible to the team, so that it serves as an 'information radiator' about the bigger picture for the team; there when they want it, but easy to ignore when they don't. This version is for the current work at HinH.

Figure 5-21- User Story Mapping at HVAC in a Hurry

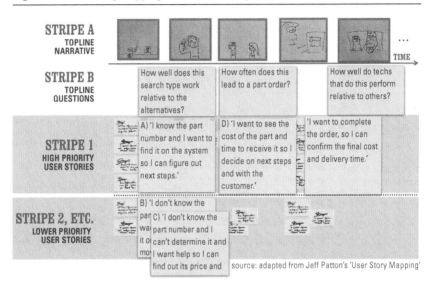

source: adapted from Jeff Patton's 'User Story Mapping'

Teams will approach the particulars differently, but the basic idea is to have a top 'stripe' that describes the larger arc of the team's target UX, using storyboard squares. These should show the user *in situ*, not, for example, wireframes of the current or proposed UI. From there user stories are aligned vertically in prioritized 'stripes'. For example, in the case of HinH, their subject interviews (for developing and testing their Right Problem hypotheses) suggested that most of the time, techs have the part number in question, so that's their highest priority search-related story. The others are in lower stripes. The team should work to a point of view on a complete 'stripe B' of highest priority stories for a complete UX, get those through the product pipeline observing the results, infer what they have learned from this, and then decide what's next.

Experiment cadence isn't math or physics—teams should adaptively find the particular cadence that works for them. For example, in a more dynamic environment, it might make sense to look at the 'macro' metrics monthly. In a team that's just starting a new concept, they may run a series of weekly design sprints for 90 days before they decide on a focal JTBD:VP pairing. All that said, consistency is important. As a team lead, you'll know if you're getting to successful practice if:

1. you need relatively few status/project meetings during the week
2. when you talk to technical specialists, they have a comfortable understanding of what constitutes success for their execution
3. in general, the team is getting better and better at minimizing waste and maximizing wins

In the next section, you'll learn about how to instrument the necessary Observations to answer these 'micro' questions with Google's tool chains, which are a popular choice for doing this particular set of jobs.

How to Acquire Observations

While there are many tools out there to do this, Google Analytics (GA) is a popular choice. While the transition from their v3 to v4 (GA3 to GA4) has been rocky for many,[25] between the alternatives you're likely to either be using GA or something else heavily influenced by the same prevailing concepts.

Regardless of the product you're using, analytics tools will always be a kind of Swiss Army Knife, offering many options and ways to do things. A good one makes all those options easy to try, but rarely do they do much that's useful in the way of helping you ask the right questions. Given this,

---

25 This is a lively discussion about the transition from practitioners: "Y Combinator," Y Combinator, accessed July 25, 2022, https://hdd.works/3J4cVMw This includes a discussion of emerging alternatives like Matomo and Fathom.

it's important to start with a clear Experiment Design and work from there on how to implement what you need for it in your analytics suite. Setting up analytics is like finger painting–easy to do, hard to do well.

That said, as long as you start with a clear intention and your tool isn't too obscure, a few Google searches on 'how to', and you'll get great results. And, of course, it gets easier with practice. This is how we'll approach using GA—by focusing on approach and fundamentals.

Let's start with how to set up and measure our DV's. Regardless of the tool, this is generally a good place to start setting up your infrastructure for Observation and measurement, in the sense that it's good to work backward from the outcome you want. We'll specifically look at the DV's associated with this epic user story from HinH:

I want to see the pricing and availability of the part so I decide on next steps and get agreement from the customer.

For that we had these notes on the analytical question we want to answer:

Are the tech's finding and accessing these pages?

:: How many new users are able to at least try it out?

DV: New Users with >0 Parts Lookups/Signups

:: Of the users that have tried it, how often do they use it?

DV: Lookups/Active User

To keep the example nice and specific, let's have a look at how you'd instrument an Observation so we know whenever a technician completes a successful part lookup, which is the numerator (top) of this ratio from above–'DV: Lookups/Active User'.

We'll do this in three steps:

1. defining the Observation in the analytics suite
2. getting our application to create or send data to trigger the Observation in the analytics suite
3. making sure #1 and #2 are working as we expect.

Your particular tool might frame these activities differently, and that's fine, these are fairly generalizable to analytics in general. Also, as soon as you integrate it into your application, your analytics suite will start collecting a lot of data points–it's part of their job. Will it be collecting everything you need? Not always, and so as you're getting started it's good to a) make sure you can get what you want and b) make sure you know how to make that happen. For you and your particular team, you can judge an analytics suite on how easy it makes that.

We'll start with #1, defining the Observation we want in our analytics suite. We need to define this Observation in our analytics app so we know we can come back and measure it. In our specific example of instrumenting Observation for HinH in GA4, we'll make the worst case assumption we have to explicitly, even though it collects many behaviors by default.

In the screenshot below, I've defined an 'Event' to record parts lookups. Basically, what you're seeing is the server side configuration of what we're after with this Observation. I've added a GA4 Event where basically what I'm saying is "GA, I'm going to send you an Event in the format you require, and I want you to recognize this as a part lookup. You will know it by its name: 'lookup'."

Figure 5-22: Creating a Custom Event in Google Analytics

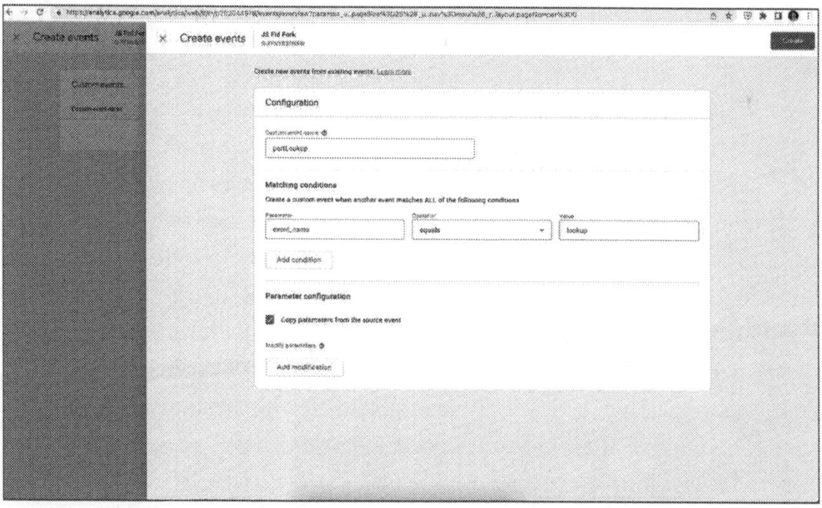

We might want to add additional parameters like part number, but this gets us the basics.

An 'Event' in GA essentially serves the purpose of having GA record any user behavior or attribute that it doesn't record by default. You can see a view in GA of the reporting on them here–HinH events for search, lookup, and order:

Figure 5-23: Event Reporting in Google Analytics (Time Series)

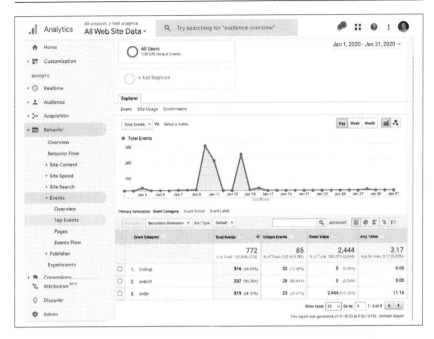

Now, what we're after is the DV 'Lookups/Active User' and so we have a little more work to do to create a composite view that, say, shows us that ratio over time. At this point, though, we know we're observing the lookup event and the rest of the work generally follows a similar pattern.

When does this Event record? We want it to record whenever a technician completes a 'valid' or successful parts lookup. How do we make that happen? Here again, the analytics suite may by default have access to enough about the app's behavior to consistently record what we want. Or it might not. Here again, let's make the worst case assumption that we need to include a function in our own code to do this so we can control how these Observations are recorded.

Basically, we just need a function that deals with sending the event parameters from above to the GA application in the way that it wants (per its API). As part of the normal process of setting up Google Analytics on your application, which basically just involves including a small JS snippet in your pages, you'll have the 'gtag' function available to send events. Its basic form is:

```
gtag('event', <action>, {
  'event_category': <category>,
  'event_label': <label>,
  'value': <value>
});26
```

'Event' is the event you want to record, 'lookup' in our case. <event-params> is an optional set of key-value pairs you can send if you want. For example, if we were interested in the part number and the customer whose job the tech was completing, then the function call might look like this:

```
gtag('event', 'lookup', {
  event_category: lookups,
  event_label: searchByPN,
});
```

With all that up and running, once there's some traffic recorded, we can go to a report like the one you see which shows the occurrence of Events and, in typical GA style, let's you slice and review the particulars as you like.

GA, or really any analytics application, is its own application with its own MVC. The data model from our perspective is all the stuff our web application sends it; the Views are the various reporting screens, and the Controllers it uses to make most of that happen are pretty opaque since that's up to Google and we're just users of this product. It's certainly the gorilla in its category, but it's not magic. It only knows what we tell it. More specifically, it only knows whatever it's decided to send itself through the JS base lib they gave us to include, and any custom Events we decide to send it. One implication of this is that it doesn't have any historical data for our application from before we added GA to it.

Other than the Events we send it, what kind of things does the base GA set up give us? What are the IV's we have to work with? The other big items are:

1. Attributes for Visitors/Users

   It records the user's (general) location, whether they're new

---

26 "Measure Google Analytics Events : ; Universal Analytics for Web (Gtag.js) :   Google Developers." Google Developers. Accessed August 2, 2022. https://hdd.works/3PTxs8Z. https://hdd.works/3PTxs8Z

or returning, and what browser and device they're using (mobile, computer, etc.), among others. Periodically, Google also adds other things about the users. Obviously, they know a lot of stuff about everyone.

2. Referral Sources

Where are the visitors coming from? For example, did they just type your web address into their browser, or are they following a 'like' from Twitter, Facebook, another site, etc.? Also, if you add any parameters to your URLs for tracking (ex: https://www.alexandercowan.com/?utm_source=digital-skills-thing&utm_medium=email&utm_campaign=online), GA will record these and organize the parameters they carry with the rest of your data.

3. Page Views by Session

It stores the pages your user clicks on and the progression (including time on page) between the pages for each user's session on the site.

4. On Page User Events

This might be user clicks, watching a video, doing a search, etc.

GA is pretty focused on what we generally call 'descriptive analytics': describing the data as it is. They do some 'diagnostic analytics', like noticing that your pages are loading slower and how that's affecting traffic, and it even attempts some 'prescriptive analytics', like recommending you try to make a certain page load faster. To run the A/B tests we mentioned above, they have another tool called Optimize.

Instrumenting Observation in Google Optimize

Basically, Google Optimize allows you to configure, run, and analyze the results of A/B tests. You can decide what versions of a page you want to allocate what portion of that page's traffic to, and off it goes. It even has a nifty visual editor you can use to make the changes, which you can see here.

Let's say we're interested in how having that third search type affects onboarding and engagement. We could code that user story and then make it a 'B' treatment to the site. In fact, there's even a lean UX approach called the 'fake feature test' where we add the button, see if anyone clicks on it, and if they do just give them an error or 'temporarily unavailable, etc.'. What I've done here with Google Optimize is add the third search (get help) in Optimize and allocate it to a third of that page's traffic.

Figure 5-24: Google Optimize

Common Anti-Patterns and Failure Modes

This is mostly a recap of what you've learned. That said, here's a summary of a few things to watch for and avoid.

1. Inferences without Actionability

   Hire an analyst and they're going to analyze. But just like hiring a developer to build software without a clear charter, this is likely to lead to waste, work that's disconnected from what matters to your user, and demoralized employees. Instead, integrate analytics (Hypothesis Testing) into your pipeline such that it's decisive to what the team focuses on and why for each agile sprint.

2. Not Creating an Explicit Experiment Design

   This is arguably just a symptom of #1 above, but in practice it's important to work backwards from actionability to an Experiment Design that has an explicit 'line in the sand' on both effect size and the confidence you feel you need on both alpha and beta.

3. Not Considering Effect Size (Power)

   Particularly prevalent with frequentist approaches, this is a common failure mode and not infrequently related to the items above. Regardless of which statistical approach you're using, make sure effect size is part of your Experiment Design and carried forward to the Observations you acquire.

4. Over or Under Powering a Study

   Without an explicit Experiment Design, it's highly unlikely that you don't collect either too many or too few Observations. While teams and companies that are in the habit of experimenting get better at it over time, making it easier, one common thread for the practice of HDD is 'do fewer things but better' and that certainly applies to Hypothesis Testing.

5. Not Taking Advantage of all Feasible Experiment Design Patterns

   In digital applications, this often means getting comfortable

running Retrospective Case Controls as a preliminary
Experiment Design.
6. Not Taking Advantage of Thompson Sampling or Similar
   While this or something like it using Bayesian approaches
   is pretty well baked into popular tools like Google Optimize
   and Optimizely, if you're not taking advantage of this
   in your Hypothesis Testing, you're missing out on an
   economic powerhouse.

What We Learned

Hypothesis-Driven Development offers one of the most promising avenues
for creating a durable culture of experimentation. This means marrying
qualitative and quantitative evidence in service of the actionable,
small batch, inferences that supercharge a practice of agile. We started
with some points of contrast between how a high-functioning vs. low-
functioning team might operate with regard to HDD. Then we learned
about pairing customer questions with experiment designs, applying
statistical reasoning with an economic lens, and how to link Continuous
Design to your Hypothesis Testing. Your job, should you choose to accept
it, is to move your teams from an output-driven mindset to an outcomes-
driven mindset. This chapter, and the recommended practices below will
give you the tools you need to get you and your teams there.

Recommended Practice & Supplemental Resources

1. Practice and Apply Innovation Analytics to Your work
My top recommendation on this is just to start framing and testing what you and your team are doing. The early results might be hard won and modest, but this is the best way to make sure that whatever additional material you decide to learn is applicable and going to stick with you in actual practice.

That said, this link will take you to a set of resources for more depth on what you learned in this chapter. It includes cases, online readings, books, and online courses with notes on how to figure out which one might be the best fit for you: https://hdd.works/3vhZNxB.

2. Design & Conduct an Experiment
Specifically on the topic of designing an experiment, my first recommendation is to finish the next chapter, which compliments this one. However, this link will take you to templates and resources to help you get started: https://hdd.works/3b67K2a/.

3. Understand Frequentist vs. Bayesian Statistical Reasoning
In general, I've focused these sections on getting to practice, but stats can be a lot and if you'd like to get a little more depth on some of the topics here, this link offers a portfolio of readings, books, and online courses: https://hdd.works/3vdyZi5.

Guest Editors

This chapter and the next are kind of a 'package' and I worked with both Casey and Eric on them. While we met working together at UVA, both have a solid footing in both industry and academic practice.

Guest Editor: Casey Lichtendahl

Casey and I first met through students who had taken both our courses. His elective in data science (est. 2014) offered Darden's MBAs a new type of experience, and we were both passionate about taking the MBA students we so admired and making sure they had the creative confidence to really get in the game in tech, taking traction roles in applied general management and analytics. For the MBA of today, we think the best roles are in product development, working with an interdisciplinary team of, say 7-12 on iterative improvements. This means being able to create focus relative to a company's strategy, but also collaborating closely on a product pipeline, including intuition on how data and analytics can move the needle on outcomes. Casey has remained determined to stay on top of practice, academic research, and effective teaching. After a 15-year career at Darden, he recently transitioned to Google as a staff data scientist.

Three questions with Casey

What led you down the path to data science?
I have this habit of questioning assumptions. Getting my MBA at Darden, I learned about decision analysis and I started to wonder "What if we used a different set of assumptions?". I got really interested in answering that question and ended up at Stanford doing a masters in management science and then statistics. That taught me how to look under the hood and tinker with the statistical plumbing. After that, I learned more about the current practice of what we call data science teaching the subject and now working in industry practicing it.

What have we learned about the right entry points and engagement models for a generalist who collaborates with data scientists on the job?
The methods and topics are different, but essentially I think it's the same as what we've learned about helping them engage with software engineers–that they need creative confidence. They need to learn and maybe continually learn enough about the work those teams are doing to engage in a way where they can frame goals and ask the right questions about approach and what's feasible. For example, an analyst could deliver a model of churn that's 75% accurate and have it be pretty useful. What if they're interfacing with a manager who's convinced the accuracy has to be at 99%? Best case, you have an analyst that can help the general manager better understand the model's actionability–but that's putting a lot of onus on the analyst to do something that's mostly in the general management domain. More likely, they're going to end up with waste where instead they could be working on their next win together.

What are you most excited to learn about next?
Recently, I've been really interested in approaches where a Frequentist's p-value and a Bayesian's probability to be best are equivalent. Basically, both approaches are trying to do the job of helping a manager decide which version of a given UX is the best. To the extent there's some equivalence, I think that can help bridge the gap between Frequentists and Bayesians in data science. There's a real gap there that seems unnecessary to me. This is an unresolved issue that came up in the experiments course I co-developed with Eric Tassone. In that course, we teach both Frequentist and Bayesian approaches to designing and analyzing experiments.

Guest Editor: Eric Tassone

Eric and I met through our mutual friend
and collaborator, Casey Lichtendahl.
Professionally, Eric has followed a winding
path which has led him to where he is now:
the center of practice in data science and
analytics, both academic and professional.
His educational journey started with
undergraduate and masters degrees in mathematics, proceeded to a
J.D. (law degree), and then to a PhD in biostatistics, where he learned
about the experiment patterns you saw in this chapter. While he's
tagged in to teach various classes at UVA and elsewhere, most recently
Eric spent nearly 12 years at Google across teams working on their
core Search property, YouTube, and product ecosystem teams. An
expert at the integrated practice of data science at the intersection
between machine learning and statistics, Eric remained doggedly
curious about the larger portfolio of scientific techniques to draw
inference, including use of the experiment patterns you learned about
in this chapter.

Three questions with Eric

*In 1999 you were practicing law in Florida. How did you get interested
enough in statistics to get a PhD?*
Before that I was an undergraduate mathematics major, focusing
on pure math. During law school I took a break to do a Master's in
Applied Mathematics, during which I was exposed to (1) computer-
based mathematical modeling and (2) graduate-level statistical theory
(in excellent courses by professors Dr. James Keesling and Dr. Brett
Presnell at the University of Florida). "Data Science" wasn't a popular
term at the time, but looking back I think it was kind of a proto data
science degree–using computers, data, and stats models to frame
decisions under uncertainty.

There I am in Florida in 1999 practicing law, and I found myself missing my quantitative roots. While I was visiting a friend working on a Ph.D. in Biostatistics at Emory, I saw an excellent seminar by Dr. Lance Waller, who would later become my dissertation advisor, about statistical methods for assessing environmental justice. That topic and the possibility of researching it as part of a Ph.D. is what nudged me into leaving the practice of law, even though the firm was terrific and supportive. The focus of my Ph.D work was the development of statistical methods you could implement with big data and heavy computing power, which was pretty 'data-sciency' at the time

What did you learn that you most value working as a data scientist at Google?
Google is blessed with a terrific, open culture. This means you have access to curious peers who you can learn from and who value your point of view. In terms of day-to-day substantive work, I'll try to combine two ideas into one so I meet the 'most' part of your question: I learned that quantitative problems are embedded in engineering problems, which are in turn embedded in business problems. So instead of merely coming up with a putatively 'best' solution from one (often narrow) perspective, data scientists have to draw from our collective breadth and come up with solutions at various levels of accuracy, speed, interpretability, complexity, and so on. And then we must develop the judgment to make appropriate, and at times difficult, tradeoffs to select the solution that works best given the operational reality of the embedded problem.

What are you learning about now?
In light of those embedded problems mentioned in the previous answer, I am trying to learn more about problems that sit at the intersection of data science and business. One frame for thinking about this is the difference (if any) in the practice of data science between the types of problems involved in running a business (e.g., controlled experimentation, forecasting, capacity planning, churn analysis, and so on) versus the types of problems that arise in products (e.g., recommendation systems, ranking, on-the-fly image

classification, and the like). In the former category the fruits of data science are often used to aid human decision making whereas in the latter category we are often looking to build systems that make decisions without human supervision. I'm interested in the differences between these categories – Do we need different training for data scientists? Different data collection and privacy policies? Different ethical practices? Different engineering and business cultures? Anyway, these are the sorts of things I am thinking about and trying to learn about right now in my role as an Associate Professor of Data Science at the University of Virginia School of Data Science who also teaches at UVA's Darden School of Business.

6

FROM INFERENCE TO YOUR NEXT PRODUCT PRIORITIES

Figure 6-1: Hypothesis Testing & HDD

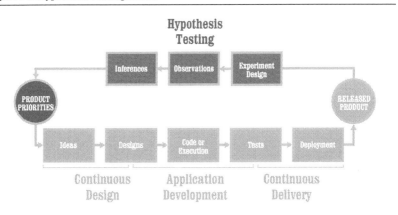

How do you decide where to experiment next? This is a question your team should revisit every iteration/sprint, and it should be one where you, as the product person, regularly invest substantial energy and consideration. Your answer should have a durable context, one that allows you to answer the question: "How do I establish a consistent context for what we might focus on and why, even as our results drive us to vary that focus sprint to sprint?"

Figure 6-2: Iterating Between Continuous Design & Hypothesis Testing

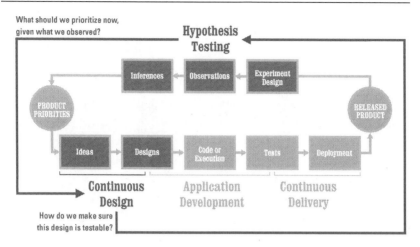

We have previously discussed how to unbundle and sequence testing related to product/market fit. In particular, I hope you took home the uncomfortable reality that a team can build a highly usable, highly reliable product or feature that no one wants. Any given concept should only move from left to right across the double diamonds or Right Problem and Right Solution on the basis of successful testing, or the team incurs an undue risk of creating waste and diverting resources from another concept that is ready to be a big win. In this chapter, we're specifically focused on instrumenting Observation into the working software you're going to deploy.

Like explorers mapping out new territory, you need to decide what's important to explore while you're still drawing the map. This will change, and it should change as you learn more, particularly in the early days of a new undertaking. What helps is having a Customer Experience (CX) map that makes it easy for the team to navigate your current understanding of what outcomes you're after. Success here means that in the context of their particular focus, week to week, sprint to sprint, that your team knows what user behavior they're trying to improve and how what they're doing will contribute to that.

In agile, a visual item that helps a team's shared understanding is called an 'information radiator'. Back to the 'blue button moment', what you want is a situation where your colleagues are asking these questions and finding answers on their own initiative—instead of meetings where the team is supposed to 'get on the same page'.

Given this, as the HinH team unpacks their CX map, it's important that it motivates the team to ask the hard questions even at inconvenient times. For example, if churn is high, rather than throwing more money at acquisition or grinding out more features from the backlog, the team may need to more fundamentally revisit how customers (or users) are engaging with the product's value propositions.

In order to create a little distance between the details (features, code, testing, analytics) that everyone's working on day to day, and the actual user experience, I like to start a new CX map with a storyboard that steps through trigger, action, and reward/conclusion for the focal JTBD:VP pairings that the team is working. For HinH, one such JTBD is 'getting replacement parts to a job site' for Trent the Technician by way of a self-service parts ordering application. Economically, this ties back to the team's current objective: 'Automate and standardize the best of what the company has learned to improve user outcomes and their current KR's (key results):

KR1: Deploy the parts ordering app in {month 1 of the quarter}

KR2: Onboard at least 100 users for the test cohort

KR3: Achieve >80% of parts ordered through the app with the test cohort

How do you create such a storyboard?

Mapping the Customer Experience

You can see the team's working view on Trent, the JTBD, and the team's VP here. But how does this happen? Where does the JTBD start? End? Here is a simple storyboard that sketches out a take on the experience for Trent the HVAC Technician. The trigger is that he decides he needs a replacement part to complete a repair; the action is that he remembers there's a new app and tries it out. The reward is that he's able to self-service the part order and plan out his next steps with the customer without having to spend time on the phone, etc. coordinating and handing off the next steps with others.

Figure 6-3: A JTBD:VP Mapping for Trent the Technician

PERSONA, JTBD, AND VALUE HYPOTHESES AT HVAC IN A HURRY

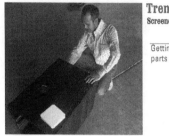

Trent the Technician

Screener How many HVAC repairs did you do last week?

JTBD	ALTERNATIVE	VALUE PROPOSITION
Getting replacement parts to a job site	Call the office and request the part then wait for an update on the phone or through a call-back	If we automate parts lookup and ordering online, then the tech's will use it and it will improve outcomes.

Figure 6-4: Storyboarding the CX for Self-Service Parts Ordering

As you can see, there's nothing particularly notable about my drawing skills. Like a bad but enthusiastic dancer, I am trying to give you permission to go to the whiteboard and without reservation put yourself and the rest of the team in the user's shoes. You can do this anywhere— whiteboard, collaboration tool like MURAL, Miro, etc. This version I did on paper with a Sharpie, and then I dropped the image into Keynote (Apple's PowerPoint-like app) to add the text. If you're still not convinced about the value of storyboarding, ask yourself: How engaging was your last meeting?

Depending on where and how you use the table, you may also find it useful to extend it with a table like the one below that describes the UX in more detail and is also a place to make note about open questions and focal Observations you'd like to have on user behavior.

Table 6-1: Notes on CX Storyboard

Panel	Notes	Questions & Observations/Metrics
A	Trigger: Trent finds in his troubleshooting that a part needs replacing.	During discovery interviews with techs, we found most of the time the part number is printed on the part and question and that sometimes they have to look it up based on the make and model of the equipment. In rare cases, they aren't sure and have to send a photo to dispatch.
		How might we translate these searches to a digital UX? How do we make sure we see how it's working?
B	Action: He gets on to the system, finds the part, and orders it.	We need to carefully instrument Observation so we know how many cases are dropping out (and the tech has to use the old processes by hand). We should make sure we can ID the users, as well, so we can retread with discovery interviews if we need.
C	From there, Trent's able to sort out his next step with the customer.	Same here: Is Trent able to finish in this way/get this reward? Or are there other logistical or admin. hurdles that end up preventing him?
D	Trent makes a habit out of self-servicing his replacement part orders. He makes materially fewer calls to dispatch.	We need to be able to easily observe, possibly by segment and cohort, but TBD: the extent to which, after trying the system, the techs tend to continue to use it and jump on the question of why not if we don't see that use. Are we able to mediate the call logs from the call center by tech to specifically measure this?
E		
F	Does this actually make Trent better off? HinH?	Does this help increase billable hours for Trent? Customer satisfaction for the relevant customers? Does Trent like it?

While storyboarding, try to stick to the essentials from the user's perspective. If it's unclear whether or not you know something from primary sources (your own interviews) or secondary sources (data you think/hope the company has), just make a note of that and continue on. Remember, you're not storyboarding to prove a point, you're storyboarding to: 1) facilitate shared understanding and focus within the team, and 2) get the right questions in the foreground for the team to consider. Without the level of specificity a storyboard provides, it's hard for teams to converge enough focus for a durable approach to evidence-based application development.

Following the storyboard, we have the job of unpacking the specifics of the CX for quantitative observability and useful experimentation. This has to include a point of view on metrics that are amenable to the analytical methods you have available while also linking as directly as possible with the company's operational objectives, expressed as OKR's, for instance. The tendency in the data science community is to measure the correctness of a model. However, what the team really should care about is the expected economic value the model could generate. For example, if we're forecasting how much inventory or capacity we need, we can make sure our model's statistically valid, but what's economically important is balancing stock outs with the cost of excessive inventory. If we're creating a model of churn, we could create a model that designs interventions to reduce that, but the economic consequence you care about is maximizing the economic value of the customers you're acquiring. This is where the CX map comes into play.

Mapping the CX for Focused Experimentation

Now that our storyboard has helped us think about the particulars, how might we create measured Observations of the various behaviors we described so we can make specific Inferences, Inferences that adaptively make our product priorities smarter? Let's say you're Frangelico and one of the district managers tells you, "The techs don't like the new tool. Not sure what to do."

What should Frangelico do then? He could and probably should pick up the phone and talk to this important collaborator about what he or she has observed about the lack of user engagement with the new tool. But they have a day job, too. We can be a lot smarter about what we do next if we know specifically what those techs have or have not done with the tool. For example, do they just not like the idea and decide not to really try it? Did they try it but give up because it wasn't easy enough to use? Or, did they give it a solid try and then just find that it wasn't helping them? These all have different implications for what we need to learn and test next if we want to maximize outcomes and minimize waste.

For this purpose, I like to take what's described in a storyboard and map it to a CX sequence that answers the questions you see here.

Table 6-2: CX Mapping

Question	Acquisition	Onboarding	Engagement	Outcomes	Retention
What does this mean?	How does the customer go from not knowing about our product or feature to being able to use it?	What is the absolute minimum set of actions that lead to some first tangible reward for using the feature or product?	At what point has the user made a habit out of—or 'standardized on'—our feature or product's value proposition for the JTBD in question?	When and how do we observe whether the user has gotten the outcomes they wanted from the product or feature?	Based on our particular engines of growth, what are successful customer behaviors from our perspective?

These particular terms, this particular funnel framework, isn't that important. However, there are three things about it that are important to get right–specifically, that it:

1. **Has Definitions that are Complete and Mutually Exclusive**

   The terms should be as complete and as mutually exclusive as possible. Picture this: You're Frangelico and you're walking in to meet with the person who manages all the HVAC tech's in St. Louis. You ask her how things are going with the new tool. She says, "Not great." Do you have background data to at least know where things went wrong? Did only a few of the tech's try the tool? Did they try it but find out they weren't able to look up a part? Did they actually give it a good try and use it for a while and then stop using it? This is crucially important to figuring out how you're doing and where a given team needs to focus.

In practice, what it requires is that both in terms of qualitative understanding or 'ground truth' as well as specific metrics, there's a minimum of ambiguity about which state a given user has progressed to–onboarding, engagement, etc. With a basic digital analytics set up like Google Analytics, this is usually pretty self-evident and doable with the exception of Outcomes.

With an internal app like HinH's, you'll probably have access to the data you need to calculate Outcomes. However, if you're, say Fitbit and you have a customer that's focused on lowering their blood pressure, you may not. You may have to measure Outcomes with an indirect instrument like a survey, meaning that you'll have to work with a lot less than 100% coverage of all your users and with self-reported data that may be subject to bias. This may also be the case with denominating Engagement–you need to know the users total activity for the given JTBD. Let's say you're AirBNB and you want to know how well you're doing at getting more of a given traveler's overnight stays. You have their AirBNB bookings, but how many nights of hotel stays do they have per year? You may need to find proxies for this or supplement your estimates with surveys.

All this is manageable, and I would generally sketch your CX Map with whatever Outcome definition you think will serve you best, then find proxies or other vehicles to estimate for that definition as need be.

2. Describes a Single JTBD:VP Pairing

A given CX Map can describe a single JTBD: Value proposition pairing–for example, 'Getting Replacement Parts to a Job Site: Parts Ordering Application' in the case of HinH. Given that you can factor JTBD at various levels of abstraction, this still leaves you a lot of discretion about scope. However, particularly if you have a product suite with a lot of discrete VP's, it's not necessarily the place you should capture topline metrics like monthly active users or gross revenue. The main job of the CX Map is to help isolate and unpack user behaviors in context vs. provide a single business-wide view of what's happening.

3. **Describes a Single User**

You can top down this or bottom up it, but these definitions apply to the behavior of an individual user.

From these definitions, we'll frame a specific DV for each step for each individual user. Let's say you're talking with a founder working toward product/market fit, and they tell you "We acquired 1,087 new users yesterday!" Is that fantastic, good, just OK, or bad? If they had 2,000 visitors to the site and 1,087 of them signed up, it's fantastic, at least by most standards. If they had 100,000 users visit, it's probably less than fantastic.

For this essential reason, your DV for each leg of the CX map should be a rate or ratio. That rate or ratio should allow you and your team to assess, from one sprint to another, whether a given change (IV) has improved the DV or not. For example, in the expanded CX Map below for HinH, you can see that the DV for Engagement is 'Parts Ordered Online/Parts Ordered by Tech'. This tells us the extent to which a given tech has standardized on the app for the JTBD of getting replacement parts.

Table 6-3: CX Map for HinH Self-Service Parts Ordering (Full)

CX Map for Getting Replacement Parts to a Job Site using New Parts Ordering Application

Question	Acquisition	Onboarding	Engagement	Outcomes	Retention
What does this mean?	Signing up for an account	Ordering one part	Consistently using the tool to look up and order parts	The tech finds it's making their job easier.	Reducing the overhead to complete a job & increasing customer satisfaction.
How do we observe this? What's the DV?*	Number of Signups/ Number of Visitors	Users with >0 Parts Lookups/ Signups Signups/ Users with >0 Orders	Parts Ordered Online/ Parts Ordered by Tech	Reduced Time to Repair Increased billable/total hours	Steady to increasing Parts Ordered Online/ Parts Ordered by Tech Increase in customer satisfaction/ job
What is the cut off for a transition?	3 days from applicable event (email, etc.) or 30 minutes in the case of a web visit	1 day from Acquisition	30 days post Onboarding	90 days post Onboarding but also ongoing	90 days post Onboarding but also ongoing
What is our 'Line in the Sand' threshold?	>50%	>66%	>50%**	Time to Repair: >20% decrease relative to baseline Billable Hours: >10% increase	Portion of Tech's who increase usage: >75% Satisfaction: >20% increase

Question	Acquisition	Onboarding	Engagement	Outcomes	Retention
How might we test this? What new IVs are worth testing?*	Mandating use of the app vs. not Intro/training workshops vs. not. Live chat concierge test	Observing cohorts across onboarding programs & product iterations	Observe cohorts across onboarding programs & product iterations and see where we can get to >80%	Observe outcome metrics across cohorts	Observe outcome metrics across cohorts
What's tricky? What do we need to watch out for?	We don't know yet.	Optional vs. mandatory training	Engagement vs. Outcomes with pulling vs. pushing	We're not sure yet, but we'll know much more after we get going.	We're not sure yet, but we'll know much more after we get going.

* DV is 'dependent variable' and IV is 'independent variable'
** Just in case this is confusing relative to the 30-50% we discussed in the last chapter, this is a ratio of all the parts a tech orders online relative to all the parts they order. The last ratio had to do with the techs behavior on a given visit and was the ratio of visits to a parts page that resulted in an order relative to all visits to that page.

The next item describes how long it takes to get an Observation. In practice, establishing a metric here is pretty important for getting to a functioning CX Map with your infrastructure for Observation. Consider onboarding–at what point do you decide a new user just isn't going to progress from Acquisition to onboarding? When do you decide they're churned, and have abandoned the product entirely? Even if you're not immediately sure, it's useful to take a best guess and be ready to revise it. It's also worth noting that this is designed to be at a level of detail that serves a whole team as a general purpose focal point.

The next item, your 'Line in the Sand', is where the rubber hits the road. I learned this phrase from the book *Lean Analytics*. One of their core takes is that good analytics are analytics that change your behavior, and that if you don't have a 'line in the sand', you won't have the impetus you need to start operating that way.[1] So, this is a practical vs a theoretical finding, but a minimum viable CX Map should have lines in the sand, which are your best guesses for what constitutes the user behavior you can reasonably get to with a strong execution.

Does that mean you can't change the line in the sand if you learn something different about the underlying ground truth on those activity cadences? No. It just means that at any given time, you should be closing your loop on Hypothesis Testing with explicit lines in the sand.

For an excellent example of adaptively pairing what we're calling Continuous Design and Hypothesis Testing, the authors of Lean Analytics (Croll and Yoskovitz) offer the story of a startup called Highscore House. The team there was working on an app to help parents manage their children's chore lists at home. As well they should, they set a 'line in the sand' about what constituted Engagement- four interactions with the app per week. Most users fell below this. The team started testing various changes across the CX to boost Engagement. The results weren't great. Then they made some time to do subject interviews with users who were somewhat engaged, but below the line in the sand. What they essentially found was that these users were well engaged with the app, using it to do the applicable JTBD, in our terms–the line in the sand was just a little too high. Likewise, with a Retrospective Case Control for example you can readily compare users to calibrate and texture your lines in the sand as you learn more about your user personas.

The last two rows, 'How might we test this? What are the big IVs worth flexing?' and 'What's tricky? What do we need to watch out for?' are usually the most ongoing. This is where you note ideas you have for Hypothesis Testing and particular challenges you have on getting the Observations you need. For a minimum CX Map where you can start accruing a baseline, you don't need these, so you can defer them if you're pressed for time at the start. It's worth noting that by 'IV' here we specifically mean 'new alternative CX's' instead of, say, an IV we can't change directly, like seasonality.

Once you sketch a CX Map, then what? From there, this map serves as a focal point and 'information radiator' for the team to use as they decide where to experiment and how the results of past experiments inform their

---

1   Alistair Croll and Benjamin Yoskovitz, "Lean Analytics: Use Data to Build a Better Startup Faster," (O' reilly, 2013), chapter 2.

product priorities. Ideally, it's up on a wall or generally in some spot where it's highly visible to the team if you're in a shared office or if you're hybrid or remote, on a pinned thread in Slack, in a Google Doc, etc.. While the idea with the CX map is that it's a relatively durable view from sprint-to-sprint of the target UX and user behaviors, that doesn't mean it can't or shouldn't change. A healthy, useful CX map is viewed a lot and consistently serves as the repository for changes in points of view as the team's understanding evolves.

Being consistent with framing the team's work this way is easier said than done. Most people are either a) heavy on the quantitative side, b) heavy on the qualitative side, or c) just don't focus with this level of detail. Your job as a product or business lead is to do strong, consistent work across qualitative and quantitative Observations, making actionable inferences on an adaptive, agile cadence.

Framing & Testing Acquisition

In general, by 'Acquisition' we're answering this question: How does the customer go from not knowing about our product or feature to being able to use it? For a music streaming service like Spotify, this would mean getting users to create a trial account to use the service. For a consumer product with a physical component like a Fitbit, this would mean both getting the customer to buy a Fitbit and getting them to create an account to start using the service.

At HinH, it means getting technicians to create an account so they can try out the new parts ordering app. However, this is somewhat unique to our story being about the very first feature on a brand new product. In a more mature product or IT system, it would be more normal to have an acquisition item that just has to do with trying out a new capability.

What you're after here is a set of acquisition recipes that work economically, not just in terms of this one step, but in the rest of the context downstream in the whole CX arc the map describes. For example, you may find a set of AdWords on Google that are cheap and have good click-through rates (CTRs), but if those users perform poorly across the rest of the CX and stop using the product or feature prematurely, then they won't make sense economically. And this is crucial to the practice of CX mapping—while it helps us focus from sprint-to-sprint, it also helps us frame Experiment Designs that deliver Inferences that both address the job (or metric) at hand, but with an awareness of its overall context for the CX.

The DV for Acquisition that we identified in the CX Map is 'Number of Signups/Number of New Visitors'. What we're essentially asking is, 'Of all the people who visit the site, how many sign up to have an account to use the app vs. decide it's not worth it for some reason and bounce?' This seems like a reasonably good choice of DV for experiments since it's a ratio, as are most good DVs in HDD. Number of visits is a terrible metric—who even knows if those were HVAC technicians vs. bots? And what we care about is getting them to the next step, but signups by itself is a terrible metric as well; what if 200,000 techs visit the site but only two hundred sign up? That's a bad result and that's why, with regard to Acquisition, the team is focused on the ratio of Number of Signups/Number of New Visitors.

You may have heard the term 'vanity metric', which means a metric that is simple and likable but does not tend to be informative or actionable. Just looking at visits or just looking at signups are both examples of vanity metrics.

What IVs might they test? The CX map noted the idea of trying out training or intro sessions and seeing if that improves on this ratio. To do that, we'd need a way of identifying those session participants later when they (hypothetically) sign up, but that's generally feasible with URL parameters. If the team experiments and finds a material difference between techs who go to such a session and those who don't, that's economically actionable in that they might then invest in such intro sessions across the board. They might also tie in some qualitative research on what the successful registrants learned at the session that got them to register to see if there's a way they can improve the UI/UX to make those sessions less necessary.

Another IV that's available with just about any analytics package is the entry page for these new users. The team has made the assumption that it's okay to make users sign up for an account before they try out the app, and would expect to see a nice tidy page progression from the home page to the registration page. But what if, for example, the techs are texting each other links to parts, but the recipients of these aren't usually motivated enough to create an account to see the one part. That's something the team should then consider for a change.

Framing & Testing Onboarding

By 'onboarding' here we mean: 'What is the absolute minimum set of actions that lead to some first tangible reward for using the feature or product?' For Spotify, this might mean that, following Acquisition, the user is able to find and play their favorite song. If the user wanted the service specifically to listen to music on-demand while they drive to work, it might additionally mean getting the service working the way they want in their car. With a physical+digital product like a Fitbit, it might mean recording your first workout and seeing how many calories you burned.

At HinH, they've unpacked onboarding and observed it in two steps with two corresponding DVs: first, a user finding pricing and availability for a part (which can be useful by itself) and then second, ordering that part through the app. The DVs are:

1. Signups/
   Users with >0 Parts Lookups
2. Signups/
   Users with >0 Orders

In other words: first, how many of our newly signed up users are able to look up and find at least one replacement part and then, second, of those, how many order at least once?

These onboarding steps are progressive—a user has to look for and find a part before they can order it. In metrics-speak, we'd say that the part lookup's metric is leading and the orders are lagging. If we think usually Trent the Technician looks up a part, gets the O.K. from a customer, and then orders it on the spot, the distinction isn't that actionable, other than observing whether users get stuck for some reason after the look up. If, however, we think Trent may end up looking up the part and then later coming back to find it again and order it, then that could be actionable. For example, putting a 'recent searches' element on the first page of the UI he sees on a return visit may be useful. If the company is operating at enough scale, it might even be actionable for a supply chain process where HinH proactively makes sure the right replacement part inventory is in the right place.

Regardless, generally speaking, the selection of leading vs. lagging indicators across your CX map is highly important if you want to accelerate learning on how a change is performing. For example, if you offer a SaaS product with a free trial and you know that after two weeks of active Engagement users convert to the paid plan at a rate of 81% in week 5, then that's a great leading indicator of how you're doing with those customers, as opposed to just looking at a lagging indicator like conversions to paid plans.

Let's take a closer look at specifically how we'd acquire the Observations for these two onboarding DVs at HinH. After creating an account and logging in (Acquisition), the user sees HVAC parts and can search/filter for the part of interest:

Figure 6-5: HVAC Parts Page (No Filter)

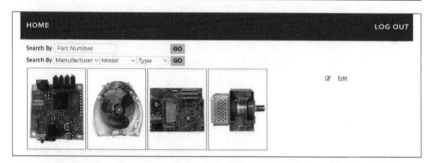

Figure 6-6: HVAC Parts Page (Search by Part Number)

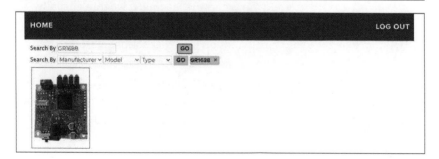

If they click on the part above, they'll see a page with details on the part including its pricing and availability:

Figure 6-7: Part Detail Page

The first time a new user gets to one of these pages, we increment the number of 'lookups', using, say, an Event in Google Analytics and that way we can properly calculate '>0 Parts Lookups' for our first DV: 'Signups/ Users with >0 Parts Lookups'.

Following this, a user that's ready to order would add the part to their cart, check out, and then complete the order:

Figure 6-8: Ordering a Part

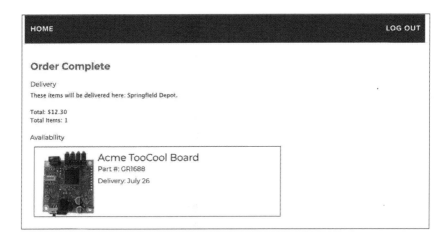

The first time a user gets to this page with a complete order is what we'd want to see to increment our second DV: Signups/Users with >0 Orders. Why not when the user clicks the 'finalize order' button in the last screen? Well, what if the order fails for some reason? That's certainly not out of the question for a new application like this. While we'd certainly want to know about those ordering errors, analytically we wouldn't want to consider those users part of our population that successfully onboarded; in fact, quite the opposite. Even in these seemingly obvious analytics configurations, it's important to think in terms of specific, testable Controllers.

When and why does this particular section of the CX Map matter? If you're Acquiring a lot of users but not getting them to Engagement, meaning for example they churn or are considered inactive relative to the Observation internals you set, then the team's focus should probably be somewhere between onboarding and Engagement. In such a situation, for example, you'd probably see a good-to-OK cost per acquisition (CPA) but a lot of churn.

What IVs might the team want to test here? The CX map mentions, 'Observing cohorts across onboarding programs & product iterations'. What that means, for example, is that we might want to tag or otherwise analytically separate a set of users who onboarded in one way vs. another so we can run Prospective Cohort Studies (PCS) if it's an opt-in treatment or a Randomized Control Experiment (RCE) if the treatment is assigned at random. For example, we might want to test the effect of training on onboarding as well as Acquisition. Another IV might be sets of users who were mandated to use the tool vs those that weren't: how much more likely did that make it that these users would at least get their first order done on the app?

Framing & Testing Engagement

Here, what we're asking is: 'For users that get onboarded, how many make a habit out of using our application?' For Spotify, this would mean that the service is now the user's go-to place for listening to music, at least wherever they regularly did that before–on their Alexa at home, on their phone in the gym, or in their car, for example. For a Fitbit, it would mean that the user is tracking all their fitness activity with the Fitbit. This means more or less 'owning' the JTBD or JTBDs in question, and so it requires being able to denominate the natural cadence of that activity, which can be challenging and may require estimation. For example, how does Spotify know how often a given user listens to music? They don't. However, they do know that if a user is using Spotify 4-5x per week and then that stops happening, they've probably lost Engagement, and it's a leading indicator that the user will churn off the service.

In the case of HinH, we defined this DV for Engagement: 'Parts Ordered Online/Parts Ordered by Tech' starting 30 days after they've onboarded. The idea with engagement is that we've seen the user make a regular habit of using our application, standardizing their behavior on it. In the case of HinH, we're assuming that on their existing systems they can track which parts a tech orders so they can fairly exactly denominate engagement on the new app.

Another classic example in the enterprise would be observing whether users are still engaging with workarounds like spreadsheets vs. using the enterprise application. That can be difficult to measure. In many such cases, it's necessary to take a best guess about the natural cadence of the JTBD as a whole, set a line in the sand, and then see how things look after a couple of iterations. If the results are still puzzling, you might need to do some user discovery interviews to learn more about the natural activity cadences.

What IVs might the HinH team want to test here? The onboarding programs and product iterations are clearly still relevant. They could also try sending reminders or 'tips' to the techs on email and see if that helps. What else? What if there remains large populations of techs who aren't engaging and the team isn't very confident about why? This is an example of a situation where you'd want to consider going back to some of the fundamental Right Problem/persona research you started with; interviewing a few folks in both of those populations is a great way to effectively find the IVs that are going to move the DV.

Framing & Testing Outcomes

Here, what we're asking is: For the users that make a habit of using our app, are they better off in the way we told them they'd be? For something like Spotify, they might frame their parent JTBD as 'enjoying more music'. How do you know if this is happening for a user? A popular approach is sending out surveys or prompting users at key moments to rate the app. This is not a terrible way to go as long as users do it, but in general, observing what users do vs. what they say is better practice. Often, measuring

Outcomes is easier for more concrete, component JTBDs. For example, Spotify recently introduced a discovery tool for podcasts—tell us about yourself, and we'll make some suggestions. This obviously creates much stronger opportunities to compare user intent with user behavior and, more directly, outcomes. If a user starts and finishes one of the suggested podcasts, that's an excellent sign. If their engagement improves when they use that same tool or related discovery UX, that's even better.

Back to the Fitbit example, the easiest way for them to measure my outcomes is to have me set a goal for something they can measure directly with their device during onboarding. How hard should you push the user to set such a goal during onboarding—you have to experiment and see, but this is a good example of how items in the CX Map relate to each other and why it's important to track individual users so that, for example, you can see if adding a little more friction in onboarding pays off downstream to retention.

In this example, my goal is to lower my blood pressure and that's not directly measurable. However, I'm mostly doing that by losing weight and while this isn't directly measurable with their device either, it's relatively straightforward to self-report or, in some cases, automatically report with a compatible wifi-enabled scale. You can see an example of the option to set this goal in Figure 6-9.

Figure 6-9: Fitbit Homepage

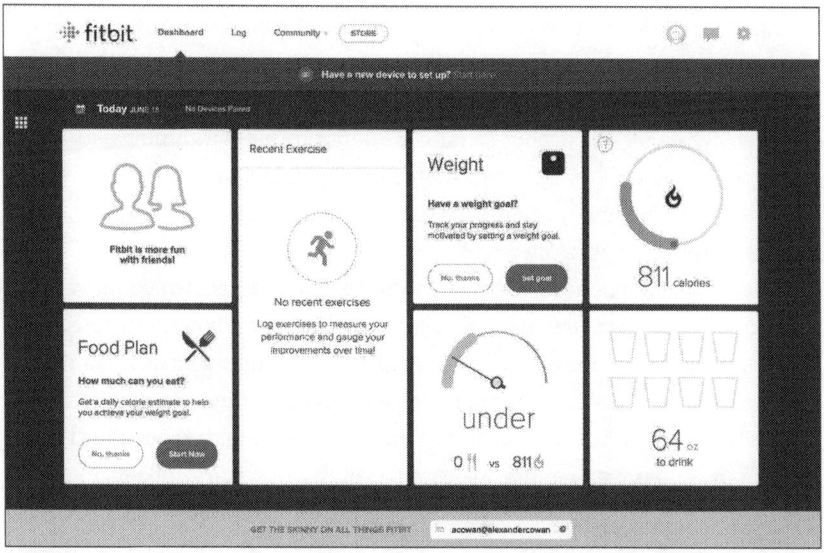

For outcomes at HinH we have:

    1. Reduced Time to Repair: For techs using the application for over 80% of their parts orders (those that are Engaged), how has the time from when a customer requests a repair to when that repair is completed change relative to the ~6 months before they created an account on the platform? The team's line in the sand here is that they want a 20% decrease.

    2. Increased billable/total hours: This is a ratio where we're assuming the HinH team has existing baselines for each tech from, say, their workforce management application, and what we're looking for is an improvement in this ratio. That indicates that the tool is helping reduce overhead, particularly the non-billable kind. Their line in the sand is that they'd like to see a 10% improvement here.

    3. Increased Customer Satisfaction/Job: Again, assuming the HinH team has a baseline for jobs each tech completed, does using the parts tool help improve this? Their line in the sand here is a 20% improvement.

For internal products like HinH, you can generally arrange to measure outcomes fairly directly. If you're a third party, it's hard–but it's important. If you're a B2B product or a B2C product of a 'practical' nature, like Highscore House or TurboTax, then you want this key leading indicator of whether or not you're really fulfilling your promises and your product premise across personas.

    What if you're a product that's primarily for entertainment–a video game or a service like Instagram? While it's not uncommon to see such products primarily focus on what we're mapping as engagement and retention, outcomes still matter if you want a durable customer relationship. For example, games like World of Warcraft have created enormously productive franchises by understanding what outcomes players are invested in achieving over time and designing around those. For example, such games often have sophisticated infrastructure for facilitating a social experience with a particular group, or improving the experience and prestige of a player's character.

At this phase, we have a user that's Engaged. What experiments and what IVs might the team consider? In retention, we'll look at all the things we want happy users to do to support our business model design. However, since here what we're specifically looking at is whether they got their target outcomes, a good candidate for experimentation (and qualitative discovery) is to understand the differences between users who 'Engaged' according to how we defined that on the CX map, and got to those positive outcomes, vs. those that did not. What are the traits of users who try it for 30 days (in our definition of engagement) and then stop? How do we fix that?

Framing & Testing Retention

Is the user exhibiting the behaviors we need to hit our OKRs and help make the company's business model work? For one product team of many, how do we cascade the company's topline OKRs down to a specific set of testable retention behaviors? In his book, *The Lean Startup*, Eric Ries offers the idea that choosing a principal 'engine of growth' is crucial to deciding which user behaviors a product should prioritize. He describes three:

1. Paid

   We're mostly using paid channels (ads or commissions, for example) to drive growth. Our principal retention behavior is transactional, making sure that we're taking in more revenue for a given customer than we spent to acquire them.

2. Viral

   We're mostly using organic (unpaid) channels for growth. Our principal retention behavior has to do with happy users sharing our product or service to others. For example, if we're Dropbox, we care a lot how many new users a current user brings in by sharing files to them via Dropbox.

3. Sticky

   However we Acquire a user, we're mostly focused on being able to cross-sell, upsell, or repeat sell them more of what we offer. Our principal retention behavior is share of wallet and repeat purchases.

Since HinH's audience is internal, they're probably pretty happy if the techs keep using the tool, and get the outcomes the team had in mind, and, ideally, seem to be recommending the tool to the other tech's they work with. In the CX map, we have the following DVs:

1. Steady to increasing Parts Ordered Online/Parts Ordered by Tech
2. Increase in the same for peer techs

Given the situation at HinH, there probably aren't a lot of experiments they'll run here—most of them would probably be more related to outcomes. The exception here would be if they started to see techs disengage with the tool after the 90 days. This is also true if, say, HinH started offering their applications to other HVAC service companies: if users start disengaging, your economic buyer (the person paying the SaaS fees) may not notice for awhile, but that is a leading indicator that you're about to have churn. Salesforce, for example, was an early pioneer in paying attention to the behavior of enterprise users who weren't themselves paying customers but rather users within a paying customer.

We are Each a Cohort of One

For many, looking at aggregate metrics that show few or no relationships between customer behaviors isn't just a matter of convention–it's all they've ever known. After all, it's relatively recent that we have this surfeit of richly detailed, interconnected data on customer behavior. It takes awhile for habits and practice to catch up. And if your job is to sell bars of soap, it may not seem like that big a deal, especially if things are going all right.

However, like so many other areas you've learned about, with a little extra work these disruptive times can very much work to your advantage if you're ready to adapt. Most fundamentally, this means thinking from the individual on upward to what you can generalize, vs. starting from monolithic aggregates like total users, or even sales. Not only are we trying to scale user behaviors which will change over the course of their experience with the product, but the general movement of individuals in and out of a given aggregate metric will inevitably confound any question about how you're really doing with customers.

Consider, for example, a classic failure mode: good acquisition with high churn. For some reason, maybe a cool story, maybe a lot of ad spending, or maybe great *problem*/market fit, you're acquiring a lot of users. You have something they think they want. But after a few weeks, these new acquisitions stop engaging. Let's say their engagement by week looks something like this:

Figure 6-10: Activity Over Time for a Single User

Let's say, though, that even as they're failing on engagement, they're doing great on acquisition–this schedule, for instance:

Table 6-4: New Adds for Cohort Example

	Jan 1	Jan 8	Jan 15	Jan 22	Jan 29	Feb 5	Feb 12	Feb 19	Feb 26
New Adds	100	200	300	400	500	500	550	600	600

In that case, if you just look at daily or monthly activity, things might still look terrific, something like this:

Figure 6-11: Total User Activity (Whole Userbase)

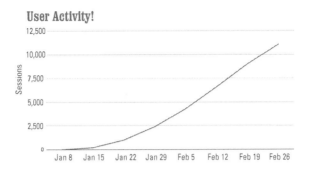

I think most generalists would look at that graph and say 'Great! Let's pour fuel on the fire!' The problem is that this could easily be a graph of an economically insolvent set of CXs, one that's actually composed of lots of little curves that show users consistently coming, trying, and leaving. This is what the curve above looks like if you assume that peak and decline user activity profile we considered above.

Figure 6-12: Total User Activity (Whole Userbase) by Cohort

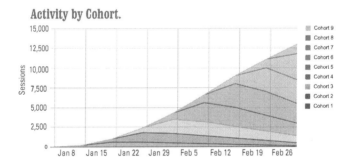

However, the team that's working against a CX Map, or something like it, will notice this fairly readily: their metrics on Engagement would be way under their 'line in the sand' threshold.

This is true whether you're getting paid by individual users or an enterprise buyer, though those two situations may have longer feedback loops on retention behaviors, in this case subscribing and paying. While a company might take awhile to decide that a B2B application isn't working for them, they will eventually. This may be a blessing in the short term if you lose course and need to correct, but it can be a curse if the only thing the company's sensitive to observing is a decline in lagging metrics like recurring revenue.

Debugging User Behavior

An experienced coder will tell you that to code is to debug, that debugging isn't something that happens when things go wrong—it's just a natural part of the process. Innovation is the same. While the Lean Startup popularized the idea of driving to a 'pivot or persevere' moment, in practice knowing what that specifically means for your product and how to make the right pivot, large or small, requires thoughtfulness, consistency, and practice.

I mentioned that the Lean Analytics authors state that good metrics change your behavior. Another way of saying this relative to a practice of HDD is that the Inferences from your Hypothesis Testing should support deliberate, relevant, intentional debugging across your CX Map. In practice, this requires careful discernment about how you'll invest your team's time to minimize 'F'. That might mean a design sprint, dedicating a whole sprint to Continuous Design, it might mean new features, or it might require improving your infrastructure for either deploying changes (Continuous Delivery) or testing them (Hypothesis Testing).

The worst possible response to bad results (or call them 'negative Inferences' if that stings less!) is reflexively cramming more content into Application Development, hoping that something will stick. With blind intuition, the odds these new features will face of being successful aren't great, and the whole while you're exhausting the team, accruing technical debt, and overcomplicating the product, creating UX debt.

The best possible reaction to bad results should be to frame key questions and bracket them between Continuous Design and Hypothesis Testing with Application Development and Continuous Delivery as a means to those ends.

It's not always tidy. Your hypotheses will be proven false, and while that's somewhat expected, knowing what to do next and how to keep it from demoralizing a team is hard. Messier still, sometimes the experiments and testing themselves will fail! You'll make a mistake on Google Analytics, you'll ask (in retrospect) the wrong questions of your subjects, the results of your MVP test are all over the place and don't make sense. Just like a serious coder, a serious innovator learns from experience what to do when things break.

Whether you should debug from the bottom up or the top down is kind of a 'thing' in engineering. For example, when I got my Cisco certification for networking, their point of view was that you should always debug from the bottom up. If a network connection is failing, first make sure the router is plugged in, then check whether it can reach the Internet, then look at the particulars of the connection that's failing– a connection to download files from a secure network at another office, for example. Debugging from the top down would mean that you first see if there's something going on with the application you're using or connecting with on the far end, then checking your Internet connection, then making sure the router is plugged in.

The sections that follow will help you more purposefully consider how you debug your product outcomes using HDD across your product pipeline. Whether you're going to go bottom up or top down in any given situation, it's important to know your 'stack'—where the top and bottom are and what they mean–and that you're consciously *either* going bottom up or top down. The diagram here offers a view on this for the product pipeline we've been using.

Figure 6-13: Debugging Outcomes with the Product Pipeline

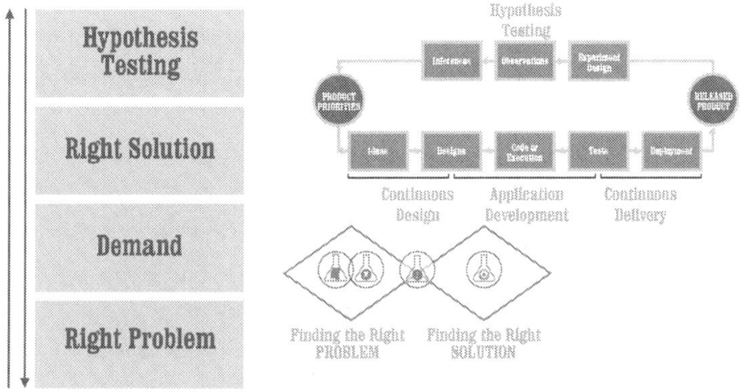

I flipped a coin, and the result is: we'll start at the top of the stack.

Hypothesis Testing

There's no shortage of technical things that can go wrong with an Experimental Design–test infrastructure is misconfigured, sample populations

are a mismatch, etc. In fact, in his book *Trustworthy Online Controlled Experiments* Ron Kohavi and his coauthors[2] lay out a 'sample ratio mismatch test', popularly known as 'A/A testing'. The basic idea is that in many circumstances you should test *how* you select your sample populations–that the results you get are close to 50/50 so you know when you introduce a 'B treatment' so that you're probably looking at a truly random population.

All that said, the failure mode I see most is a lack of economic actionability. If the results aren't informing a decision that drives revenue or a goal on user behavior related to growth, then what is the economic purpose of the experiment? Even if the Inference itself is valid, if the results aren't informing a decision, running experiments is just another waste of energy, resources, and credibility.

Why does this happen so often? It's because not enough people have read this book. I kid, but I do think the reason lies in the fact that this is where the team has to admit that things might not go according to a predictable plan, and that they might have to find they're wrong to get to what's next. It's messy, confusing, and if there isn't a strong culture of experimentation, then it's also embarrassing.

> *"Your job is to make sure that not just the Experimental Design makes sense and is tied to a decision or decisions, but also that your team celebrates their accomplishments in experimentation and learning."*

Observations break, too. While today's tool chains do a pretty good job of helping avoid this, applications like Google/Facebook/LinkedIn Ads, Google Analytics, Optimizely, and Mailchimp, the various configurations you might want for a given Experiment Design leave plenty of room for mistakes, both technical and experimental.

---

2 Ron Kohavi, Diane Tang, and Ya Xu, *Trustworthy Online Controlled Experiments: A Practical Guide to A/B Testing* (Cambridge, United Kingdom: Cambridge University Press, 2020).

For example, consider the following pipeline where a user goes from seeing an ad they can click, to a landing page where they can sign up to hear more about it via email, to then completing the final objective of purchase. Even in a relatively simple, off-the-shelf, set up like this, there's plenty that can go wrong. Some of those things are more technical, like the integration with the landing page and the email system not working, and some of them are more experimental, like disabling an underperforming ad, page, or email variant.

Figure 6-14: Acquisition Pipeline

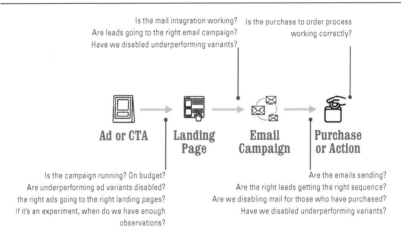

For the generalist or product lead who wants to foster a culture of experimentation, making this infrastructure the domain of specialists or having elaborate change management procedures is not the right answer. Whether you call it 'growth hacking' or 'RevOps', successful growth programs in digital usually depend on refactored, interdisciplinary roles and practices. For example, Booking.com is often lauded for their culture of experimentation and they freely share that they achieved this by allowing anyone in the company to launch an experiment without permission from management.[3]

For how to work toward strong practice, we can also take a page from the DevOps movement—encourage action and experimentation, but limit the 'blast radius' of changes and specifically respond to issues as they

---

3   Stefan Thomke, "Introduction," in *Experimentation Works: The Surprising Power of Business Experiments* (Boston, MA: Harvard Business Review Press, 2020).

arise. While the particulars of this will vary, the way successful teams get there has a lot in common. Rather than having managers issue general edicts, teams calmly, constructively, and collaboratively diagnose the root cause of issues and consider adapting or changing specific practices to avoid them in the future. To the extent there are speciality teams or departments, they define their success in terms of delivering useful self-service infrastructure for product teams.

One final note on dealing with Observations: While digital infrastructure has made it easy for teams to spin up new experiments, it's a mistake to underutilize the data you already have in hand. For example, a Retrospective Case Control can be a great way to quickly explore associations between a target DV and various IVs in order to make better decisions about where to invest in experimentation.

Our final step in the job of Hypothesis Testing is Inference. Since this is the last step, 'bugs' rooted in other areas may easily cascade down to looking like Inference problems. For example, not pairing action with Inference is an issue with Experimental Design, not Inference. The same is true of having too many or too few Observations.

Model selection is important here, and you've probably heard the phrase 'correlation does not equal causation', or more generally, association[4] doesn't equal causation. This is important with regard to Inference in both directions. First, you don't necessarily need to prove causation to make an economically actionable decision. Second, it's important and useful to keep the team (and yourself) focused on what you have proven vs. what you haven't. Given that not all of us are particularly numerate, using the right terms and taking reasonable amounts of time to explain Hypothesis Testing to your stakeholders and team is probably a worthwhile investment toward creating a high-functioning culture of experimentation.

With Hypothesis Testing we've considered more of a general purpose section of the pipeline. The user behavior we observe is the aggregate of whether we've adequately validated our Right Problem hypotheses, Demand hypotheses, and Right Solution hypotheses. In the next three sections, we'll look at how to isolate observed 'bugs' on user behavior to one of these more specific domains, so you can focus on the right fix.

---

4 that correlation deals with linear associations where association deals more generally w/ the
   relationship between a DV and IV's

Right Solution Testing

How do we know if we have the right solution or whether we need to iterate on it? What if, instead, an issue upstream in the Continuous Design process is the real problem? For example, what if the UI is fine

but we don't fundamentally have demand for the Value Proposition we're delivering on with our UI? Or, what if they're both irrelevant because we're addressing a JTBD that doesn't matter much to our customer? For example, in Laura Klein's 'jobs for pets' example, no matter how usable we make our interface, pet owners won't be putting their pets to work.

We'll answer these questions with the elements you already know from Chapter 2 on going from Idea to Design: user stories, prototyping with comparables and patterns, usability testing, and the particular application analytics you can use to hypothesis test your solution.

Figure 6-15: Continuous Design and the Usability Hypothesis

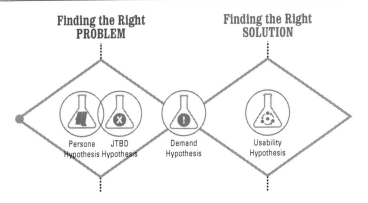

Source: adapted from the UK Design Council & 'The Design of Everyday Things'

Let's start with user stories and how, in HDD, they help us transition from a validated Demand Hypothesis to a testable set of Usability Hypotheses. In HDD, only after we have results over our 'line in the sand' threshold for an MVP test would we transition to building a solution. For example, the team at Aardvark, a social search startup sold to Google in 2010, smoke tested and eliminated six unrelated startup ideas before they arrived at what became Aardvark through promising demand testing with various 'smoke test' MVPs.[5]

If you release a product or feature that just doesn't see any visits from the users you identified as valuing the solution's proposition, that's a likely indicator that a constructive next step in your debugging is to take a closer look at how you tested your Demand Hypothesis. This might feel like 'going backward' for you or your team. If so, consider emphasizing the iterative nature of any innovation project—you're not going backward, you're iterating forward with HDD, and the Demand Hypothesis is the next place to focus.

Figure 6-16: Debugging with Continuous Design

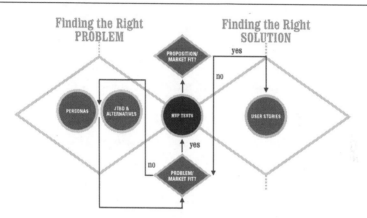

What if the bounce rate is high? Say, you're getting users in the door, but then they're walking right out. Your first priority should be to see if this happens as soon as possible, as uncomfortable as that may be. The user story map, contoured by a CX map that decomposes the overall customer journey is a useful place to start, particularly for making sure that you're releasing batches of features to maximize learning.

---

5   "Aardvark," Aardvark - Case - Faculty & Research - Harvard Business School, accessed July 17, 2022, https://hdd.works/3II50Ex.

Figure 6-17: User Story Map

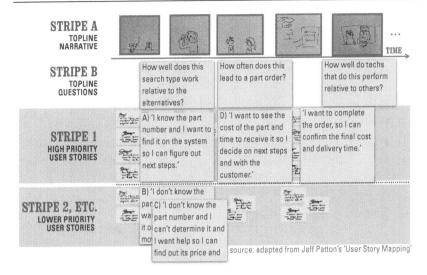

source: adapted from Jeff Patton's 'User Story Mapping'

In our HinH example, the team takes its best guess about the most important search feature (by part number) and leaves the other search features (filtering by make, model, submitting a photo) until after they were able to release a version of the solution that allowed a technician to get all the way, *hypothetically*, to some tangible reward. That reward is finding info on the part's pricing and availability for the JTBD in question.

At Aardvark, even after they started building their solution, the team left part of the social search process to manual 'Wizard of Oz' MVPs where they employed temporary help. Why layer in all that automation if it turns out nobody cares about social search?[6]

How do you act on a result where your users seem to care, walking in the door, but then they walk right back out? This may be evidence that you have a proposition of interest to users, but that your current implementation of that proposition, your current solution, is not a fit for the users you're acquiring.

Donald Norman's 7-step model is a useful way to focus your diagnosis and debugging so you make sure you're not wandering in circles.

---

6   "Aardvark," Aardvark - Case - Faculty & Research - Harvard Business School, accessed July 17, 2022, https://hdd.works/3II50Ex.

Figure 6-18: Donald Norman's 7-Step Model of User Cognition

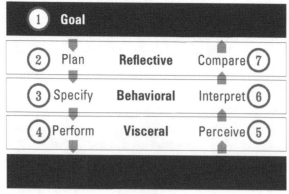

source: adapted from 'The Design of Everyday Things'

To recap, the process starts with a Goal, Step 1 in Donald Normal's 7-step model. For the HVAC in a Hurry example with their JTBD of 'getting replacement parts to a job site', there are actually two goals: 1) finding the part's pricing and availability so they can get agreement from the customer and then 2) placing an order so they know they're set for the repair.

What's the right proposition? Based on some testing inside the enterprise, the digital team at HinH is reasonably confident it's a self-service parts ordering application they can use on their mobile devices. Rightly or wrongly, they think they've progressed beyond MVP testing and want to build a 1.0 solution.

What's the Right Solution? Based on their initial research and testing, they think they can get a reasonable 1.0 that will deal with enough cases to observe engagement by just implementing search by part number, deferring search by manufacturer, make, and model or photo until they see if they achieve some initial engagement.

What if they're wrong? What if the actual truth is that the team has a failed problem/solution hypothesis–specifically, that they're only going to get substantial engagement if the techs can search by both part number and manufacturer, make, and model? What would that look like? Assuming they're not wrong about some non-trivial population of tech's wanting to search by part number, they'd probably see some techs successfully onboard because, say, when they try that tool what happens to be in front of them is a part where they have the part number. However later these same tech's would again visit the part search page but abandon it with no search, and then not visit again, or maybe taper off their visits. If the team has a strong suspicion about this, they could release their 1.0 with a small B-treatment where users see an option to search by manufacturer, etc. that actually doesn't work, returning an error like 'sorry- currently offline; please search by part number if possible'. This could at least show the team they're specifically off on the overall problem/solution fit. Whether that's the right answer for you in a similar situation is a matter of judgment–the main thing is to stay aware of where you are in your stack while debugging and what you do or don't have evidence to Infer.

What if they're *right* about being able to get to substantial engagement with just the search by part number but the UI is bad or the search performs poorly? Then we'd get slightly different observations– techs entering part numbers and attempting part number searches, but not clicking on any results and abandoning.

A notable corner case of this diagnosis is where users express interest in a solution, but aren't finding it in the product's UI. Drew Houston, founder & CEO of Dropbox, addressed this problem and how their team monitors for it: "We get feature requests for things we already have. These are particularly bad because it means that even though we've implemented something, our users can't find it. We pay close attention when that happens."[7]

How do product teams reliably get to good answers on this? In a sense, the practice of parallel prototyping is starting the debugging process early. By beginning with the assumption that no one can always get to the right solution, teams encourage the idea that experimentation pays, a finding supported by research at Stanford[8] and by practitioners at innovation powerhouses like Google.[9] By making a habit out of trying more than one approach, the team is ready to be wrong, which is important particularly in an area like designing for usability where things don't break as overtly as they do with the software itself.

---

7 Jon Ying et al., "Meet the Team! (Part 1)," RSS, accessed July 14, 2022, https://hdd.works/3O8xDM0.

8 Steven P. Dow Stanford University et al., "Parallel Prototyping Leads to Better Design Results, More Divergence, and Increased Self-Efficacy," ACM Transactions on Computer-Human Interaction, December 1, 2010, https://hdd.works/3O6XhB4.

9 www.facebook.com/startingatechbusiness, "Josh Andrews (Google) on Killing Complexity," Alex Cowan, October 29, 2017, https://hdd.works/3o68IOS.

In Chapter 2, we focused on using HDD to design and test your way to reliable usability. If you test early, often, and reasonably well, then it's hard to get too surprised by your results. The diagnoses we've considered so far were more foundational and anchored in choosing the right user stories to deliver on your problem/market fit and your proposition/ solution fit. The diagram here pairs a few key questions with the three components we've used to focus implementation and testing of UIs to deliver on those user stories.

Figure 6-19: Unpacking Usability

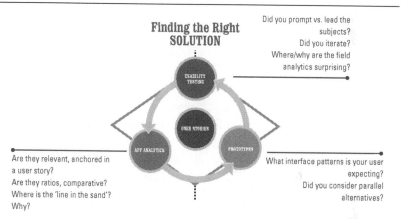

Let's say you're puzzled or surprised by the UI you just released–the app analytics are below the threshold you wanted. First, I would make sure those app analytics are clearly, explicitly connected back to the rest of your understanding about the user through user stories. If not, you'll lack a strong foundation to ask the right questions. From there, I would consider whether the ratios are contextualized with proportions. For example, in the case of HinH, I would make sure I'm considering the number of site visits relative to the number of successful parts lookups, as opposed to a total which may be misleading if you happen to be having a particularly large or small number of visitors to the relevant pages.

Finally, I would make sure you confirm that the rest of your customer discovery supports your point of view on what constitutes a good baseline or 'line in the sand' as the 'Lean Analytics' authors put it.

What about the interface patterns themselves? As we move from step (2) to step (3) in Donald Norman's 7-step model, our user is applying the existing models of how similar UIs work to engaging with your product. If user interactions look patchy, consider whether you've been explicit about that and whether the interface patterns are something they've seen. Also, make sure to socialize this idea with your team. I was once involved with a social media startup where one of the executives confidently told me, "Our designers are the best. They have thought of ways to search that no one has ever considered." Users don't want novelty—they want to achieve their Goal with a minimum of friction and get on with the rest of their lives.

Finally, single subject, live usability testing is kind of the connective tissue between your design ideas and the user. Like a statistician, your job is to make good choices about how to make sure the test set up is approximating as best as possible the environment your 'real' users will see out in the wild. Make sure you're prompting vs. leading subjects. For example, if you're telling a subject to 'show me how you would click on the big red button you see here', they will click on that button but you may be getting a false positive about usability. Finally, unlike statistics, it's OK to revise a lot while you're testing with live, individual subjects. With the exception of very late stage user testing, you're definitely not looking to collect a statistically actionable set of Observations—that's what app analytics are for. Finally, it's worth mentioning that as a bridge between live subject testing and the cold hard facts of an analytics system, some teams find 'real time analytics' helpful. These are services like Clicky and Mouseflow that allow you to view visual recordings[10] of user behavior.

This diagram summarizes the three general user behaviors we reviewed, the hypothetical diagnosis, and how to proceed with debugging.

---

10 Technically, they're assembled from component parts vs. a true screen recording. Also, there is some controversy about their fidelity since they have to use cursor position as a proxy for eye position.

Figure 6-20: Debugging from Demand to Solution Design

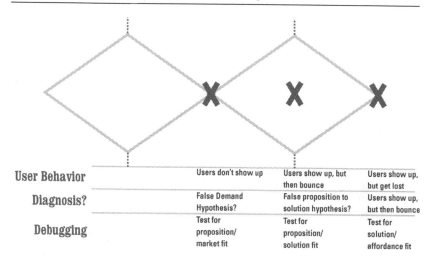

User Behavior	Users don't show up	Users show up, but then bounce	Users show up, but get lost
Diagnosis?	False Demand Hypothesis?	False proposition to solution hypothesis?	Users show up, but then bounce
Debugging	Test for proposition/ market fit	Test for proposition/ solution fit	Test for solution/ affordance fit

Demand Testing

How do you debug false—or possibly worse—confusing results from testing your Demand Hypothesis? This happens a lot. While producing excellent work, the community of practice around Lean Startup tends to be singularly focused on testing ideas with MVPs. This is a great thing to do and I love what it's done for those of us in the startup and innovation communities.

Demand Testing

MVP Results?
Problem/Market vs.
Product/Market?
Cohorts Across UX Map?

However, I see a lot of MVP tests where the team gets confusing results. Most often, this is the unsurprising result of having a loose or non-existent Right Problem hypotheses about who the proposition is for and what job it does for the customer. For example, if I want to use a concierge MVP to test a meal plan service for working parents, and I just grab whatever subject doesn't pepper spray me off the bat in the parking lot of a grocery, then the likelihood that I start to see much in common with the test results is vastly lower than if I find subjects in a way that lets me screen them with a simple question like, 'How many times last week did you prepare dinner for your kids after work?'.

Below are the three MVP types we focused on earlier, the questions they're good at answering, and where they fit in the Continuous Design process.

Figure 6-21: Debugging Demand

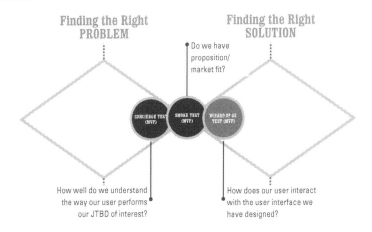

Finding the Right **PROBLEM**

Finding the Right **SOLUTION**

Do we have proposition/ market fit?

CONCIERGE TEST (MVP)

SMOKE TEST (MVP)

WIZARD OF OZ TEST (MVP)

How well do we understand the way our user performs our JTBD of interest?

How does our user interact with the user interface we have designed?

Very much by design, these bleed into the transition between Right Problem testing and Right Solution testing. This might seem like it will make testing your Demand Hypotheses messy. It does! But that messiness is intrinsic to the innovation process and the best way I've found to manage it. Let's take a look at how to interpret and act on both false and ambiguous testing across these three MVP patterns.

Given how observation-intensive they are, debugging the concierge MVP involves the least guesswork. If your results aren't converging, make sure you're starting with a strong screener, linked to your Right Problem hypotheses. Depending on your subject recruitment vehicle, you may also need to screen for the relevant trigger events. For example, if I used the screener above in the grocery store parking lot, got a positive, but then the parent is just picking up cough medicine, having them play along like they're really shopping for dinner (to get a Starbucks gift card, be nice, etc.) will deliver low fidelity results. You'd be better off just doing a simple subject interview as you might have for your Right Problem hypotheses.

Don't overdrive the visibility of this particular experiment vehicle. It's a great way to learn more about how your target user engages with the JTBD that interests you, and you can take that forward to tighter smoke test experiments and Right Solution testing. It is not a good way to test demand for your proposition or even for problem/market fit. If I spend 30 minutes in the grocery store with a subject, hand them a $20 gift card, and ask how much they liked what we did, I'll get a 'it was great, thanks' or something like it ≈100% of the time. For testing your core Demand Hypothesis, you'll want to use the Smoke Test MVP.

A positive Smoke Test excites and energizes a team—you're about to build something you already know has promise! As you know if you've done it, getting there typically requires a few iterations. If you can't shake CTRs, etc. which come in below your thresholds, sometimes it's time to pivot and congratulate yourself for running a disciplined process that minimizes waste. If you think you're missing something, though, you may also be right.

In these cases, the most common fix I see working is to tighten the Right Problem hypotheses and try again. For example, if you were advertising a meal plan service for working parents, try sub-segmenting that based on other features you observed on the part of your subjects during discovery—just dads, trying to eat organic without breaking the bank, etc. Generally, this means making sure you have a tight screener and going out and interviewing more subjects. In some cases, you may be able to identify a key feature of your users from analytics, such as geography, device type, etc.

Another intriguing case for debugging is where you're seeing positive results in the early part of your Smoke Test pipeline, but not the later parts. The diagram here shows what those results mean, and the right move is probably to pivot accordingly.

Figure 6-22: An Acquisition Pipeline relative to Product/Market Fit

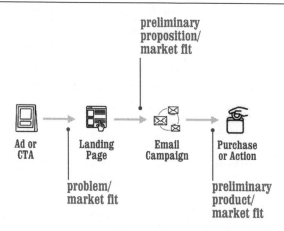

For example, when I first began to explore taking my Coding for MBAs course online, I wanted to start with an online but synchronous (live) format. I ran tests with my Coursera learners and saw strong (passing) CT rates on the emails and the landing page where interested learners could sign up.[11] However, when it came time to purchase, conversions were terrible—way, way below the line in the sand. After doing a few follow-ups, it was pretty clear that these learners who came from Coursera where they could take courses on their own schedule at a very low cost didn't want our scheduled, higher cost live class, even though the topic interested them. I pivoted to a version of the course on Coursera and that's gone pretty well.

The Wizard of Oz MVP pattern's main job is to serve as a bridge between your demand testing and your usability/Right Solution testing. If you're doing a subject test as you would for usability testing (but having a Wizard respond behind the scenes) then apply the debugging we stepped through in the prior section on Right Solution testing. If you're taking part of the UI live and observing 'real' users, then apply the debugging above from the Smoke Test Pattern.

As long as you know what you're trying to test, pick a relevant MVP vehicle, and have clear thresholds, you're already way ahead of the game. Don't mix up the role of an MVP and a 1.0, even for a new feature on an existing product.

Finally, there's the question of where this all ends–for example, once you have product/market fit? In practice, for a given product, this is when you shift focus from learning to scaling. What scaling means is this area is essentially making investments to increase demand, often referred to as 'demand generation' or 'growth hacking'. The short version is that all these techniques are widely applied in those areas–there's smaller learning vs. scaling loops for just about everything you do, whether it's writing a blog post or finding your next high-performing Google AdWord.

Right Problem Testing

This is the starting point and foundation for your Continuous Design process, the last stop on top to bottom debugging of user behavior. The diverge,

Right Problem
Screeners & Specificity?
Early Market vs. Later Market?
JTBD Importance?

---

11 Yael Grushka-Cockayne and Alexander Cowan, *Growth Hacking Online Education*, Case OM-1719, Published April 29, 2021. https://hdd.works/3AOwZAo.

converge patterns matter a lot here. It's good to diverge and consider many personas and JTBD when you're first concepting a new product or feature. It's equally important to converge and focus as you move to testing your Demand Hypothesis and subsequent work.

Failure to do this is the top problem I see in this part of debugging a product pipeline, and it leads to ambiguous or failed MVP tests, products no one shows up for, and demoralized teams whose stock options aren't appreciating. While Right Problem might seem like the softer, fuzzier part of a hypothesis-driven approach to development, in fact, it anchors several crucial criteria for understanding causation laid out in the The Bradford Hill criteria, a long-standing, durable take on how to scientifically establish causality.[12]

One of those criteria is 'consistency'—the idea that the results stand up to substantial variation (people, places) *within* the contours of the established experimental criteria. In the Right Problem area, we drive to this with the screener on the Persona Hypothesis that helps us make sure we can on the one hand find a suitable pool of subjects, and on the other objectively sort out your target user from the population at large. Another of these criteria is 'coherence'—the idea that laboratory findings and epidemiological findings (in the population at large) make sense together. In our case, that means using our exploration and testing of Right Problem to make sure we understand a day in the life of our particular personas and then use that to anchor and explore the 'ground truth' of what we want to see if we can reproduce with Hypothesis Testing.

Even though your Right Problem hypotheses are the foundation of your Continuous Design process, they change out from under you. First, the relationship between your Right Problem hypothesis and your solutions will change–historically, that kind of change is inevitable as new technologies and user behaviors come online. Second, as your user base grows, you'll almost certainly be adding substantial new personas with somewhat new JTBD's. You'll need to take stock of those while making sure that the collection of users and JTBD continues to make sense as a target for an adequately focused proposition.

---

12 Kristen M Fedak et al., "Applying the Bradford Hill Criteria in the 21st Century: How Data Integration Has Changed Causal Inference in Molecular Epidemiology," Emerging themes in epidemiology (BioMed Central, September 30, 2015), https://hdd.works/3cf9uX3.

The cautionary tale of the once dominant note-taking app Evernote is how they famously floundered after adding too many features, variations, and product extensions. Trying to be something for everyone, it became relevant to no one, as the saying goes—or, more accurately, just not as competitive.[13]

Finally, as we discussed in Chapter 2, make sure you don't lead your subjects, or your actual work with subjects will just be a circular set of confirmation bias. Ask your users, 'What are the top five hardest things about getting dinner on the table for your kids after work?' Not: 'How likely would you be to buy this new meal plan service we're making.'

Without a strong culture of experimentation, companies and teams readily fall into the trap of running a 'feature factory' where the focus is simply on output rather than outcomes. The questions shift from, 'How do we know if this is working?' to 'How fast can we build this so we can get to building even more?' The team gets more stressed and less inclined toward open collaboration, the product gets cluttered, the customers get confused and just give up on you.

In Practice: How HinH experiments their way to Product/Market Fit

So far, between this chapter and the one before it, you've learned the foundations of how to:

1. link your target outcomes to DVs and frame their relationship with IVs, related DVs, models and inferences
2. describe the macro progress of a CX toward product/market fit relative to a particular JTBD:VP pairing: qualitatively with storyboards, and quantitatively with a CX map
3. describe your micro objectives for user behavior with user stories and analytics, prioritizing your development for learning with user story mapping
4. design experiments for the above and link those to Inference and economic actionability
5. implement the above in Google Analytics

---

13 David Pierce, "Evernote's CEO on the Company's Long, Tricky Journey to Fix Itself," (Protocol, December 31, 2021), https://hdd.works/3uNTq4X.

With a little practice, I don't think you'll find any of these particularly difficult. However, what's challenging for the general manager is iterating to a practice of agile where these activities are a regular and useful habit, rather than one of several dozen things you feel like you should be doing but have trouble finding time to do.

To get a sense of how these practices might work for a team, let's return to HinH and walk through how they've used experiments in their work so far, and how they might use them to work through what they think is currently between them and a strong product/market fit for their parts ordering application. This is the team's first application together, and in 'Sprint 0' Frangelico drafted a working version of their team charter. Over sprints 1-3 they used design sprints to go from a bunch of ideas that look pretty arbitrary in retrospect to their current JTBD:VP pairing.

In sprint four, they wireframed, tested, and re-wireframed a parts ordering application. In sprints 5 & 6, they iterated to a 1.0 that allows them to observe delivery of their VP with a simple web application that allows the technicians to place orders online. All the order management (everything after order submission to part delivery) is still handled manually by someone they have on loan from the dispatch team—a Wizard of Oz MVP pattern to refine their Right Solution hypotheses. This isn't scalable, but that's okay. The table below summarizes their work to date.

Table 6-4: The Work of the HinH Team: Sprints 0-7

Sprint	Focus	Outcomes
0	How do we take what we've learned at HinH and use digital to amplify it?	Frangelico drafts a working point of view and meets the new team.
1	What part of the business should we focus on? And, for that part, what's actually on their A-list?	The teams zeros in on the work of the field tech's. Instead of their initial concept of centralizing technical documentation, they observe that getting replacement parts consistently shows up as a job where the current alternative isn't great.
2	Does there seem to be demand for a self-service alternative where the tech's can order their own parts?	A combination of email tests, briefings, and soft requests for engagement from the field service managers suggest that the proposition looks generally promising.

Sprint	Focus	Outcomes
3	How well do we understand the way this parts ordering process might work?	The team applies the 'concierge MVP' pattern, shadowing some tech's and also using a text-based set up to supply parts ordering for tech's, all in order to better understand how the process might work.
		There are clearly two sequential events for self-service, both important: getting pricing and availability for a part so they can confirm (or not) with the customer, and then the order itself so they can schedule their next visit. They feel ready to start testing solution designs, including specific UI concepts.
4	How do we maximize usability?	The team anchors their Usability Hypotheses in user stories and from there tests parallel prototypes with subjects (tech's). They arrive at a preliminary design they feel is investable for a 1.0.
5	How do we get a version of this thing working?	The team pushes hard on getting a working item out the door that they can test live. They make progress but it's not there yet.
6	How do we get a version of this thing working?	The team decides to 'Wizard of Oz' the ordering functionality, handling it manually with loaner staff from dispatch, and pares down the size of their initial pilot.
7	Maybe it's a good idea to clean up loose ends and obvious tech debt while leaving headroom for the unexpected as we release to real users?	The team dedicates this week to taking a breath, dealing with obvious and immediately actionable tech debt related to observability and supportability, and making sure everyone is generally available to deal with the unexpected as they release.

As we pick up with the team in sprint 7, the big question they need to answer is whether or not anyone's really going to use this application. Why not roll it out to everyone? Haven't they tested enough? They've tested enough to roll out a 1.0 to a population they can meaningfully observe to decide what's next. To roll it out to all their regions, however, would almost certainly be highly wasteful. First, they still don't know for certain that it's the right solution. They've done what I would offer is reasonable experimentation to minimize waste relative to a testable 1.0, but that is a long way from creating a certainty.

To do more testing before releasing a 1.0 to a test audience would be too much research up front and wasteful; less would have been an irresponsible and premature investment in product development. Striking this balance is important for successful practice. The idea that you can take a completely predictable yellow brick road with no failed experiments and get to a good outcome can tank team morale–that's not how things usually go. What might adaptive, balanced decisions look like? We'll pick up with the team at sprint (week) 7 where they've had the application in front of some test populations for a week and are deciding what they can Infer and what that means for their next product priorities.

As we pick up with the team in Sprint 8, they've finished their retrospective from Sprint 7, their first week live with the 1.0.

Sprint 8

Acquisition isn't going as well as they'd like. There are too few users on the system to make any definitive conclusions, and as far as the team can see, from the Observations they've logged, those users' behavior is all over the map. Given this, they've decided that the best place to focus for the next sprint (#9) is on Acquisition, specifically improving their focal DV, Number of Signups/Number of Visitors. At 22%, they're well below their 'line in the sand' on this focal DV.

Figure 6-23: Login Page at HinH

In their UX map, HinH sketched these particulars for Acquisition.

Table 6-5: Acquisition at HinH

Question	Acquisition
What does this mean?	How we ask or require a given cohort or segment of techs to use the tool.
How do we observe this? What's the DV?*	Number of Signups/ Number of Visitors
What is the cut off for a transition?	a single web session (max 1 hour)
Line in the Sand	>50%
How might we test this? What are the big IVs worth flexing?*	Mandating use of the app vs. not Intro/training workshops vs. not. Live chat concierge test
What's tricky? What do we need to watch out for?	We don't know yet.

The first question they ask themselves is: 'What, if anything, can we learn from the data we already have about what might be driving Acquisition?' based on their field interviews, where they generally got to know the technicians and the course of their day. They've identified a few possible interventions they think might be worth testing. One of these is 'mandating use of the app or not', which refers to whether or not the technicians' management requires them to use the tool, or just announces its availability and makes it voluntary.

In sprint 6, they made the tool available in two new offices, St. Louis and Tampa. After checking in with them, Frangelico learns that In St. Louis, the general manager mandated use of the tool whereas the Tampa region announced it but did not mandate it. The team now wonders what they can Infer from differences since this was originally an IV of interest. For example, does this map to one of the experiment patterns they've been using: Retrospective Case Control (RCC), Prospective Cohort Study (PCS), or Randomized Control Experiment (RCE)?

It might map to an experiment pattern referred to as a 'natural experiment', which offers some of the features of an RCE, in particular the big one–being able to Infer causality. This concept was popularized in a famous study economists Alan Krueger and David Card conducted on the effect of a minimum wage on restaurant employment near the border of New Jersey and Pennsylvania.[14] Microeconomic theory held that since NJ had increased their minimum wage from 4.25 dollars to 5.05 dollars that they should see a decrease in employment. They didn't and the general consensus is that this was a counterfactual on cause and effect between some types of wage increase and employment levels.

This Inference was worthy of a Nobel Prize, so if the HinH team decides there weren't major confounders in play, this difference between the tool's rollout in St. Louis vs. Tampa is probably good enough for them to make a preliminary Inference about the importance of mandating vs. not. First, they need to make sure they understand the circumstances or 'ground truth' of the Observations. Sri, one of the team's developers, asks the inconvenient question: "What does 'mandating' really mean? Are they not letting them place a single order any other way? Or did they just tell the tech' 'you have to use this'?". The team decides they have a few questions to answer in order to establish the 'ground truth' of their Observations.

Looking at the region's orders, clearly St. Louis is still putting plenty of orders through the legacy system and only three of the 23 techs there have signed up for an account. Clearly, the mandate wasn't 100% enforced. To establish the 'ground truth' of what really, specifically is going on in St. Louis, Frangelico, the team lead, calls the GM and finds out that they announced mandatory use of the tool in their email (but that's not well read by the techs) and also mentioned it at the short Monday morning meeting they have where about 80% of the tech's attend. On the other hand, it turns out Tampa announced the tool in the same ways (the email and their weekly meeting) but didn't mandate it. The table here summarizes the Observations they have from their own sources and from Events in Google Analytics.

---

14 Ben Zipperer, "Equitable Growth in Conversation: An Interview with David Card and Alan Krueger," accessed July 14, 2022, https://hdd.works/3ICahgT.

Table 6-6: CX at St. Louis and Tampa for HinH

Item	Visits/ Tech's	Signups/ Visitors	Signups/ Tech
Saint Louis (23 techs)	8 43.7% (=8/23)	3 37.5% (=3/8)	3/23 13.0% (=3/23)
Tampa (25 techs)	1/25 4.0% (=1/25)	1 100% (=1/1)	1 4.0% (=1/25)

* unique visits
** St. Louis 'mandated'; Tampa did not

The managers both emailed their teams on Friday, right at the end of Sprint 5, and, based on looking at visits, it doesn't look like that drove any response. On Monday, the managers made their verbal announcement and that was associated with some difference on both the regions' tech's propensity to visit the app (visitors/total tech's; 8/23 for S.L. and 1/25 in Tampa).

What can the team infer from their natural experiment, and what, if anything, is actionable about that? There does seem to be a possible relationship between mandating (even 'soft mandating') use of the tool and sign-ups—around a third of the St. Louis tech's at least had a look vs. just 4% for Tampa. That said, the Observations are small and anecdotal, and given that the team is still learning about how the techs interact with the tool, the results are pretty uncertain.

Given the small population of users who successfully onboarded and began to engage with the tool, the team decides that the obvious thing to do is to get in touch with them for brief interviews to learn more about the qualitative or 'small data' or ground truth circumstances of how they started using the tool. What they find out in St. Louis is that one user (Pablo) liked the tool and showed his colleagues/friends David and Mike how to use it when they were out for drinks that night. In Tampa, the one user (Paula) is someone they interviewed during their early user discovery, and so she was just especially curious to try it out. With regard to Signups, what they know from these two offices is anecdotal and seems to have a questionable relevance to the independent variable (IV) of mandating the tool vs. not. However, with regard to Visits, the results are a little more interesting, 34% vs. 4% of the techs at least taking a look.

The team decides the bar incident is interesting, particularly since all four of the tech's who signed up onboarded, ordering at least one part, and are engaged, now ordering parts through the tool. Acquisition still seems to be the right place to focus given that a) they still have relatively few users and b) the initial results for onboarding and engagement are solid, though small and certainly not conclusive. Their hypothesis is, 'If we offer a short onboarding session in a region that's mandating use of the tool, then it will increase Acquisition.'

Sprint 9

The team picks another region, Albuquerque, and a Prospective Cohort Study. This is an experiment where the participants opt-in to one experience vs. another and the team observes how that associates with some outcome, in this case signing up for an account. Through the manager in Albuquerque, the team offers a 30-minute onboarding session, hoping that at least coffee, donuts, and a break from physical labor and dealing with customers is appealing enough for the techs. The question the team wants to answer is whether this concierge onboarding associates with increased signups and onboarding. You can see the results in the table here.

Table 6-7: CX at Albuquerque

Item	Session	No Session
Total Techs (Albuquerque)	27	
Signups for Onboarding Session	10 37.0% (=10/27)	17 63.0% (=17/27)
Show-ups for Onboarding Sessions vs. total techs	8 29.6% (=8/27)	19 n/a

Item	Session	No Session
Successful Onboardings vs. cohort size (session vs. no)	8 100% (=8/8)	2 11.8% (=2/17)
Successful Engagements (still ordering parts +2 weeks post onboarding) vs. cohort size (session vs. no)	7 87.5% (=7/8)	2 100% (=2/2)

Going into the study, the team had three questions. First, would at least 25% of the techs show up? Check. Second, would the techs actually use it after the concierge onboarding? Check. Third, if the concierge onboarding checks out on the first two questions, what can the team learn from this to scale onboarding? The logistics, economics, not to mention the optics, of flying around the country to teach techs how to use a tool that was supposed to be self-service are unworkable.

The session suggested an association between participating in the session vs. not with regard to Engaging with the parts ordering application. While two techs heard about the tool without the session and started using it, that's just around 12% of the applicable techs, where almost 90% of the techs who showed up to the session onboarded. This comparison is somewhat confounded by the likely bias of those who showed up to the sessions to use the tool in general, but so far in their prior experience without the event, the tool doesn't get much uptake with the technicians.

The team decides to briefly follow up with the successfully engaged Albuquerque techs by phone to see what they hear from them about going from not knowing about the tool to making a habit of using it. What they hope to get out of talking with the techs are a few focal points they can then use to somehow come up with a more scalable onboarding recipe. It works. The follow-up's boil down to three essential findings:
1. the weekly emails the techs get from management are always too long and too irrelevant and no one reads them
2. the digital team didn't do any better: the copy they put together for Albuquerque didn't get any more tech's Acquired than in other markets

3. what mattered to the techs was finding out that they could order parts themselves in 30 seconds and that using the app was pretty easy, particularly relative to what the techs have seen from IT in years past

The team decides to test a more scalable refinement in their next test in Sprint 10.

Sprint 10

Based on what they learned in Sprint 9, the team has two new treatments (IV's) they want to test:

1. Revised Email to Techs Announcing Tool at their Branch
   While the team had at first thought it would be best to reach the techs through the weekly email they got from management, they've learned from the regional offices that the medium has gone stale—no one reads it. These come with a standard subject line at the same time every week, and it's not the case that the tech's never read any correspondence from the company. Given this, the digital team wants to test a standalone streamlined email to the technicians with the subject line 'order parts yourself in 30 seconds' and a few focused sentences and images on what the tool does and how they can use it.

2. Concierge Chat on the Site for New Users
   The team feels they've learned enough where they can do the concierge onboarding over chat and, when necessary, screen sharing. They have some JS and a third party tool that lets them present a chat affordance to new users and conduct a help session for them.

Since they have two treatments and each needs a control, they'll need 2x2 'cells' or treatment groups as follows:

Table 6-8: Experiment Design- Tabulation

Treatment	Chat		No Chat	
	Email	No Email	Email	No Email
Number of Tech's	20	20	20	20
Successful Onboardings vs. cohort size (session vs. no)	?	?	?	?
Successful Engagements				
(still ordering parts +2 weeks post onboarding) vs. cohort size (session vs. no)	?	?	?	?

While their line in the sand for effect size is fairly high, a 40% lift, and that reduces the number of Observations they need, they want 20 techs per 'cell' and so they plan to *randomly* assign technicians to a cell across the techs in three different offices: Houston, Cincinnati, and Fresno.

What's the actionability of these results? The best possible Observations would suggest the new email is enough to get them over their line in the sand. Given the steady, incremental improvements they've been making in the UI, they think this is plausible. If this is the case, they'll accelerate the rollout schedule, continuing to refine the email and the product.

Next best would be that the new email along with the chat gets them over their line in the sand. In that case, they'll continue to staff the assisted chat and roll out somewhat slower with more focus on improving the transition from onboarding to engagement.

If none of the treatments get them over their line in the sand, they'll zoom out and probably run a design sprint to either learn more about what didn't work for the tech's or, possibly, test product updates they think are investable based on what they observe.

Antipatterns & Failure Modes

Here are a few things to watch for and avoid.

1. **Big Ideas**

   It's ok to have a big vision, in fact that's probably good. But having ideas that you can't unpack, sequence and test in small batches is unnecessary risky. Very few ideas *can't* be tested this way. As serial CTO Darren Bauer Kahan, says: "You can't take a nine month idea, slice it into one week iterations, and get agile." Using the techniques of Continuous Design to unpack your ideas for testability is an economic superpower in the sphere of digital innovation.

2. Big Design, Big Dev Up Front

3. Weirdly, sometimes even when we aren't obliged to use big ideas, we still want to be done with one part or another and so we make a plan and do big batch design, big batch development, and probably big batch release, too. There's rarely a need. Particularly if you aren't obliged to big ideas, try to find ways to sequence and test your work to minimize waste and create more opportunities for wins.

4. **Murky Experiment Design**

   While we covered this pretty extensively in the last chapter, crisp, intentional Experiment Designs are crucial to actionable Inferences. And sometimes you even find with RCE's that the test population randomly or unintentionally had some kind of imbalance that confounds the results. In these cases, teams can use the 'A/A' testing you heard about earlier in the chapter.

5. **Decoupling Experimentation from Economic Actionability and Decision Making**

   In the practice of HDD (and, really, in a business context) experiments are for decisions. If the results won't inform the team/org of a decision, why are you investing there?

6. **Wanting to be Done**

   This is a pretty 'low level' behavior that arguably drives a lot of things we've covered, but I think it's worth mentioning:

people HATE uncertainty. We love to feel we've done good work and for most of us that's work that's done and crossed off the list. In practice, it's important to associate experiment designs with a feeling of 'done' for the team—you considered carefully, designed a good experiment, and it's running. When the experiment finishes and you get your results, you'll know what to do next because you have a line in the sand. Now, it's time to move on to something else or relax a little.

7. Being a Jerk

I'm not a management guru and I'm sure I've been a jerk on more than one occasion. None of us are perfect, but it's important to be... nice! We're all just hairless apes that want to be loved. Even being right won't get you to a good outcome if the team doesn't feel their contributions matter or that they're contributing to something they don't' like.

What We Learned

Using CX mapping helps us apply HDD to whatever is happening with product/market fit, whether it's testing for a new one or scaling an existing one. If you're practicing HDD, 'debugging' user behavior should be a regular and natural part of your agile cadences—be those weekly, bi-weekly, etc. The CX Map offers a way to consistently, intentionally monitor user behavior and link that to crisp prioritization decisions, which are rarely easy. We stepped through how you might create a CX Map of your own. We then looked at what 'debugging' might mean across the Continuous Design process. We closed with a specific example how HinH used this CX map across sprints to move the needle on the user behaviors they want.

Recommended Practice & Selected Resources

1. Sketch a CX Map

Pick a specific JTBD:VP pairing and sketch how you'd unpack the customer experience from Acquisition to Retention. What are the specific behaviors you'd watch for and how would you measure them? You'll find a tutorial and a template here:
https://hdd.works/3PSFxuD

2. Take Your Metrics and Make them Better

Do you have focal metrics for your team? Are they aware of them and are they relatable to the work, day to day? Are they readily measurable? For key outcomes, are there leading metrics that might work better or complement lagging ones? This page has a reference and a few checklists to help you get started:
https://hdd.works/3zOAHt2

Guest Editors:

Casey and Eric are the guest editor for both this chapter and the last.

7

YOU, THE HYPOTHESIS-DRIVEN DEVELOPER

As a generalist in digital, your job is to develop winning product experiences. That might mean a hit new software application, but it also might mean a truly useful implementation of some 3rd party software to help your colleagues do their job smarter. Hypothesis-Driven Development will help you cohere the diverse portfolio of skills and activities required for a modern digital execution. As you decide where to upskill and look for opportunities for high quality directed practice, HDD is an excellent way to focus what you'll learn next and make sure that you don't underdo it or overdo it.

Everything you've learned here is an applied science, meaning that fluency comes from practice. This has a few implications for what you do next. First, the first time you try to code your own prototype or run your own survivability analysis, don't expect it to go smoothly. It will be more like learning to ski or surf—kind of messy in the early days, but increasingly enjoyable. Second, it's important to pair what you learn with high quality opportunities for practice, work that feels relevant. Ideally, you can find this in your day job, but, if not, my advice is to charter a small but specific side project that interests you and use that for practice. You can pick up anytime and refresh your memory about HDD with this consolidated reference: https://hdd.works/book.

But, specifically, where do you start? How do you prioritize? How do you 'manage upward' to arrive at team, business line, or company-wide charters that are HDD-friendly? In the next few sections, we'll unpack that.

How do I develop myself with HDD?

My hope is that the book has given you a foundation understanding of how to approach product development and generally how the various 'digital' topics you'll encounter fit into its practice. As you start putting this understanding into practice, as I hope you do, Figure 7-1 offers a point of view on how you might think about focal points for what you're learning, and where those are taking you.

Figure 7-1: HDD Skills Stack

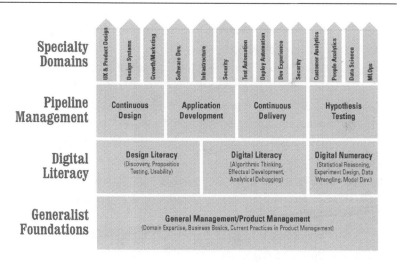

There's no single right sequence to work through these items. However, other than the 'Generalist Foundations' I generally recommend proceeding from the top downward in vertical slices, particularly if you're currently on the job (vs. a student). This might seem counterintuitive—shouldn't you walk before you run? However, the reality is that you'll probably find the material much more interesting and job-relevant if you start from the type of work that you do now. By contrast, even a diligent student is at high risk of losing steam if they feel they're working to learn topics they aren't applying and don't immediately matter to them professionally.

Let's consider a specific example: you're a user experience (UX) designer and you want to learn more about using experiments and big data to test ideas and build products powered by machine learning (ML). In a bottom up approach, you might start by taking a statistics or data science course online. That is fine as long you get through it. However, instead, I would first consider sitting in on, assisting with, or otherwise learning about the work of a team or individual at your company that does this. You should actively participate if at all possible–offer to help with the grunt work! Earmark plenty of extra time to learn about new topics as you encounter them and then consider what course of study you might want to undertake to learn more. This way, you have a stronger sense of actual practice and hopefully a place to apply what you learn.

Let's say you can't find such a project or a worthwhile collaboration within one. I see this happen plenty and my advice is always the same: create your own side project (personal or otherwise) and use that to get the experience you want. This works well and is fairly commonplace in innovation hotspots like Silicon Valley. One key facet of doing this successfully is intentionally prioritizing what you want to learn about, and this is particularly important if you have collaborators. For example, if the project is about learning to go from design to code, don't worry too much about testing and validating the idea as if it was a startup. On the other hand, if your experience is in software development and you want to see what it's like to test new ideas from scratch, don't spend a lot of time engineering the thing up front.

A great way to steward this kind of focus in a side project is to think about a portfolio entry you might create at the end of the project, something like what you see in Figure 7-2. Regardless of the side project's economic outcome, could you clearly explain the project's intention, methods, outcomes, and a retrospective on what you learned? This page has a few tutorials you can use as a starting point: https://hdd. works/3PDbqqv.

Figure 7-2: Personal Innovation Portfolio Entry

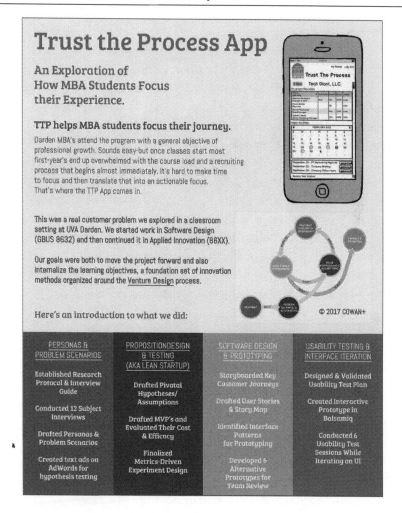

Trust the Process App

An Exploration of How MBA Students Focus their Experience.

TTP helps MBA students focus their journey.

Darden MBA's attend the program with a general objective of professional growth. Sounds easy—but once classes start most first-year's end up overwhelmed with the course load and a recruiting process that begins almost immediately. It's hard to make time to focus and then translate that into an actionable focus. That's where the TTP App comes in.

This was a real customer problem we explored in a classroom setting at UVA Darden. We started work in Software Design (GBUS 8632) and then continued it in Applied Innovation (86XX).

Our goals were both to move the project forward and also internalize the learning objectives, a foundation set of innovation methods organized around the Venture Design process.

Here's an introduction to what we did:

© 2017 COWAN+

PERSONAS & PROBLEM SCENARIOS	PROPOSITIONDESIGN & TESTING (AKA LEAN STARTUP)	SOFTWARE DESIGN & PROTOTYPING	USABILITY TESTING & INTERFACE ITERATION
Established Research Protocol & Interview Guide	Drafted Pivotal Hypotheses/ Assumptions	Storyboarded Key Customer Journeys	Designed & Validated Usability Test Plan
Conducted 12 Subject Interviews	Drafted MVP's and Evaluated Their Cost & Efficacy	Drafted User Stories & Story Map	Created Interactive Prototype in Balsamiq
Drafted Personas & Problem Scenarios	Finalized Metrics-Driven Experiment Design	Identified Interface Patterns for Prototyping	Conducted 6 Usability Test Sessions While Iterating on UI
Created text ads on AdWords for hypothesis testing		Developed 6 Alternative Prototypes for Team Review	

How do I help my team apply HDD?

The hardest thing about innovation programs in general, be they digital transformations or agile implementations, is creating an interdisciplinary focus such that individuals within teams can self-organize around an outcome. Specifically, without a clear view of what user outcome constitutes success and how to test that in small batches, most managers will fall back on a command and control approach of prescribing work, and most individuals will cling to the safety and comfort of doing things how they've always done them in the past.

The need to create 'pull' around outcomes vs. just push work to individuals means that most teams are best off starting with work on Continuous Design. Do they have a 'Right Problem' hypothesis, complete with personas and jobs-to-be-done? Have they gotten outside the conference room and interviewed these people? How can they test new ideas in one week instead of nine months by using MVPs? And rather than big batch development, how do they create an environment where they can test usability early and often? Now, it may not be practical for a manager or individual to drop everything and do design sprints for multiple iterations. That's OK. My advice is do a little at a time, picking and choosing practices that you think can most help in the short term. Show vs. tell on the kind of work you want to be doing, and progressively you'll get there.

How do I help my business as a whole apply HDD?

The good news here is that you've already learned about a great starting point for this in Chapter 1: the Business Model Canvas. The key thing is to get to a place where you can define the business' point of view on their current or hypothetical product/market fit using Customer Segments and Value Propositions. Even if you're not in charge of 'strategy', the great thing about the Canvas is that it's so easy to sketch on, even if you're just asking the parties concerned about the current business model design so you can understand it better.

Figure 7-3: The Business Model Canvas

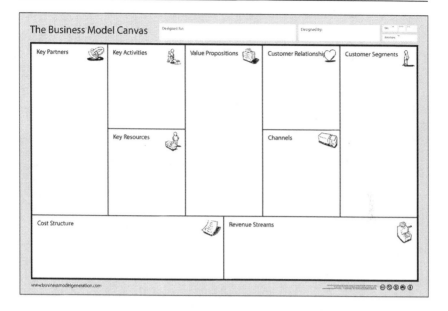

How do I develop my product portfolio?

For large companies with multiple lines of business, companies where those lines of business are distinct enough to have their own Business Model Canvas, for example, another level of abstraction is helpful as a way to drive focus and cohesion. For this I like to use the Corporation Innovation Canvas, which you can see here in Figure 7-4.

Figure 7-4: The Corporate Innovation Canvas

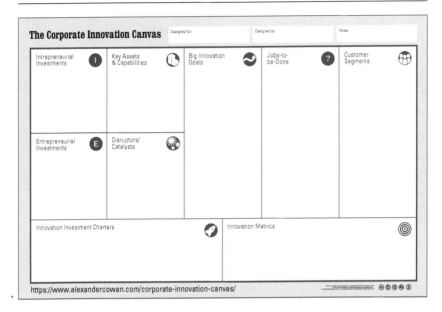

For large firms, the 'Innovator's Dilemma' is often the default—large firms have trouble investing money and management attention in small new ventures.[1] Shaking this tendency requires intention and discipline. The idea with the Corporate Innovation Canvas is to create an 'innovation strategy' that's simple and highly visible. What segments and JTBD does the firm think are important? What disruption catalysts are acting on the existing businesses? And what existing assets can the firm bring to bear on new opportunities? Given all this, what are the company's innovation goals? And finally, how might the company unpack them into specific, testable charters they can use to steward and govern a series of small bets?

In summary, what's important is a clear definition of success that cascades from the company to different lines of business (if you have more than one) to teams to individuals. Crucially, you should be able to then observe the relevance of outcomes from each bottom up.

---

1 Clayton M. Christensen, *The Innovator's Dilemma: The Revolutionary Book That Will Change the Way You Do Business* (New York: Harper Business, 2011).

Figure 7-5: Corporate Innovation Stack

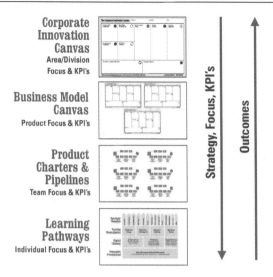

Corporate
Innovation
Canvas
Area/Division
Focus & KPI's

Business Model
Canvas
Product Focus & KPI's

Product
Charters &
Pipelines
Team Focus & KPI's

Learning
Pathways
Individual Focus & KPI's

Strategy, Focus, KPI's

Outcomes

In Closing...

I'd love to hear how things go with your practice of HDD. At this point, we've spent more time together than I have with most people I've met. I'd love to hear your HDD stories if you'd like to share them. Tag me on LinkedIn, @ me on Twitter (@cowansf), or just drop me a plain old email at acowan@alexandercowan.com.

Recommended Practice

Summary Reference for the Book
As you may have noticed if you checked any of the links in these sections, the book reference exists on a single, consolidated page. For this page, the main link to remember is: https://hdd.works/book.

Create a Personal Innovation Portfolio (Recap)
As a reminder from Chapter 2, there's a reference with examples, tutorials, and templates here: https://hdd.works/3PDbqqv.

Draft an Agile Team Charter

While there are few universal practices in agile, having teams create and maintain their own charters is one I've found particularly useful, particularly relative to the idea of creating 'pull' around user empathy and testable outcomes. This page offers tutorials, templates, and examples: https://hdd.works/charter.

Sketch a Business Model Design (Recap)

As a reminder from Chapter 1, there's a reference with examples, tutorials, and templates here: https://hdd.works/3cgjn6N. Regardless of whether you're the 'strategy person', this is a great way to facilitate meaningful discussions about business model design and how to align the target outcomes for various teams with that design.

Charter a Company Innovation Strategy with the Corporate Innovation Canvas

For a large company with multiple lines of business, the Corporate Innovation Canvas can be a helpful way to untangle all the things that the company's stakeholders want to have happen with innovation, and consider how they align and what that means for focus and investment. This page has tutorials, examples, and templates: https://hdd.works/3TJXHRA.

P.S.

Also, if you enjoyed the book and don't mind leaving a review, those are tremendously helpful. In any case, best wishes for your practice of HDD and thank you for your interest in the book.

ABOUT THE AUTHOR

Alex first started trying to make money with computers at 19 and he's been at it for the last 25 years. Through new ventures, 'intrapreneurial' ventures inside existing companies, and three successful exits as both founder and investor, he's never stopped wondering how to do it better. Now a professor at the University's Darden School of Business, he's helping to rethink the way we prepare leaders for successful careers in tech. With over 500,000 courses sold, his approach has become popular with practitioners worldwide.

He is also a silly goose.

Made in the USA
Middletown, DE
15 November 2024

64648836R00181